INTRODUCTION TO FINANCIAL ACCOUNTING

INTRODUCTION TO FINANCIAL ACCOUNTING

Bernard Nabarro

Kruger Brentt
Publishers
2024

Kruger Brentt Publishers UK. LTD.
Company Number 9728962

Regd. Office: 68 St Margarets Road, Edgware, Middlesex HA8 9UU

ISBN: 978-1-78715-252-6

Disclaimer:

Every possible effort has been made to ensure that the information contained in this book is accurate at the time of going to press, and the publisher and author cannot accept responsibility for any errors or omissions, however caused. No responsibility for loss or damage occasioned to any person acting, or refraining from action, as a result of the material in this publication can be accepted by the editor, the publisher or the author. The Publisher is not associated with any product or vendor mentioned in the book. The contents of this work are intended to further general scientific research, understanding and discussion only. Readers should consult with a specialist where appropriate.

Every effort has been made to trace the owners of copyright material used in this book, if any. The author and the publisher will be grateful for any omission brought to their notice for acknowledgement in the future editions of the book.

For information on all our publications visit our website at http://krugerbrentt.com/

Preface

Financial accounting is a fundamental branch of accounting that plays a critical role in capturing, summarizing, and reporting the financial transactions and performance of a business or organization. It provides essential information to various stakeholders, enabling them to make informed decisions about the entity's financial health, performance, and future prospects. The primary purpose of financial accounting is to present a clear and accurate picture of an organization's financial activities, primarily through the preparation of financial statements. These financial statements include the balance sheet, income statement (also known as the profit and loss statement), cash flow statement, and statement of changes in equity. Each statement offers unique insights into different aspects of the organization's financial position and performance. Financial accounting plays a crucial role in the world of business and finance. Its importance stems from the value it adds to various stakeholders, providing them with essential information for decision-making, financial analysis, and accountability. Here are some key reasons why financial accounting is important:

Financial accounting enables businesses to produce accurate and reliable financial statements, such as the balance sheet, income statement, and cash flow statement. These statements provide a comprehensive view of the company's financial performance and position, fostering transparency and accountability to investors, creditors, and other stakeholders. Business owners, management, and investors heavily rely on financial accounting data to make informed decisions. Whether it's assessing profitability, identifying cost-saving opportunities, or evaluating investment options, financial accounting provides the necessary information to guide strategic choices. For investors, financial statements are vital tools to assess the financial health and potential risks of a company. Transparent financial reporting enhances investor confidence and encourages investment, as it demonstrates the company's commitment to openness and compliance with accounting standards.

Creditors, such as banks and suppliers, use financial accounting information to assess the creditworthiness of a business. By analyzing financial statements, creditors can determine the company's ability to repay loans or fulfill payment obligations, which affects credit decisions and interest rates. Companies are required by law to maintain accurate financial records and report their financial performance as per the applicable accounting standards and regulations. Financial accounting ensures compliance with these rules, promoting ethical practices and reducing the risk of fraudulent activities. Financial accounting allows companies to compare their financial performance over time and against industry peers. Benchmarking against competitors helps identify areas for improvement and highlights the company's relative strengths and weaknesses. When businesses seek to merge, acquire, or be acquired, financial accounting data is crucial for valuation purposes. Proper valuation ensures fair deals and minimizes the risk of over- or underpaying for assets and businesses. Financial accounting forms the foundation for calculating taxes and ensuring compliance with tax laws. Properly recorded financial transactions and statements help businesses accurately report income and expenses, reducing the risk of tax-related penalties. For efficient resource allocation, companies need to understand their financial position. Financial accounting enables businesses to allocate resources effectively, optimize spending, and allocate funds to areas that contribute most to their success. Financial accounting provides a common language for communication between a company and its stakeholders. Through financial statements, companies can effectively communicate their financial performance, achievements, and future prospects. Financial accounting is essential for maintaining accurate records, supporting decision-making processes, complying with regulations, and fostering transparency and trust among stakeholders. It forms the backbone of the financial management system and significantly influences the success and sustainability of businesses and organizations.

The book "Introduction to Financial Accounting" appears to be a comprehensive guide that covers various essential aspects of financial accounting. It caters to both service and merchandising businesses and helps readers grasp accounting principles using both cash and accrual basis methods. By exploring assets, liabilities, and stockholders' equity in detail, the book equips readers with a solid foundation to analyze and interpret financial statements effectively. The inclusion of capstone experiences adds a practical dimension to the learning process, making it a valuable resource for students, aspiring accountants, and anyone seeking to understand financial accounting principles. We are grateful to all those persons as well as various books, manuals, periodicals, magazines, journals etc. that helped in the preparation of this book. In spite of the best efforts, it is possible that some errors may have occurred into the compilation and editing of the book. Further queries, constructive suggestions and criticisms for the improvement of the book are always welcome and shall be thankfully acknowledged.

Bernard Nabarro

Contents

PREFACE V

1. ACCOUNTING CYCLE FOR THE SERVICE BUSINESS—CASH BASIS 1

1.1 Introducing accounts and balances 1

1.2 Net income—a critical amount 3

1.3 The mechanics of the accounting process 3

1.4 Financial statements 14

1.5 Asset, liability and stockholders' equity accounts 28

1.6 Account wrap-up 34

1.7 The accounting equation 35

1.8 Changes in stockholders' equity 42

1.9 Wrap up 47

2. ACCOUNTING CYCLE FOR THE SERVICE BUSINESS—ACCRUAL BASIS 49

2.1 Accrual basis of accounting 49

2.2 Matching principle 49

2.3 Adjusting entries 54

2.4 Adjusting entries—deferrals 73

2.5 Adjusting entries—accruals 78

3. ACCOUNTING CYCLE FOR A MERCHANDISING BUSINESS........................ 91

3.1 Introduction 91

3.2 Merchandising income statement 93

3.3 Basic merchandising transactions (perpetual inventory system) 95

3.4 Transportation costs for merchandising transactions 100

3.5 Basic merchandising transactions (periodic inventory system) 106

3.6 Closing entries for merchandising accounts 109

4. ASSETS IN MORE DETAIL 115

4.1 Inventory 115

4.2 Cash 128

4.3 Note Receivable 134

4.4 .Uncollectible Accounts 139

4.5 Fixed And Intangible Assets 152

4.6 Summary 164

4.7 Gains And Losses On Disposal Of Assets 166

4.8 Gains And Losses On The Income Statement 179

4.9 Investments 185

4.10 Investments In Bonds 202

5. LIABILITIES IN MORE DETAIL 227

5.1 Sales Tax 227

5.2 Payroll 228

6. STOCKHOLDERS' EQUITY IN MORE DETAIL 261

6.1 Accounting Equation 261

6.2 Corporations And Stockholders' Equity 262

6.3 Issuing Stock For Cash 265

6.4 Issuing Stock For Non-Cash Assets 267

6.5 Cash Dividends 272

6.6 Stock Dividends 273

6.7 Stockholders' Equity Section Of The Balance Sheet 275

6.8 Stock Splits 276

6.9 Cash Dividends Calculations 276

7. CAPSTONE EXPERIENCES: STATEMENT OF CASH FLOWS & FINANCIAL STATEMENT ANALYSIS 283

7.1 Financial statements 283

7.2 Statement of cash flows 283

7.3 Financial statement analysis 302

7.4 Summary 331

7.5 Accounting as a profession 331

INDEX 337

01 Accounting Cycle for the Service Business—Cash Basis

1.1 INTRODUCING ACCOUNTS AND BALANCES

Accounting may be defined as the process of analyzing, classifying, recording, summarizing, and interpreting business transactions. One of the key aspects of the process is keeping "running totals" of "things." Examples of items a business might keep track of include the amount of cash the business currently has, what a company has paid for utilities for the month, the amount of money it owes, its income for the entire year, and the total cost of all the equipment it has purchased. You want to always have these running totals up to date so they are readily available to you when you need the information. It is similar to checking what your cash balance in the bank is when deciding if you have enough money to make a purchase with your debit card.

We will now refer to these "running totals" as balances and these "things" as accounts. Any item that a business is interested in keeping track of in terms of a running dollar balance so it can determine "how much right now?" or "how much so far?" is set up as an account. There are five types, or categories, of accounts.

WHAT IS A CATEGORY?

A category is a classification that generally describes its contents. The table below shows three column headings in bold: Planets, Colors, and Food. These are sample categories

PLANETS	COLORS	FOOD
Saturn	Red	Pizza
Venus	Green	Brownies
Mars	Yellow	Chicken
Earth	Blue	Eggplant

Below each column heading is a list of four items that are actual examples of items that fall into the respective category. If "Red" appeared under the "Planets" heading, you would immediately assume there was an error. It does not belong there.

There are many items that businesses keep records of. Each of these accounts fall into one of five **categories.**

1. **Assets:** Anything of value that a business owns
2. **Liabilities:** Debts that a business owes; claims on assets by outsiders
3. **Stockholders' equity:** Worth of the owners of a business; claims on assets by the owners
4. **Revenue:** Income that results when a business operates and generates sales
5. **Expenses:** Costs associated with earning revenue

Different accounts fall into different categories. **Cash** is an account that falls in the **asset** category. The Cash account keeps track of the amount of money a business has. Checks, money orders, and debit and credit cards are considered to be cash.

Other than Cash, we will begin by covering accounts that fall into the **revenue** and **expense** categories.

Revenue is income that results from a business engaging in the activities that it is set up to do. For example, a computer technician earns revenue when they repairs a computer for a customer. If the same computer technician sells a van that they no longer needs for his business, it is not considered revenue.

Fees Earned is an account name commonly used to record income generated from providing a service. In a service business, customers buy expertise, advice, action, or an experience but do not purchase a physical product. Consultants, dry cleaners, airlines, attorneys, and repair shops are service-oriented businesses. The Fees Earned account falls into the **revenue** category.

Expenses are bills and other costs a business must pay in order for it to operate and earn revenue. As the adage goes, "It takes money to make money."

Expense accounts differ from business to business, depending on individual company needs. The following are some common expenses that many businesses have:

Wages Expense	Cost of paying hourly employees
Rent Expense	Cost for the use of property that belongs to someone else
Utilities Expense	Costs such as electricity, water, phone, gas, cable TV, etc.
Supplies Expense	Cost of small items used to run a business
Insurance Expense	Cost of protection from liability, damage, injury, theft, etc.
Advertising Expense	Cost of promoting the business
Maintenance Expense	Costs related to repair and upkeep
Miscellaneous Expense	Costs that are minor and/or non-repetitive
ANY Expense	Any cost associated with earning revenue

A **chart of accounts** is a list of all accounts used by a business. Accounts are presented by category in the following order: (1) Assets, (2) Liabilities, (3) Stockholders' equity, (4) Revenue, and (5) Expenses.

CHART OF ACCOUNTS (PARTIAL)

The following table summarizes the categories and accounts discussed so far:

ASSETS	REVENUE	EXPENSES
Cash	Fees Earned	Wages Expense Rent Expense Utilities Expense Supplies Expense Insurance Expense Advertising Expense Miscellaneous Expense

1.2 NET INCOME—A CRITICAL AMOUNT

The difference between the total revenue and total expense amounts for a particular period (such as a month or year), assuming revenue is higher, is **profit.** We will now refer to profit as **net income.** The following is a key calculation in determining a business's operating results in dollars:

Revenue - Expenses = Net Income

Net income is determined by subtracting all expenses for a month (or year) from all revenue for that same month (or year). A **net loss** results if total expenses for a month (or year) exceed total revenue for the same period of time.

Net income is a result that business people are extremely interested in knowing since it represents the results of a firm's operations in a given period of time.

1.3 THE MECHANICS OF THE ACCOUNTING PROCESS

1.3.1 The Journal

Financial statements are key goals of the accounting process. In order to prepare them at the end of an accounting period, individual financial transactions must be analyzed, classified, and recorded all throughout the period. This initially takes place in a record book called the **journal,** where financial events called **transactions** are recorded as they happen, in chronological order.

When a transaction occurs, two or more accounts are affected. There is also a dollar amount associated with each of the accounts. Determining which accounts are impacted, and by how much, is the first step in making a journal entry.

This is a sample of a few rows in a journal. It has five columns: *Date, Account, Post. Ref., Debit, Credit.*

Date	Account		Debit	Credit

In the journal, the column heading **Debit** means "left" and **Credit** means "right." There are other familiar interpretations of these words, so don't be confused: the terms here only have to do with whether a dollar amount is entered in the left or the right number column.

These words may also be used as verbs: To "debit an account" means to enter its amount in the left column. To "credit an account" means to enter its amount in the right column.

1.3.2 Rules of Debit and Credit

Whether a particular account should be debited or credited is based on (1) the type of account it is and (2) whether the account is increasing or decreasing.

RULES OF DEBIT AND CREDIT	
for Cash and Revenue and Expense accounts	
Debit CASH when you receive it	Cash increases
Credit CASH when you pay it out	Cash decreases
Debit EXPENSES when you incur them	Expenses increase
Credit REVENUE when you earn it	Revenue increases

1.3.3 Journalizing Transactions

We now will come to one of the most important procedures in the recordkeeping process: journal entries. It involves analyzing and writing down financial transactions in a record book called a journal. Financial events are evaluated and translated into the language of accounting using the process of **journalizing.**

Select two accounts and, according to the rules of debit and credit for cash, revenue, and expense accounts, decide which account to debit (left column) and which to credit (right column). The debit entry is always listed first. No dollar signs are required in the journal.

Journalizing involves the following steps:

1. Select two (or more) accounts impacted by a transaction.
2. Determine how much, in dollars, each account is affected. Often times the amounts are given; other times the amounts must be calculated based on the information provided.

3. Based on the rules of debit and credit, decide which account(s) is debited and which is credited.
4. Enter the date on the first line of the transaction only.
5. Enter the account that will be debited on the first line of the transaction. Enter its amount in the Debit column on the same line.
6. Enter the account that will be credited on the second line of the transaction. Enter its amount in the Credit column on the same line.

NOTE: Indent the credit account name three spaces.

SAMPLE TRANSACTION #1:

On 6/1, a company paid rent of $2,000 for the month of June.

Date	Account		Debit	Credit
6/1	Rent Expense		2,000	

PARTIAL TRANSACTION

- *Rent Expense* is an expense account that is increasing. Therefore, it is debited. The account with the debit amount is entered first.

Date	Account		Debit	Credit
6/1	Rent Expense		2,000	
	Cash			2,000

COMPLETE TRANSACTION

- *Cash is an asset* account that is decreasing. Therefore, it is credited. The account with the credit amount is entered next.

SAMPLE TRANSACTION #2:

On 6/5, a customer paid $800 cash for services the company provided.

Date	Account		Debit	Credit
6/5	Cash		800	
				2,000

PARTIAL TRANSACTION

- *Cash is an asset* account that is increasing. Therefore, it is debited. The account with the debit amount is entered first.

Date	Account		Debit	Credit
6/5	Cash		800	
				8,00

COMPLETE TRANSACTION

- Fees Earned is a revenue account that is increasing. Therefore, it is credited. The account with the credit amount is entered next.

In practice, each transaction follows immediately after the previous one, as shown here.

Date	Account		Debit	Credit
6/1	Rent Expense		2,000	
	Cash			2,000
6/5	Cash		800	
	Fees Earned			800
6/8	Wages Expense		500	
	Cash			500
6/10	Cash		600	
	Fees Earned			600

The same journal continues on from period to period. You do not start a new\ journal for a new accounting period (month or year).

1.3.4 Ledger

The **ledger is** the second accounting record book that is a list of a company's individual accounts list in order of account category. While the journal lists all types of transactions chronologically, the ledgers separate this same information out by account and keep a **running balance** of each of these accounts.

Each account has its own ledger page. The account name appears across the top. The ledger form has six columns: *Date, Item, Debit, Credit, Debit, Credit.* The first set of Debit and Credit columns are where amounts from the journal transactions are **copied.** The second set of Debit and Credit columns are where the account's running total is maintained. An account's **running balance** typically appears in either the Debit or the Credit column, not both. The following is a sample ledger for the Cash account.

		Cash			
Date	Item	Debit	Credit	Debit	Credit
6/1		12,000		12,000	
6/2		2,000		14,000	
6/3			3,000	11,000	
		Copy amounts from journal (use either column)		BALANCE columns (use one of the two)	

IMPORTANT: Information entered in the ledger is always copied from what is already in the journal.

1.3.5 Posting

The process of copying from the journal to the ledger is called posting. It is done one line at a time from the journal. Here are step-by-step instructions for doing so.

1. Take note of the account name in the first line of the journal. Find that ledger account.
2. Copy the date from the journal to the first blank row in that ledger.
3. Leave the Item column blank in the ledger at this point.
4. Take note of the amount on the first line of the journal and the column it is in.
5. Copy that amount to the same column in the ledger on the same line where you entered the date.
6. Update the account's running balance. Take note of the previous balance in the last two columns of the ledger, if there is one. Do one of the following, based on the situation.
    a. If there is no previous balance and the entry is a Debit, enter the same amount in the Debit balance column.
    b. If there is no previous balance and the entry is a Credit, enter the same amount in the Credit balance column.
    c. If the previous balance is in the Debit column and the entry is a Debit, add the two amounts and enter the total in the Debit balance column.
    d. If the previous balance is in the Debit column and the entry is a Credit, subtract the credit amount from the balance and enter the difference in the Debit balance column. *
    e. If the previous balance is in the Credit column and the entry is
    f. Credit, add the two amounts and enter the total in the Credit balance column.
    g. If the previous balance is in the Credit column and the entry is a Debit, subtract the debit amount from the balance and enter the difference in the Credit balance column.

- Note: The only exception to the above is the rare occasion when one of the calculations above results in a negative number. No negative amounts should appear in the ledgers. Instead, the balance will appear in the opposite balance column.

7. Go back to the journal and enter an "x" or checkmark in the PR column to indicate that you have posted that line item.
8. Repeat the process for the next line in the journal.

Every time an account appears on a line in the journal, its amount is copied to the proper column in that account's ledger. A running total is maintained for each account and is updated every time an amount is posted.

The example that follows shows a journal with five transactions that involve Cash. On each row where Cash appears in the journal, the amount on the same line is copied to the same column in the Cash ledger, in either the first Debit or the first Credit column. Superscripts are used here to match each Cash amount in the journal to its posting in the ledger. For example, the first debit to Cash in the journal for $6,000 is copied to the debit column in the ledger (#1). The next time Cash appears in the journal is a credit for $2,000, so that is copied to the first credit column in the ledger (#2).

JOURNAL

Date	Account		Debit	Credit
6/1	Cash	x	6,000[1]	
	Fees Earned			6,000
6/2	Rent Expense		2,000	
	Cash	x		2,000[2]
6/3	Wages Expense		1,000	
	Cash	x		1,000[3]
6/4	Cash	x	5,000[4]	
	Fees Earned			5,000
6/5	Wages Expense		1,000	
	Cash	x		1,000[5]

LEDGER

Date	Item	Debit	Credit	Credit
6/1		6,000[1]		6,000
6/2			2,000[2]	4,000
6/3			1,000[3]	3,000

Date	Item	Debit	Credit	Credit
6/4		5,000[4]		8,000
6/5			1,000[5]	7,000
6/4	Cash	x	5,000[4]	
	Fees Earned			5,000
6/5	Wages Expense		1,000	
	Cash	x		1,000[5]

As shown in the previous example, the first entry in the ledger indicates which of the two final columns will normally be used to maintain the accounts running balance. For the Cash account, the first entry is in the first Debit column, so the running balance begins accumulating in the second Debit column. On the first row, the amounts in the two Debit columns will be the same. In this case, the amount is $6,000 in both. After the first entry in the ledger, subsequent debit entries are added to the previous debit balance, and subsequent credit entries are deducted from the previous debit balance.

GETTING THE JOB DONE

You can go to an ATM to withdraw cash from your checking account. The first steps are to insert your debit card into the ATM machine and select the amount you would like to receive. If that is all you do, no money will come out no matter how long you stand there. In order to get the job done, you also need to enter your PIN. The goal is to withdraw cash, and if you do not complete that step, it is not going to happen.

Similarly, there is a goal to preparing the journal and ledgers – to maintain a running balance of each account your business has. If you enter a transaction in the journal, you are off to a good start, but if you don't complete the step of posting the journal entry to the ledgers, the correct balances are not going to happen.

1.3.6 Normal Balance

The last two Debit and Credit columns in the ledger are where a running total (balance) is maintained for each account. An account's running balance will accumulate in EITHER the Debit balance column OR Credit balance column (two far right columns), but rarely both. The **normal balance** is also whatever it takes to increase that type of account, either Debit or Credit. The normal balance for an account is the column in which its running total is maintained.

An example of a journal and ledgers follows. Try to follow how the numbers from the journal on the left appear in the ledgers on the right and how the running balances in the ledgers are determined.

JOURNAL

Date	Account		Debit	Credit
6/1	Cash	x	2,000	
	Fees Earned	x		2,000
6/2	Supplies Expense	x	300	
	Cash	x		300
6/3	Cash	x	500	
	Fees Earned	x		500
6/4	Supplies Expense	x	200	
	Cash	x		200
6/5	Cash	x	800	
	Fees Earned	x		800
6/6	Supplies Expense	x	400	
	Cash	x		400
6/7	Cash	x	600	
	Fees Earned	x		600

LEDGER

Date	Item	Debit	Credit	Debit	Credit
6/1		2,000		2,000	
6/2			300	1,700	
6/3		500		2,200	
6/4			200	2,000	
6/5		800		2,800	
6/6			400	2,400	
6/7		600		3,000	

Fee Earned

Date	Item	Debit	Credit	Debit	Credit
6/1			2,000		2,000
6/3			500		2,500
6/5			800		3,300
6/7			600		3,900

Supplies Expense

Date	Item	Debit	Credit	Debit	Credit
6/2		300		300	
6/4		200		500	
6/6		400		900	

The first entry in each ledger, either Debit or Credit, dictates whether the running balance will appear in the Debit or the Credit balance column. If the first entry is a Debit, the running balance accumulates in the Debit balance column. A debit is the "positive" for this type of account; any subsequent debit entries are added and credit entries are subtracted from the running balance. Conversely, if the first entry is a Credit, the running balance accumulates in the Credit balance column. A credit is the "positive" for this type of account; any subsequent credit entries are added and debit entries are subtracted from the running balance.

The grayed column above in each ledger represents the balance column that will normally remain blank.

The total of all the Debit balances in the ledgers MUST EQUAL the total of all the Credit balances in the ledgers. If this is not the case, there is a recording error that must be located and corrected. In the example above, the ledgers balance: 3,000 + 900 (debit balances) = 3,900 (credit balance).

The same ledgers continue on from period to period. You do not start new ledgers for a new accounting period (month or year).

To summarize the two record books, the journal first records all types of transactions chronologically, in time sequence order. The ledgers separate the same information out by account and keep a balance for each of these accounts.

IMPORTANT: If you are making entries in the ledgers, you must be COPYING from the journal.

CAN I HAVE THE RECIPE?

I have a great recipe for chocolate chip cookies. Here are the ingredients. At this point you must be confused, or think I am crazy. The cookies could not possibly be the result of those ingredients—the input does not match the output. Anyone who knows anything about cookies can see that.

It is the same with the accounting process. It is not possible to have a correct ledger and/or financial statement balances if the input in the journal has errors. Yet some students "know," or copy from others, what the correct results should be in spite of incorrect journal entries. This violates the process of posting to the ledgers, which is carrying over what is in the journal.

It is more correct for an error to carry through to all parts than for one part to be incorrect and subsequent parts to be correct. To your accounting instructor, a correct balance based on a faulty journal is as unlikely an outcome as is chocolate chip cookies from taco ingredients. It just can't happen!

If there is an error in the journal, procedurally the mistake should carry through to the ledgers and the financial statements.

1.3.7 Trial Balance

The total of all the debit balances in a company's ledger accounts must always equal the total of all the credit balances. A **trial balance** is a list of all a business's accounts and its current ledger balances (copied over from the ledger accounts). A trial balance may be generated at any time to test whether total debits equals total credits. It is simply a worksheet to check for accuracy before preparing financial statements. If both of the Total columns do not equal, there is an error that must be found and corrected.

The example that follows is for a company with only four accounts. The trial balance on the left lists these accounts and their corresponding balances at the end of the month, which are copied over from the ledgers on the right.

TRIAL BALANCE

Account	Debit	Credit
Cash	3,000	
Common Stock		2,000

Account	Debit	Credit
Fees Earned		1,900
Supplies Expense	900	
TOTAL	3,900	3,900

LEDGERS

Date	Item	Debit	Credit	Debit	Credit
6/1		2,000		2,000	
6/2			300	1,700	
6/3		500		2,200	
6/4			200	2,000	
6/5		800		2,800	
6/6			400	2,400	
6/7		600		3,000	

Common Stock

Date	Item	Debit	Credit	Debit	Credit
6/1			2,000		2,000

Fees Earned

Date	Item	Debit	Credit	Debit	Credit
6/3			500		500
6/5			800		1,300
6/7			600		1,900

Supplies Expense

Date	Item	Debit	Credit	Debit	Credit
6/2		300		300	
6/4		200		500	
6/6		400		900	

1.4 FINANCIAL STATEMENTS

The goal of journalizing, posting to the ledgers, and preparing the trial balance is to gather the information necessary to produce the **financial statements.** The **time period** concept requires companies produce the financial statements on a regular basis over the same time interval, such as a month or year. Most of the amounts on these statements are copied directly from the trial balance, and then appropriate calculations and summary amounts are also displayed. The first of the four financial statements will be discussed here.

1.4.1 Income Statement

The **net income** from a business's operations for a period of time is so important to business people and investors that one financial statement—the **income statement**—is dedicated to showing what that amount is and how it was determined. The income statement is a report that lists and summarizes revenue, expense, and net income information for a period of time, usually a month or a year. It is based on the following equation: **Revenue - Expenses = Net income** (or Net loss). Revenue is shown first; a list of expenses follows, and their total is subtracted from revenue. If the difference is positive, there is a profit, or net income. If the difference is negative, there is a net loss that is typically presented in parentheses as a negative number.

SAMPLE INCOME STATEMENT

Jonick Company
Income Statement
For the Month Ended June 30, 2018

Fees Earned		$30,000
Operating expenses:		
Salaries expense	$2,500	
Wages expense	2,200	
Rent expense	2,000	
Insurance expense	1,900	
Supplies expense	1,800	
Advertising expense	1,700	
Maintenance expense	1,600	
Utilities expense	1,400	
Vehicle expense	1,100	
Miscellaneous expense	800	
Total operating expenses		17,000
Net income		$13,000

FORMATTING TIPS

- Complete heading: Company Name, Name of Financial Statement, Date

- Two Columns of numbers—left one for listing items to be sub-totaled; right one for results
- Dollar signs go at the top number of a list of numbers to be calculated
- Category headings for revenue and expenses only if there is more than one item listed in the category
- Expenses listed in order of highest to lowest dollar amounts, except for Miscellaneous Expense, which is always last
- The word "Expense" on expense account names
- Single underline just above the result of a calculation (two of these)
- Dollar sign on final net income number
- Double underline below the final net income result

The income statement answers a business's most important question: How much profit is it making? It is limited to a specific **period of time** (month or year) from beginning to end. The income statement relies on the **matching principle** in that it only reports revenue and expenses in a specified window of time. It does not include any revenue or expenses from before or after that block of time.

You have just learned about the income statement—the accounts it displays and its format. We will hold off for now on the other three financial statements—the retained earnings statement, the balance sheet, and the statement of cash flows —and learn about those later.

1.4.2 The Accounting Cycle

Accounting is practiced under a guideline called the time period assumption, which allows the ongoing activities of a business to be divided up into periods of a year, quarter, month, or other increment of time. The precise time period covered is included in the headings of the income statement, the retained earnings statement, and the statement of cash flows.

Therefore, the accounting process is cyclical. A cycle is a period of time in which a series of accounting activities are performed. As was just stated, the typical accounting cycle is a year, a month, or perhaps a quarter. Once the current cycle is completed, the same recording and reporting activities are then repeated in the next period of time of equal length.

In accounting, journalizing and posting transactions to the ledgers are done every day in the cycle. Financial statements are typically prepared only on the last day of the cycle. Once the financial statements are complete, the process continues on into the next accounting period, where again the financial statements are the goal of the recordkeeping process.

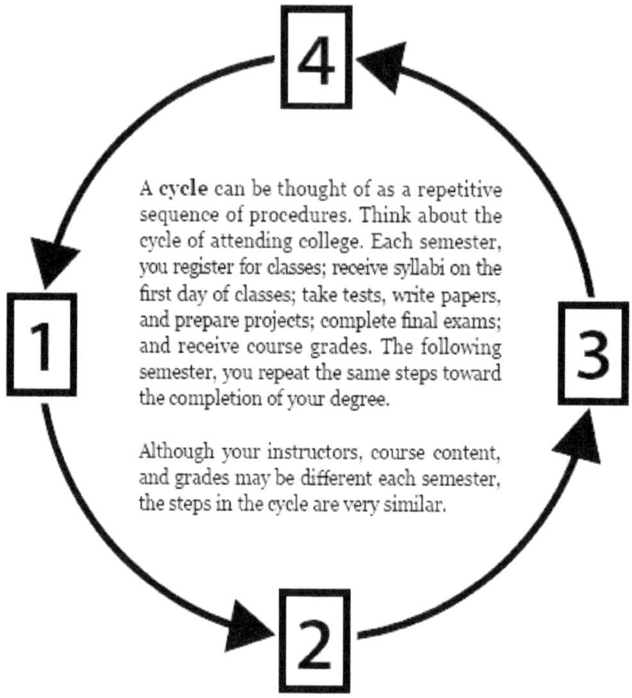

1.4.3 Temporary Accounts

The accounts on the income statement are called **temporary** accounts. They are used to record operational transactions for a specific period of time. Once the income statement is prepared to report the temporary account balances at the end of the period, these account balances are set back to zero by transferring them to another account. When the next accounting period begins, the beginning balances of the temporary accounts are zero, for a fresh start.

1.4.4 Closing Entries

The financial statements are the goal of all that is done in the accounting cycle. However, there are some steps that need to be taken once those reports are completed to set up the ledgers for the next cycle. These steps involve closing entries.

Closing entries are special journal entries made at the end of the accounting period (month or year) **after the financial statements are prepared** but before the first transaction in the next month is recorded in the journal. The purpose of closing entries is to set the balances of income statement accounts back to zero so you can start fresh and begin accumulating new balances for the next month. This process ensures that the balances on the second month's income statement do not include amounts from transactions in the first month.

Profit at the end of the accounting period is transferred into a new account called **Retained Earnings** when the revenue and expense accounts are closed out. The Retained Earnings account is only used for closing entries.

Closing entries transfer the balances from the revenue and expense accounts into *Retained Earnings* in preparation for the new month. *Retained Earnings* is an account where profit is "stored." Think of the retained earnings balance as "accumulated profit," or all the net income that the business has ever generated since it began operations.

Assume a business's accounting period is a month. For the first month in which the business operates, the beginning retained earnings balance is zero since there were no previous periods and therefore no previous profits. At the end of the first month, the retained earnings balance equals the net income for the month.

After the first month, when closing entries for the current month are journalized and posted, the additional net income for the next month is added to any net income already in Retained Earnings from previous months. Since *Revenue - Expenses = Net Income,* moving revenue and expense balances into Retained Earnings is the same as moving the net income.

RUNNING IN CIRCLES

A track star is practicing running a lap at a time around the track. He has a timekeeper with a stopwatch timing each lap. The timekeeper clicks "Start" and the runner takes off. He crosses the finish line in 50 seconds, the time elapsed as shown on the stopwatch when "Stop" was clicked.

The runner rests, drinks, and decides to try again to see if he can do better. The timekeeper clicks "Start" and the runner takes off, running even faster. He crosses the finish line in 95 seconds, the time elapsed as shown on the stopwatch when "Stop" was clicked.

What is wrong with this picture? Was he so much slower? He did not have a poor sprint; he had a poor timekeeper! This person did not reset the stopwatch to zero for the second run, so the 50 seconds from the first run was included with the 45 seconds from the second run. The runner can subtract the 50 from the 95, but who wants to do math on the track? That is what the reset button is for, and it enables the results of both runs to be easily compared.

Similarly, income statements include revenue and expense amounts for a period of time—a month or a year. After one month is reported, the ledger balances of these accounts must be reset to zero so that the next month's income statement does not include amounts from the previous month. This is done by closing out the revenue and expense ledger balances and resetting their balances to zero.

The *Retained Earnings* account is not closed out; instead, revenue and expense accounts are closed out into it. The effects are that the credit balance in *Retained Earnings* increases each month by the month's net income amount, and the balances of *Fees Earned* and all the expense accounts become zero.

Closing entries are entered in the same journal that was used for the general entries during the month. The first closing entry is journalized right after the last general entry. Closing entries must be posted to the ledgers to impact the revenue, expense, and *Retained Earnings* account balances.

As an example, assume that on 6/30 *Fees Earned* has a credit ledger balance of $2,100 and Rent Expense (the only expense account) has a debit ledger balance of $500. Net income is therefore $1,600. The closing entry process would be as follows:

1. **Zero out the Fees Earned account** (and any other revenue accounts, if there are others.) Debit Fees Earned for its credit balance of $2,100 to close it out and bring its balance to zero.

Credit Retained Earnings for the same amount.

Date	Account		Debit	Credit
6/30	Fees Earned		2,100	
	Retained Earnings			2,100

- Fees Earned is a **revenue** account that is **decreasing.**
- Retained Earnings is an equity **account that is increasing.**

2. **Zero out the Rent Expense account** (and any other expense accounts, if there are others.) Credit Rent Expense for its debit balance of $500 to close it out and bring the balance to zero. Debit Retained Earnings for the same amount.

Date	Account		Debit	Credit
6/30	Retained Earnings		500	
	Rent Expense			500

- Retained Earnings is an equity account that is decreasing.
- Rent Expense is an expense account that is decreasing.

Once posted, these two closing entries above increase the Retained Earnings balance by $1,600, which is $2,100 - $500. The balances in Fees Earned and Rent Expense are now both zero.

EXAMPLE

One month to the next WITHOUT closing entries on 6/30

The following journal shows five June transactions. (There would be more, but we will just use five for the example.) These are posted to the ledgers on the right. The running balance in Fees Earned as of 6/30 is a $2,100 credit. The running balances of Rent Expense and Wages Expense as of 6/30 are a $500 debit and a

$300 debit, respectively. These three amounts would be reported on the income statement in arriving at a net income of $1,300 for June.

Then July begins and the journal also shows the first three July transactions. Once again Rent Expense on the first of the month is $500, the first Fees Earned transaction is $900, and Wages Expense is $300. Both amounts are posted to their respective ledgers, as is shown in the following example.

JOURNAL

Date	Account		Debit	Credit
6/1	Rent Expense	x	500	
	Cash	x		500
6/5	Cash	x	600	
	Fees Earned	x		600
6/8	Wages Expense	x	300	
	Cash	x		300
6/20	Cash	x	700	
	Fees Earned	x		700
6/29	Cash	x	800	
	Fees Earned	x		800
6/29	Cash	x	800	
	Fees Earned	x		800
7/1	Rent Expense	x	500	
	Cash	x		500
7/2	Cash	x	900	
	Fees Earned	x		900
7/7	Wages Expense	x	300	
	Cash	x		300

Retained Earnings					
Date	Item	Debit	Credit	Debit	Credit

Fee Earned					
Date	Item	Debit	Credit	Debit	Credit
6/5			600		600
6/20			700		1,300
6/29			800		2,100
7/12			900		3,000

Rent Expense					
Date	Item	Debit	Credit	Debit	Credit
6/1		500		500	
7/1		500		1,000	

Wages Expense					
Date	Item	Debit	Credit	Debit	Credit
6/8		300		300	
7/1		300		600	

Now there is an inconsistency. When the 7/1 Rent Expense debit is posted, the running balance becomes $1,000. According to procedure, that final balance would be copied to July's income statement. That report would indicate that it cost the company

$1,000 in rent during July, which is clearly not true. It only cost $500 for rent in July. The problem is that the $500 in June became a part of the July running total.

The same issue is true for Fees Earned. Only $900 was earned in July so far as of 7/2, but the running balance is showing $3,000. That is because the running total to date in July also includes the $2,100 that was earned in June.

The **matching principle** in accounting states that the revenue earned in a period must be reported in conjunction with the expenses incurred in that same period. The period we are now referring to is the month of July in this example. However, June's revenues and expenses are still included in the balances in the ledgers. Closing entries on 6/30 here would have avoided this situation but were omitted, so the July balances erroneously contain amounts from June as well.

EXAMPLE

One month to the next WITH closing entries on 6/30

The following journal has similar transactions to the previous example PLUS it has the necessary closing entries in red for the three income statement accounts. It also shows how posting the closing entries impact the ledger account balances: revenue and expense balances are now zero on 6/30, and the Retained Earnings balance has increased from zero. Closing entries are shown in red in the following example. It is a good idea to enter the word "Closing" in the Item column in the ledgers to indicate that a closing entry has been posted.

JOURNAL

Date	Account		Debit	Credit
6/1	Rent Expense	x	500	
	Cash	x		500
6/5	Cash	x	600	
	Fees Earned	x		600
6/8	Wages Expense	x	300	
	Cash	x		300
6/20	Cash	x	700	
	Fees Earned	x		700
6/29	Cash	x	800	
	Fees Earned	x		800
6/30	Fees Earned	x	2,100	
	Retained Earnings	x		2,100
6/30	Retained Earnings	x	500	
	Rent Expense	x		500
6/30	Retained Earnings	x	300	
	Wages Expense	x		300
7/1	Rent Expense	x	500	
	Cash	x		500
7/2	Cash	x	900	
	Fees Earned	x		900
7/7	Wages Expense	x	300	
	Cash	x		300

LEDGERS (EXCEPT CASH)

Retained Earnings					
Date	Item	Debit	Credit	Debit	Credit
6/30	Closing		2,100		2,100
6/30	Closing	500			1,600
6/30	Closing	300			1,300

Fees Earned					
Date	Item	Debit	Credit	Debit	Credit
6/5			600		600
6/20			700		1,300
6/29			800		2,100
6/30	Closing	2,100			0
7/2			900		900

Wages Expense					
Date	Item	Debit	Credit	Debit	Credit
6/8		300		300	
6/30	Closing		300	0	
7/1		300		300	

Notice when the first July transactions are posted to the income statement accounts, the amounts are added to previous balances of zero. When the first July transaction is recorded in these accounts, it becomes the beginning balance for the new accounting period.

By doing this, the income statement for June reports only June transactions, and the income statement for July reports only July transactions. The income statements for the two months can then easily be compared.

The following table summarizes information about the accounts you know so far:

ACCOUNTS SUMMARY TABLE

Account type	Accounts	To increase	To decrease	Normal balance	Financial statement	Close out?
Asset	Cash	debit	credit	debit	Balance Sheet	NO
Stockholders' Equity	Retained Earnings	credit	debit	credit	Balance Sheet	NO
Revenue	Fees Earned	credit	debit	credit	Income Statement	YES
Expense	Wages Expense Rent Expense Utilities Expense Supplies Expense Insurance Expense Advertising Expense Maintenance Expense Miscellaneous Expense	debit	credit	debit	Income Statement	YES

1.4.5 Revenue Transactions on Account

When a business provides a service to a customer, the customer may immedi- ately pay with cash. You record the transaction with the following familiar journal entry:

EXAMPLE

6/1 Provide a service to a customer for $100 and receive cash.

Date	Account		Debit	Credit
6/1	Cash		100	
	Fees Earned			100

- Cash is an **asset** account that is **increasing.**
- Fees Earned is a **revenue** account that is **increasing.**

The 6/1 transaction is complete on that day. The company provided the service, and the customer paid cash in full for that service.

A second possibility involves the business sending a bill, or invoice, to the customer and typically giving the customer thirty days to pay. This is a revenue transaction **on account.**

The business records earnings and credits Fees Earned when it provides the service, regardless of when it receives the payment. When Fees Earned is credited because revenue is earned, there are now two possible debit accounts: Cash (paid on the spot), or **Accounts Receivable** (to be paid in the future).

Accounts Receivable is an asset account that keeps track of how much customers owe because a business sent invoices for goods or services to the customers rather than immediately receiving cash from them. This account is used as a substitute for a debit to Cash when a company provides services to customers and bills them on account rather than receiving cash right away.

When the customer pays the invoice and the business receives the cash payment, Cash is debited and Accounts Receivable is credited. The customer's Accounts Receivable balance becomes zero now that they have paid in full.

The rules of debit and credit for Accounts Receivable are the same as they are for Cash since both are asset accounts.

RULES OF DEBIT AND CREDIT	
Debit ACCOUNTS RECEIVABLE when you invoice a customer	Accounts Receivable increases
Credit FEES EARNED when you provide a service to a customer	Fees Earned increases
Debit CASH when the customer pays the invoice	Cash increases
Credit ACCOUNTS RECEIVABLE when the customer pays	Accounts Receivable decreases

The journal and the Accounts Receivable ledger below illustrate a revenue transaction on account for a business.

EXAMPLE

Debit ACCOUNTS RECEIVABLE when you invoice a customer

Credit FEES EARNED when you provide a service to a customer

JOURNAL

Date	Account		Debit	Credit
6/1	Accounts Receivable	x	200	
	Feed Earned	x		200
6/30	Cash	x	200	
	Accounts Receivable	x		200

LEDGER

Date	Item	Debit	Credit	Debit	Credit
6/1		200		200	
6/30			200	0	

- Accounts Receivable is an **asset** account that is **increasing.**
- Fees Earned is a **revenue** account that is **increasing.**
- Cash is an asset account that is **increasing.**
- Accounts Receivable is an **asset** account that is **decreasing.**

In the 6/1 transaction, the company provided the service, but the customer has not paid yet. When the customer does pay on 6/30, both parties in the 6/1 transaction have received what they are due.

Stated another way, the company debited Accounts Receivable in the journal when cash was due from a customer and later credited it when the cash was received from the customer. By 6/30, the two Accounts Receivable entries negate one another (one debit and one credit to the same account for the same amount), resulting in a zero balance in that account on 6/30. If the Accounts Receivable entries are crossed out in the journal since they wash out to zero, notice you are ultimately left with a debit to Cash and a credit to Fees Earned. Both parties have received what they are due from the transaction by 6/30: the company received cash and the customer received service.

1.4.6 Expense Transactions on Account

When a business purchases a product or service, it may pay immediately with cash and record the transaction with the following familiar journal entry:

EXAMPLE

6/1 Purchase supplies for $100 and pay cash.

Date	Account		Debit	Credit
6/1	Supplies Expense		100	
	Cash			100

- Supplies Expense is an expense account that is increasing.
- Cash is an asset account that is decreasing.

The 6/1 transaction is complete on that day. The company received the product or service and paid cash to the vendor at the same time.

The second possibility involves the business receiving a bill, or invoice, from the vendor when goods or services are received and typically being given thirty days to pay. This is an expense transaction on **account.**

The business records the expense and debits the expense account when it receives the product or service, regardless of when it pays. When any expense account is debited because it is incurred, there are now two possible credit accounts: Cash (paid on the spot), or Accounts Payable (to be paid in the future). Accounts

Payable is a liability account that keeps track of how much a business owes because it was billed by vendors rather than immediately paying cash. A liability is a debt a business owes. The **Accounts Payable** account is used as a substitute for Cash when a business purchases something or receives a service from a vendor and does not pay cash immediately, but instead is billed on account (sent an invoice).

When the company later pays with cash, Accounts Payable is debited and Cash is credited.

The following are the rules of debit and credit for transactions involving Accounts Payable and Cash.

RULES OF DEBIT AND CREDIT	
Debit an EXPENSE when you incur it by buying a product or service	Expense increases
Credit **ACCOUNTS PAYABLE** when you are billed on account	Accounts Payable increases
Debit **ACCOUNTS PAYABLE** when you pay down what you owe	Accounts Payable decreases
Credit **CASH** when you pay off the account	Cash decreases

The journal and the Accounts Payable ledger that follow illustrate an expense transaction on account for a business.

EXAMPLES

6/1 Purchase supplies for $200 on account and receive an invoice from the vendor.
6/30 Pay on account for the 6/1 purchase.

JOURNAL

Date	Account		Debit	Credit
6/1	Supplies Expense	x	200	
	Accounts Payable	x		200
6/30	Accounts Payable	x	200	
	Cash	x		200

- Supplies Expense is an expense account that is increasing.
- Accounts Payable is a liability account that is increasing.
- Accounts Payable is a liability account that is decreasing.
- Cash is an asset account that is decreasing.

LEDGER

Date	Item	Debit	Credit	Debit	Credit
6/1			200		200
6/30		200			0

In the 6/1 transaction, the company has received the product or service but has not paid for it yet. When the company does pay on 6/30, both parties in the 6/1 transaction have now received what they are due.

Stated another way, the company credited Accounts Payable when it received the product or service and later debited it when it paid the cash to the vendor. By 6/30, the two Accounts Payable entries negate one another (one credit and one debit to the same account for the same amount), resulting in a zero balance in that account on 6/30. If the Accounts Payable lines are crossed out in the journal since they wash out to zero, notice you are ultimately left with a debit to Supplies Expense and a credit to Cash. Both parties have received what they are due from the transaction by 6/30. The company received product or service and the vendor received cash.

The following table summarizes information about the accounts you know so far:

ACCOUNTS SUMMARY TABLE

ACCOUNT TYPE	ACCOUNTS	TO INCREASE	TO DECREASE	NORMAL BALANCE	FINANCIAL STATEMENT	CLOSE OUT?
Asset	Cash					
Accounts Receivable	debit	credit	debit	Balance Sheet	NO	
Liability	Accounts Payable	credit	debit	credit	Balance Sheet	NO
Stockholders' Equity	Retained Earnings	credit	debit	credit	Balance Sheet	NO
Revenue	Fees Earned	credit	debit	credit	Income Statement	YES

ACCOUNT TYPE	ACCOUNTS	TO INCREASE	TO DECREASE	NORMAL BALANCE	FINANCIAL STATEMENT	CLOSE OUT?
Expense	Wages Expense Rent Expense Utilities Expense Supplies Expense Insurance Expense Advertising Expense Maintenance Expense Miscellaneous Expense	debit	credit	debit	Income Statement	YES

All accounts are reported on one of three financial statements. The balances of two of the five types of accounts—revenue and expenses—are reported on the income statement at the end of each accounting period. The summary number on the income statement is net income, which is revenue minus expenses.

1.5 ASSET, LIABILITY AND STOCKHOLDERS' EQUITY ACCOUNTS

The three other categories of accounts—assets, liabilities, and stockholders' equity—are reported on another financial statement called the balance sheet. Unlike the temporary accounts on the income statement, these are **permanent** accounts because they are not closed out at the end of the accounting period. Instead, the account balances of the balance sheet accounts at the end of the period are carried forward and become the starting balances at the beginning of the next period.

1.5.1 Assets

Assets are anything of value to a business, including things a business owns so it can operate. Assets are recorded in the journal at what they cost the business, or what the business paid to acquire them. This is called the **cost principle.**

The first two asset accounts are those you are familiar with so far. These are **current assets,** which means they are either cash or are expected to be converted to cash within one year.

Cash	Money a business possesses
Accounts Receivable	Amount customers owe to a business from being invoiced on account

The following assets are **fixed assets.** They are relatively expensive and will last for more than one accounting year. Therefore, they are considered assets rather than expenses, which are costs related to a particular accounting period.

Land	Real estate property a business owns
Building	Real estate property a business owns
Truck	Motor vehicle a business owns
Equipment	Electronic machinery a business owns
Furnishings	Furniture a business owns

RULES OF DEBIT AND CREDIT FOR LIABILTIES

- Debit Any ASSET when it increases
- Credit Any ASSET when it decreases

Liabilities

Liabilities are debts a business has on the assets it possesses. They are claims on the assets by people and entities that are not owners of the business. The following are liability accounts.

Accounts Payable	Amount a business owes to vendors from being invoiced
Note Payable	Loan for cash or on any of the assets owned
ANY Payable	Debt owed for a specific reason

RULES OF DEBIT AND CREDIT FOR LIABILTIES

- Credit Any LIABILITY when it increases
- Debit Any LIABILITY when it decreases

Both Accounts Payable and Note Payable are liability accounts, or debts. They are different, however. Accounts Payable is a payment agreement with a vendor who gives you time—usually thirty days—to pay for a product or service your business purchases. A note payable is a formal, signed loan contract that may include an interest rate and that spells out the terms and conditions of repayment over time.

1.5.3 Stockholders' Equity

Stockholders' equity is the stockholders' share of ownership of the assets that the business possesses, or the claim on the business's assets by its owners.

A **corporation** is a form of business that is a separate legal entity from its owners. The people and/or organizations who own a corporation are called stockholders. **Stockholders** (owners) receive shares of stock as receipts for their investments in the business. This form of business offers **limited liability** to stockholders—the owners can only lose what they invested in the business. Their other assets cannot be taken to satisfy the obligations of the company they invest in.

SOLE PROPRIETORSHIP VS. CORPORATION

Let's say you start a lawn care business and invest $500 of your own cash and spend $1,500 for lawnmowers for a total investment of $2,000. If you do not incorporate, your business is a sole proprietorship. If you do incorporate, your business is a corporation. To form a corporation, a business needs to file paperwork called **articles of incorporation** (and pay a fee) with the state in which it will be operating. The state grants the business its corporate status.

If you damage the property of one of your customers and he submits a claim against you for $10,000, the most that you can be liable for as a corporation is the amount you have invested and earned in the business. As a sole proprietorship, however, it is possible the customer can be awarded more than the value of your ownership in the business. You would then have to pay out the difference using your personal money. If you don't have enough, you could even be forced to sell some of the things you own or make payments from your future wages to pay the claim off. If you are not organized as a corporation, your risk is not limited to the amount you invested and earned in the business.

The following are stockholders' equity accounts:

Common Stock	Account that shows the value of shares of stock issued to stockholders
Retained Earnings	Account where the corporation's profits accumulate and are "stored"
Cash Dividends	Payouts of profits (retained earnings) to stockholders

Stockholders' equity is the amount of a business's total assets that is owned by the stockholders. Only two accounts fall in this category: stockholders' equity is the total of the balances in the Common Stock and Retained Earnings accounts.

Common stock is the ownership value in the business that comes from outside the company—investors who pay their own money into the business. Retained earnings is the ownership value in the business that comes from inside the company—the business makes a profit that is shared by the stockholders.

Cash dividends are payouts of profits from retained earnings to stockholders. Cash Dividends is a temporary account that substitutes for a debit to Retained Earnings and is classified as a contra (opposite) stockholders' equity account. Cash dividends will reduce the Retained Earnings balance. This is ultimately accomplished by closing the *Cash Dividends balance into Retained Earnings* at the end of the accounting period.

RULES OF DEBIT AND CREDIT FOR STOCKHOLDERS' EQUITY

Credit Common Stock or Retained Earnings when it increases Debit Retained Earnings when it decreases

- Debit Cash Dividends when it increases
- Credit Cash Dividends when it decreases

1.5.4 Balance Sheet Account Transactions

Six very typical business transactions that involve balance sheet accounts will be shown next.

1. A company purchases equipment, paying $5,000 cash.

Date	Account		Debit	Credit
6/1	Equipment		5,000	
	Cash			5,000

- Equipment is an **asset** account that is **increasing.**
- Cash is an **asset** account that is **decreasing.**

2. A company purchases equipment for $5,000 on account.

Date	Account		Debit	Credit
6/1	Equipment		5,000	
	Accounts Payable			5,000

- Equipment is an **asset** account that is **increasing.**
- Accounts Payable is a **liability** account that is **increasing.**

3. A company purchases equipment that costs $5,000. The company pays a down payment of $1,000 and takes a loan for the remaining $4,000.

Date	Account		Debit	Credit
6/1	Equipment		5,000	
	Cash			1,000
	Note Payable			4,000

- Equipment is an **asset** account that is **increasing.**
- Cash is an **asset** account that is **decreasing.**
- Note Payable is a **liability** account that is **increasing.**

NOTE: Transaction #3 is called a compound transaction because there is more than one credit. (A compound transaction could also have more than one debit, if required.) **The total of the debits must equal the total of the credits in each transaction.** In this case one asset is being purchased, but there are two forms of payment—cash and the loan.

Also notice that in transactions #1, 2, and 3 above, the account debited is **Equipment,** an asset (and not **Equipment Expense,** which would be an expense account). The same holds true for the purchase of real estate: the assets **Building** and/or **Land** would be debited (not **Building Expense** or **Land Expense**). This is because these assets will last more than one accounting period. Usually one of the first steps in starting a business is opening the business's bank account.

4. An individual invests $10,000 of his own cash to open a new corporation's checking account.

Date	Account		Debit	Credit
6/1	Cash		10,000	
	Common Stock			10,000

- Cash is an **asset** account that is **increasing.**
- Common Stock is an **equity** account that is **increasing.**

Think of common stock as a receipt for an investor infusing money or other assets into the business. It recognizes that person's ownership. A running total of all the investments that people make in a corporation is maintained in the **Common Stock** account.

Transaction #4 is recorded when an investor puts money or other assets into a corporation. There are also times when investors take money out of a business. This can only be done if the corporation has generated a profit over time, which is what the investors will draw from. The accumulated profit over time appears in the corporation's **Retained Earnings** account.

The board of directors of large corporations or the owner(s) of small, closely-held corporations may decide to pay cash dividends to stockholders if there are sufficient retained earnings and sufficient cash to do so. Cash dividends are payouts of profit to stockholders; in other words, distributions of retained earnings. Cash dividends are not paid out of owner investments, or common stock.

5. The corporation pays $1,000 in dividends to its stockholders.

It might seem logical to debit **Retained Earnings** to reduce that stockholders' equity account and credit **Cash** to reduce that asset account. That is not entirely wrong. However, we are going to reserve **Retained Earnings** for closing entries only, and payment of dividends is not a closing entry. Instead of a debit to Retained Earnings, therefore, we will substitute the **Cash Dividends** account in this transaction.

Date	Account		Debit	Credit
6/15	Cash Dividends		1,000	
	Cash			1,000

- Cash Dividends is a **contra equity** account that is **increasing.**
- Cash is an **asset** account that is decreasing.

6. The corporation closes the Cash Dividends account at the end of the month.

Finally, at the end of the accounting period (in this case a month), there is one final closing entry in addition to the ones you already know for revenue and expense accounts. This closes the Cash Dividends account to Retained Earnings, so ultimately the Retained Earnings account is reduced by the profit paid out to stockholders. The Cash Dividends account balance is set back to zero as a result.

Date	Account		Debit	Credit
6/30	Retained Earnings		1,000	
	Cash Dividends			1,000

- Retained Earnings is an equity account that is decreasing.
- Cash Dividends is an equity account that is decreasing.

The following summarizes the two cash dividends transactions in #5 and #6—paying the dividends and closing the **Cash Dividends** account at the end of the month. If the debit and credit to **Cash Dividends** is struck through since the two combined would result in a balance of zero in the **Cash Dividends** account, you are ultimately left with a debit to **Retained Earnings** (reducing it) and a credit to **Cash** (reducing it) for the payment of a dividend.

JOURNAL

Date	Account		Debit	Credit
6/15	Cash Dividends	x	1,000	
6/30	Retained Earnings	x	1,000	
	Cash Dividends	x		1,000

LEDGER

Credit Cash Dividends					
Date	Item	Debit	Credit	Debit	Credit
6/15		1,000		1,000	
6/30			1,000	0	

1.6 ACCOUNT WRAP-UP

The discussion to this point has included all five types of accounts. Asset, Liability, and Stockholders' Equity are accounts that appear on the balance sheet. Revenue and Expense are accounts reported on the income statement.

There is a hybrid version of these account types called contra accounts. The normal balance of a **contra account** is intentionally the opposite of the normal balance for a particular account classification. For example, a contra asset account has a credit balance instead of the normal debit balance for an asset account. A contra revenue account has a debit balance instead of the normal credit balance for a revenue account. This allows a company to continue to report an original amount by not making any changes directly to an account. Instead, an alternative contra account is used to report any changes. The original account and its contra account(s) are presented together on the financial statements to show original amount, total amount of changes, and the net result of the two (which is called carrying or net amount).

To recap, here is a list of the seven steps in the accounting cycle that we have covered to this point. Assume here that financial statements will be prepared at the end of each month.

Sr. No.	ACTION	WHEN	YOUR JOB
1.	Journalize transactions	Daily	THINK; analyze transactions
2.	Post to ledgers	Daily	COPY from journal; CALCULATE
3.	Income statement	End of month	COPY from ledgers; CALCULATE
4.	Retained earnings statement	End of month	COPY from ledgers and income statement; CALCULATE
5.	Balance sheet	End of month	COPY from ledgers and retained earnings statement; ADD
6.	Journalize closing entries	End of month	THINK; same three entries
7.	Post closing entries to ledgers	End of month	COPY from journal; CALCULATE

The accounting cycle involves numerous steps, yet many of them are simple copying and calculating—procedures that may be tedious, but not difficult. For the seven steps in the accounting cycle discussed so far, five of them primarily involve only copying and/or calculating.

THINKING is involved when making journal entries—you have to analyze what is happening and translate the transaction into accounting language by selecting accounts to debit and credit. You often have to calculate amounts as well. This is involved in steps #1 and #6. However, closing entries are the same three every time, so they should become relatively routine.

The following table summarizes the rules of debit and credit and other facts about the accounts that you know so far:

ACCOUNTS SUMMARY TABLE

ACCOUNT TYPE	ACCOUNTS	TO INCREASE	TO DECREASE	NORMAL BALANCE	FINANCIAL STATEMENT	CLOSE OUT?
Asset	Cash Accounts Receivable Land Truck Equipment Building Furnishings	debit	credit	debit	Balance Sheet	NO
Liability	Accounts Payable Note Payable	credit	debit	credit	Balance Sheet	NO
Stockholders' Equity	Common Stock Retained Earnings	credit	debit	credit	Balance Sheet	NO
Contra Stockholders' Equity	Cash Dividends	credit	debit t	credi	Retained Earnings Statement	NO
Revenue	Fees Earned	credit	debit	credit	Income Statement	YES
Expense	Wages Expense Rent Expense Utilities Expense Supplies Expense Insurance Expense Advertising Expense Maintenance Expense Miscellaneous Expense	debit	credit	debit	Income Statement	YES

1.7 THE ACCOUNTING EQUATION

The accounting equation is the basis for all transactions in accounting. It provides the foundation for the rules of debit and credit in the journalizing process, where for each transaction total debits must equal total credits. As a result, the accounting equation must be in balance at all times for a business' financial records to be correct. It involves the three types of accounts that do not appear on the income statement.

Assets = Liabilities + Stockholders' Equity

Businesses own assets. These may be partially owned by the owners (stockholders) and partially owned by outsiders (debtors).

When you purchase an asset, there are two ways to pay for it—with your own money and with other people's money. This concept is a simple description of the accounting equation.

BUYING A TRUCK

When you buy a truck, you can pay cash for it, as shown in the following journal entry:

Date	Account		Debit	Credit
1/1	Truck		30,000	
	Cash			30,000

If you pay in full, you own the entire vehicle and receive title to it.

Assets = Liabilities + Stockholders' Equity

30,000 = 0 + 30,000

As an alternative, you may purchase the truck by making a down payment for part of its cost and taking out a loan for the remainder. This is summarized by the following journal entry.

Date	Account		Debit	Credit
1/1	Truck		30,000	
	Cash			30,000
	Note Payable			20,000

Assets = Liabilities + Stockholders' Equity

30,000 = 20,000+10,000

This second scenario is a good illustration of the accounting equation using just one asset. The buyer receives the entire asset – the truck. The buyer must pay for this asset. They do so with two forms of payment: their own money (equity) and other people's money (the loan). The combined total of their down payment and the loan equal the cost of the truck.

The asset is the truck, the liability is the loan, and the down payment is the owner's equity.

1.7.1 Accounting Equation Broken Out

Indirectly, revenue and expense accounts are part of this accounting equation since they impact the value of stockholders' equity by affecting the value of **Retained Earnings.**

The **Retained Earnings** account normally has a *credit* balance. Closing entries move the *credit* balances of revenue accounts into **Retained Earnings** and cause that account to increase. Closing entries also transfer the debit balances of expense accounts into **Retained Earnings**, causing it to decrease

EXPANDED ACCOUNTING EQUATION

Assets = Liabilities + Stockholders' Equity
/ \
Common Stock Retained Earnings
/ \
Revenue Expenses

Common Stock plus Retained Earnings equals total stockholders' equity.

1.7.2 Accounting Transaction Grid

The following grid illustrates how familiar transactions for a new business fit into the accounting equation: ASSETS = LIABILITIES + STOCKHOLDERS' EQUITY.

Each transaction in the first column impacts two accounts. For the asset,

liability, and stockholders' equity amounts, positive numbers represent increases and negative amounts indicate decreases. The ending balances prove that total assets of $1,900 (1,500 + 400) equal total liabilities and stockholders' equity of $1,900 (100 +1,000 + 800).

Revenue and expense accounts were used temporarily and were ultimately closed to Retained Earnings. As a result, the income statement account balances were set to zero and the Retained Earnings balance increased by the net income amount of $800.

	Assets		=	Liabilities	+	Stockholders' Equity		Revenue	Expenses	
Issued stock for cash, $1,000	Cash	Accounts Receivable	=	Accounts Payable	+	Common Stock	Retained Earnings	Fees Earned	Rent Expense	Supplies Expense
Paid cash for rent, $700	1,000								(700)	(200)
Sold to customers for cash, $900	(700)							900		
Purchased supplies on account, $200	900			200						
Sold to customers on account, $500		500						500		
Paid cash on account, $200	(200)			(200)						
Purchased supplies on account, $100				100				400		(100)
Sold to customers on account, $400		400								
Received cash on account, $500	500	(500)								
Closed revenue account							1,800	(1,800)		
Closed expense accounts							(1,000)		700	300
Ending balances	1,500			100		1,000	800	0	0	0

1.7.3 Retained Earnings Statement

The retained earnings statement is a report that shows the change in the **Retained Earnings** account balance from the beginning of the month to the end of the month due to net income (or loss) and any cash dividends declared during the accounting period.

Jonick Company Retained Earnings Statement For the Month Ended June 30, 2018		
Ratained earnings, June 1, 208		$30,000
Net Income		
Less: Cash Dividends		
Increase in retained Earning	$13,000	10,000
Retained Earnings, June 30, 2018	3,000	$40,000

Sample Retained Earnings Statement

1. Start with Retained Earnings balance at the beginning of the month.
2. Add net income form the current month's income statement.
3. Subtract from net income any dividends declared during the month.
4. End with new Retained Earnings balance at the end of the month.

Profit is such an important concept in business that two financial statements are devoted to talking about it. The income statement reports net income for one period, such as a month or a year. The retained earnings statement deals with a company's net income over the entire life of the business.

The retained earnings statement is a bridge between the income statement and the balance sheet. The net income amount that appears on the retained earnings statement comes from the income statement ($13,000 in the sample above). The ending retained earnings balance ($40,000 in the sample above) feeds to the stockholders' equity section of the balance sheet.

BALANCING YOUR BANK STATEMENT

The retained earnings statement includes elements similar to those in a monthly bank statement Both statements report a beginning balance, additions, subtractions, and an ending balance.

Bank Statement (tracks your cash)	**Retained Earnings Statement** (tracks a corporation's accumulated profit)
Balance at the beginning of the month **Deposits Withdrawls** Balance at the end of the month	Balance at the beginning of the month **Net Income Dividends** Balance at the end of the month

1.7.4 Balance Sheet

The balance sheet is a report that summarizes a business's financial position as of a specific date. It is the culmination of all the financial information about the business—everything else done in the accounting cycle leads up to it.

The balance sheet is an expanded version of the accounting equation: **Assets = Liabilities + Stockholders' Equity.** The balance sheet lists and summarizes asset, liability, and stockholders' equity accounts and their ledger balances as of a point in time. Assets are listed first. Liabilities and stockholders' equity accounts follow, and these amounts are added together.

The only exception is that the amount reported on the balance sheet for Retained Earnings comes from the ending balance on the retained earnings statement rather than from its ledger. Note that **Cash Dividends** is not listed at all on the balance sheet.

SAMPLE BALANCE SHEET

Jonick Company Balance Sheet June 30, 2018					
ASSETS			**LIABILITIES**		
Cash	$15,000		Accounts payable		$5,000
Accounts receivable	10,000		**STOCKHOLDER'S EQUITY**		
Equipment	5,000		Common stock	$15,000	
Truck	30,000		Retained earnings	40,000	
			Total stockholder's equity		
			Total liabilities and stockholder's equity		55,000
Total Assets		$60,000			$60,000

BALANCE SHEET FORMATTING

- Heading: Company Name, Name of Financial Statement, Date
- Two columns: left for listing items to be subtotaled; right for results Dollar signs go at the top number of a list to be calculated
- Category headings for each account category
- Single underline below a list of numbers to be totaled
- Double underline below the final results (total assets AND Total labilities and stockholders' equity) Dollar sign on final result number

Financial Reporting

The life of an ongoing business can be divided into artificial time periods for the purpose of providing periodic reports on its financial activities.

Financial Statements Connected

Three financial statements are prepared at the end of each accounting period. First, the income statement shows net income for the month. Next, the statement of retained earnings shows the beginning and ending

Retained Earnings balances and the reasons for any change in this balance. Finally, the balance sheet presents asset, liability, and stockholders' equity account balances.

Jonick Company Income Statement For the Month Ended June 30, 2018

Fees Earned		$30,000
Operating Expenses:		
Salaries expense	$2,500	
Wages expense	2,200	
Rent expense	2,000	
Insurance expense	1,900	
Supplies expense	1,800	
Advertising expense	1,700	
Maintenance expense	1,600	
Utilities expense	1,400	
Vehicle expense	1,100	
Miscellaneous expense	800	
Total operation expenses		17,000
Net Income		13,000

Jonick Company Retained Earnings Statement For the Month Ended June 30, 2018

Retained earnings, June 1, 2018			$30,000
Net income	13,000		
Less: cash dividends	3,000		
Increase in retained earnings		10,000	$40,000
Retained earnings, June 30, 2018			$40,000

#1 The income statement is prepared first. It summarizes revenue and expenses for the month. Amounts come from the ledger balances. The result is either net income or net loss.

#2 The retained earnings statement is next. It adjusts the month's beginning retained earnings balance by adding net income from the income statement and subtracting out dividends declared. The net income of $13,000 comes from the income statement. The result is a new retained earnings balance at the end of the month.

#3 The balance sheet is prepared last. It shows assets, liabilities, and stockholders' equity as of the last day of the month. All amounts except retained earnings come from the ledger balances. The Retained Earnings amount comes from the ending amount on the retained earnings statement - in this case $40,000. The balance sheet is an exploded version of the accounting equation!

Jonick Company Balance Sheet June 30, 2018					
ASSETS			**LIABILITIES**		
Cash	$15,000		Accounts payable		$5,000
Accounts receivable	10,000		**STOCKHOLDER'S EQUITY**		
Equipment	5,000		Common stock	$15,000	
Truck	30,000		Retained earnings	40,000	
			Total stockholder's equity		
			Total liabilities and stockholder's equity		55,000
Total Assets		$60,000			$60,000

1.8 CHANGES IN STOCKHOLDERS' EQUITY

Any change in the *Common Stock, Retained Earnings, or Cash Dividends* accounts affects total stockholders' equity.

Common Stock + Retained Earnings = Total Stockholders' Equity

Stockholders' equity increases due to additional stock investments or additional net income. It decreases due to a net loss or dividend payouts. Retained earnings increases when revenue accounts are closed out into it and decreases when expense accounts and cash dividends are closed out into it. The following examples illustrate journal entries that can cause stockholders' equity to change.

1. Stockholders' equity before a business opens:

Date	Account		Debit	Credit

Common Stock + Retained Earnings = Total Stockholders' Equity
0 + 0 = 0

2. Stockholders' equity after 30 stockholders invest $1,000 each, for a total of $30,000:

Date	Account		Debit	Credit
6/1	Cash		30,000	
	Common Stock			30,000

Common Stock + Retained Earnings = Total Stockholders'
Equity 30,000 + 0 = 30,000
Each investor is now worth $1,000 in the business.

3. Stockholders' equity after one month of operations in which Fees Earned is $65,000 and total expenses are $5,000 (so net income is $60,000):

Date	Account		Debit	Credit
6/30	Fees Earned		65,000	
	Retained Earnings			65,000
6/30	Retained Earnings		5,000	
	ALL Expenses			5,000

Common Stock + Retained Earnings = Total Stockholders' Equity
30,000 + 60,000 = 90,000
Each investor is now worth $3,000 in the business.
(The original $1,000 investment plus 1/30th of the $60,000 profit, or $2,000)

4. Stockholders' equity after one month of operations and after each of the thirty investors receives a cash dividend payment of $500:

Date	Account		Debit	Credit
7/10	Retained Earnings		15,000	
	Cash Dividends			15,000

Common Stock + Retained Earnings = Total Stockholders' Equity
30,000 + 45,000 = 75,000
Each investor is now worth $2,500 in the business.
(The original $1,000 plus $2,000 profit - $500 dividends paid out)

Stockholders' equity can **increase** in two ways:

1. Owners invest in stock and Common Stock is credited and increases
2. Business generates net income and Retained Earnings is credited and increases

Stockholders' equity can decrease in two ways:

1. Dividends are paid out and Retained Earnings is debited and decreases
2. Business experiences a loss and Retained Earnings is debited and decreases

The following calculation example shows how stockholders' equity can change from the beginning to the end of an accounting period.

Beginning stockholders' equity	12,000
+ Additional investments in stock	6,000
+ Net income (or – Net loss)	**3,000**
- Dividends	- 1,000
= Ending stockholders' equity	20,000

The calculation below is the same as the one above except that net income is instead presented as revenue minus expenses.

Beginning stockholders' equity	12,000
+ Additional investments in stock	6,000
+ Revenue	**5,000**
- Expenses	**-2,000**
- Dividends	- 1,000
= Ending stockholders' equity	20,000

If net income is not given, you can solve for it algebraically using the calculations above. Assume net income is x in the first calculation above:

Beginning stockholders' equity	12,000
+ Additional investments in stock	6,000
+ Net income (or – Net loss)	**x**
- Dividends	- 1,000
= Ending stockholders' equity	20,000

Beginning stockholders' equity + Additional investments in stock + Net income - Dividends = Ending stockholders' equity

$$12{,}000 + 6{,}000 + x - 1{,}000 = 20{,}000$$
$$x = 20{,}000 - 12{,}000 - 6{,}000 + 1{,}000$$
$$x = 3{,}000$$

The highlighted accounts are the new accounts you have learned.

#1

Jonick Corporation
Income Statement
For the Month Ended June 30, 2014

Operating REVENUES:			
Fees Earned		$200,000	
Sales	$150,000		
Less: Sales returns	10,000		
Less: Sales discounts	5,000		
Net sales	135,000		
Cost of merchandise sold	55,000		
Gross profit		80,000	
Gross operating revenues			$280,000
Operating EXPENSES:			
Salaries expense		$25,000	
Wages expense		22,000	
Rent expense		20,000	
Insurance expense		19,000	
Supplies expense		18,000	
Advertising expense		17,000	
Maintenance expense		16,000	
Depreciation expense		15,000	
Taxes expense		14,000	
Utilities expense		13,000	
Payroll tax expense		12,000	
Bad debt expense		11,000	
Bank card expense		10,000	
Vehicle expense		9,000	
Delivery expense		8,000	
Amortization expense		7,000	
Miscellaneous expense		6,000	
Total operating expenses			242,000
Net income from operations			$38,000
Other revenue and expenses:			
Interest revenue		$5,000	
Interest expense		(4,000)	
Gain on sale of equipment		3,000	
Loss on redemption of bonds		(2,000)	2,000
Net income			$40,000

#3

Jonick Corporation
Balance Sheet
June 30, 2014

ASSETS			
Current assets:			
Cash		$40,000	
Accounts receivable	$28,000		
Less: Allowance for doubtful accounts	3,000	25,000	
Merchandise inventory		60,000	
Supplies		18,000	
Prepaid rent		12,000	
Prepaid insurance		6,000	
Prepaid taxes		4,000	
Note receivable		2,000	
Total current assets			$167,000
Fixed assets:			
Equipment	$16,000		
Less: Accumulated depreciation	2,000	14,000	
Van	30,000		
Less: Accumulated depreciation	5,000	25,000	
Building	200,000		
Less: Accumulated depreciation	70,000	130,000	
Land		110,000	
Total fixed assets			279,000
Intangible assets:			
Patents			14,000
Total assets			$460,000

LIABILITIES			
Current liabilities:			
Accounts payable	$14,000		
Unearned fees	13,000		
Wages payable	12,000		
Salaries payable	11,000		
Taxes payable	10,000		
Interest payable	9,000		
Notes payable	8,000		
Sales tax payable	7,000		
Social security tax payable	6,000		
Medicare tax payable	5,000		
Federal withholding tax payable	4,000		
State withholding tax payable	3,000		
Federal unemployment tax payable	2,000		
State unemployment tax payable	1,000		
Total current liabilities		$105,000	
Long-term liabilities:			
Mortgage note payable	$56,000		
Bonds payable	40,000		
Less: Discount on bonds payable	(6,000)		
Total long-term liabilities		90,000	
Total liabilities			$195,000
STOCKHOLDERS' EQUITY			
Common stock		$80,000	
Paid-in-capital in excess of par - common stock		34,000	
Preferred stock		50,000	
Paid-in-capital in excess of par - preferred stock		18,000	
Paid-in-capital from sale of treasury stock		13,000	
Retained earnings		90,000	
Treasury stock		(20,000)	
Total stockholders' equity			265,000
Total liabilities and stockholders' equity			$460,000

#2

Jonick Corporation
Retained Earnings Statement
For the Month Ended June 30, 2014

Retained earnings, June 1, 2014			$60,000
Net income		$40,000	
Less: Cash dividends	$6,000		
Stock dividends	4,000	10,000	
Increase in retained earnings			30,000
Retained earnings, June 30, 2014			$90,000

LEARNING BY DOING

I learned how to drive a standard transmission car – using a stick shift – in San Francisco. My husband is an expert at this and was in the passenger seat as my instructor. In spite of the fact that he knew how to shift and clutch, and that he was telling me (rather loudly) what to do, I still rolled backward down a hill and over a motorcycle. I can drive a stick shift perfectly fine now, but it took lots of practice and stalling to get the feel of the process.

Accounting is a skills discipline; it is also something you learn by doing. Your instructor may be an expert who explains and demonstrates, but you will only truly understand the process with hands-on practice. You have to learn it by doing it to get the feel of the process. That is how you will become an expert yourself.

1.9 WRAP UP

To this point, you have been introduced to basic concepts that pertain to business and to accounting. You have learned that businesses experience financial transactions that are recorded by selecting accounts and amounts to represent these events and entering them in the journal in chronological order. Journal entries are then copied to the ledgers to reorganize the same information by account. One of the key aspects of the process is maintaining current running balances in all of the ledger accounts. Account balances are then transferred to the income statement, retained earnings statement, and balance sheet for a professional, well-structured summary presentation that is meaningful to those reading the reports. Finally, the temporary revenue, expense, and dividends accounts are closed to Retained Earnings at the end of the accounting period to set their balances back to zero so that the cycle can begin again.

02 Accounting Cycle for the Service Business—Accrual Basis

2.1 ACCRUAL BASIS OF ACCOUNTING

The accrual basis of accounting recognizes economic events when they take place, regardless of when the related cash transactions occur. Revenue is reported in the period in which you earn it, regardless of whether you received the cash for these services yet. Similarly, expenses are reported in the period in which you incur them to produce revenues, whether or not you have paid for these costs yet.

EXAMPLE

I hire you to mow my yard this afternoon and agree to pay you $50. I am not at home when you finish the job, so you leave me a bill in the mailbox. You have EARNED $50 today, even though you have not received the cash payment yet, because you completed the work.

2.2 MATCHING PRINCIPLE

The matching principle relates to income statement accounts. It states that expenses incurred during a period should relate to (or match up with) the revenues earned during the same period. This lets you know how much it cost you to produce the revenue you generated in a given period of time, such as a month.

ANALOGY

You have probably heard that "It takes money to make money." A business person contributes financial resources and hopefully uses them effectively to generate even more value. The matching principle looks at a window of time in terms of how much income came in and how much it cost to generate that income. The key here is the "window of time," such as a month. It compares how much came in in sales in a month vs. how much was spent. Any revenue or expenses before that month or after that month are not considered.

Below is Timeline #1, which includes three months. The red bars represent revenue—three different jobs for $100 each. Job 1 was started in May and completed in June. Job 2 was started in June and completed in June. Job 3 was started in June and was completed in July. There was a total of $300 in revenue from these three jobs, but not all of it is earned in June. As you can see, only half of the revenue from Jobs 1 and 3 was earned in June.

The blue bars represent expenses. Expense 4 began in May and was incurred partially in May and partially in June. Expense 5 began in June and all of this expense was incurred in June. Expense 6 also began in June; some of it was incurred in June and some in July. There was a total of $180 of expenses, but not all of it was incurred in June. As you can see, only half of the expenses from Jobs 1 and 3 was incurred in June.

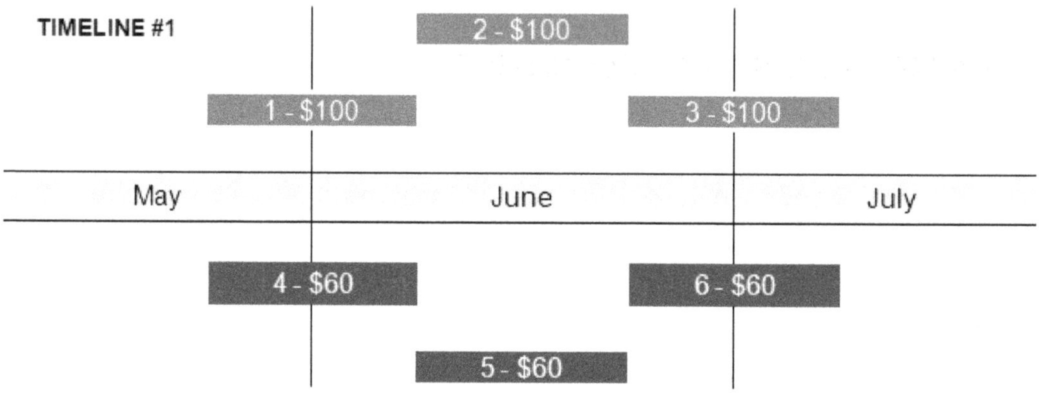

Let's say we want to produce an income statement for June, our window of time. We want to include all the revenue and expenses that occurred in June, but none that occurred in May or July. We have to "chop off" the pieces of these transactions that did not occur in June to be left with only the parts that belong in June.

The result appears in the Timeline #2 below. In June, $200 of revenue ($50 + $100 + $50) was earned and is matched with $120 ($30 + $60 +$30) of expenses that were incurred in the same month. The net income for June, therefore, was

$80 ($200 - $120).

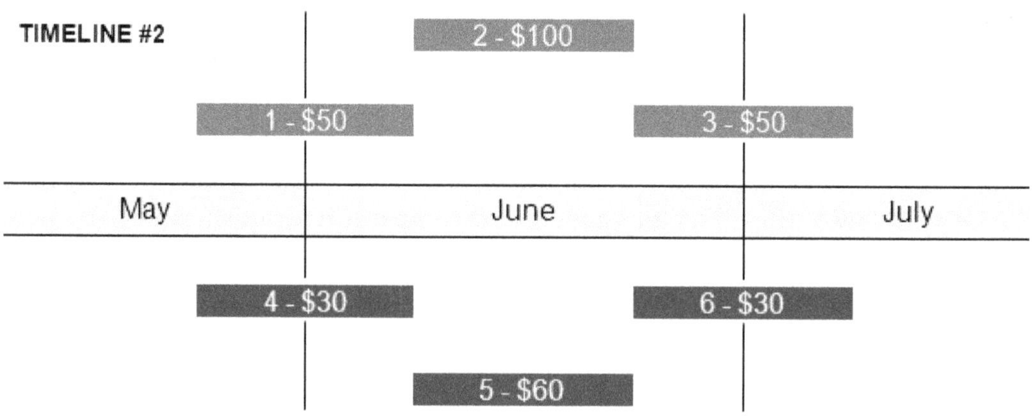

Adjusting entries, discussed next, help do the job of matching the June revenue with the June expenses by "chopping" off amounts of transactions that do not belong in a given month.

2.2.1 Adjusting Entries

Adjusting entries are special entries made just **before** financial statements are prepared—at the end of the month and/or year. They bring the balances of certain accounts up to date if they are not already current to properly match revenues and expenses. So far we have dealt with companies that did not need adjusting entries under the cash basis of accounting. Now we will see situations where they are necessary and will be using the **accrual basis** of accounting.

Many ledger account balances are already correct at the end of the accounting period; however, some account balances may have changed during the period and but have not yet been updated. This is what you will do by making adjusting entries, and this will ensure that your financial statement numbers are current and correct. Adjusting entries are typically necessary for transactions that extend over more than one accounting period—you want to include the part of the transaction that belongs in the one accounting period you are preparing financial statements for and exclude that part that belongs in a previous or future accounting period. This relates to the matching process.

IMPORTANT: Each adjusting entry will always affect at least one income statement account (revenue or expense) and one balance sheet account (asset or liability).

2.2.2 Complete Accounting Cycle

Accounting is a cyclical process. It involves a series of steps that take place in a particular order during a period of time. Once this period of time is over, these same steps are repeated in the next period of time of equal length.

The complete accounting cycle involves these nine steps, done in this order:

S. No.	Action	When	Your Job
1.	Journalize transactions	Daily	THINK
2.	Post to ledgers	Daily	COPY from journal; CALCULATE
3.	**Journalize the adjusting entries**	**End of month**	**THINK**
4.	**Post the adjusting entries**	**End of month**	**COPY from journal; CALCULATE**
5.	Income statement	End of month	COPY from ledgers; CALCULATE
6.	Retained earnings statement	End of month	COPY net income from income statement
7.	Balance sheet	End of month	COPY from ledgers; ADD
8.	Journalize the closing entries	End of month	THINK (same three entries)
9.	Post the closing entries	End of month	COPY from journal; CALCULATE

You have already learned how to complete seven of the steps. The remaining two steps, #3 and #4, are new and involve adjusting entries that update account balances that are not current just before preparing the financial statements.

IMPORTANT: Notice that **adjusting** entries are recorded **BEFORE** the financial statements are prepared and **closing** entries are recorded **AFTER** financial statements are prepared.

2.2.3 Adjusting Entry Accounts

The following list includes accounts whose balances may need to be brought up to date in the 10 adjusting entry transactions we will cover.

ACCOUNTS SUMMARY TABLE

ACCOUNT TYPE	ACCOUNTS	TO INCREASE	TO DECREASE	NORMAL BALANCE	FINANCIAL STATEMENT	CLOSE OUT?
Asset	Accounts Receivable Supplies Prepaid Rent Prepaid Insurance Prepaid Taxes Prepaid ANYTHING	debit	credit	debit	Balance Sheet	NO
Contra Asset	Accumulated Depreciation	credit	debit	credit	Balance Sheet	NO
Liability	Wages Payable Taxes Payable Interest Payable ANY Payable Unearned Fees Unearned Rent Unearned ANYTHING	credit	debit	credit	Balance Sheet	NO
Revenue	Fees Earned Rent Revenue	credit	debit	credit	Income Statement	YES
Expense	Wages Expense Rent Expense Supplies Expense Insurance Expense Depreciation Expense Taxes Expense Interest Expense	debit	credit	debit	Income Statement	YES

From this point we will go into a more detailed discussion of each of these adjusting entries above.

Here are the 10 adjusting entries we will cover.

Date	Account		Debit	Credit
6/30	Supplies Expense		100	
	Supplies			100
6/30	Insurance Expense		100	
	Prepaid Insurance			100
6/30	Rent Expense		100	
	Prepaid Rent			100
6/30	Taxes Expense		100	
	Prepaid Taxes			100
6/30	Depreciation Expense		100	
	Accumulated Depreciation			100
6/30	Unearned Fees		100	
	Fees Earned			100
6/30	Wages Expense		100	
	Wages Payable			100
6/30	Taxes Expense		100	
	Taxes Payable			100
6/30	Interest Expense		100	
	Interest Payable			100
6/30	Accounts Receivable		100	
	Fees Earned			100

- *Supplies Expense* is an **expense** account that is **increasing.**
- *Supplies* is an **asset** account that is **decreasing.**
- *Insurance Expense* is an **expense** account that is **increasing.**
- *Prepaid Insurance* is an **asset** account that is **decreasing.**
- *Rent Expense* is an **expense** account that is **increasing.**
- *Prepaid Rent* is an **asset** account that is **decreasing.**
- *Taxes Expense* is an **expense** account that is **increasing.**
- *Prepaid Taxes* is an **asset** account that is **decreasing**.
- *Depreciation Expense* is an **expense** account that is **increasing.**
- *Accumulated Depreciation* is a **contra asset** account that is **increasing.**
- *Unearned Fees* is a **liability** account that is **decreasing.**
- *Fees Earned* is a **revenue** account that is **increasing.**
- *Wages Expense* is an **expense** account that is **increasing.**
- *Wages Payable* is a **liability** account that is **increasing.**
- *Taxes Expense* is an **expense** account that is **increasing.**
- *Taxes Payable* is a **liability** account that is **increasing.**
- *Interest Expense* is an **expense** account that is **increasing.**
- *Interest Payable* is a **liability** account that is **increasing.**
- *Accounts Receivable* is an **asset** account that is **increasing.**
- *Fees Earned* is a **revenue** account that is **increasing.**

From this point we will go into a more detailed discussion of each of these adjusting entries above.

2.3 ADJUSTING ENTRIES

There are two types of adjusting entries—deferrals and accruals. Deferrals may be either deferred expenses or deferred revenue. Accruals may be either accrued expenses or accrued revenue.

1. Deferred expenses
2. Deferred revenue
3. Accrued expenses
4. Accrued revenue

2.3.1 Adjusting Entries—Deferrals

Deferrals are adjusting entries that update a previous transaction. The first journal entry is a general one; the journal entry that updates an account in this original transaction is an adjusting entry made before preparing financial statements.

Deferrals are adjusting entries for items purchased in advance and used up in the future (deferred expenses) or when cash is received in advance and earned in the future (deferred revenue).

DEFERRED EXPENSES

Deferred expenses require adjusting entries. "Deferred" means "postponed into the future." In this case you have purchased something in "bulk" that will last you longer than one month, such as supplies, insurance, rent, or equipment. Rather than recording the item as an expense when you purchase it, you record it as an asset (something of value to the business) since you will not use it all up within a month. At the end of the month, you make an adjusting entry for the part that you did use up—this is an expense, and you debit the appropriate expense account. The credit part of the adjusting entry is the asset account, whose value is reduced by the amount used up. Any remaining balance in the asset account is what you still have left to use up into the future.

These are the five adjusting entries for deferred expenses we will cover.

Date	Account		Debit	Credit
6/30	Supplies Expense		100	
	Supplies			100
6/30	Insurance Expense		100	
	Prepaid Insurance			100
6/30	Rent Expense		100	
	Prepaid Rent			100
6/30	Taxes Expense		100	
	Prepaid Taxes			100
6/30	Depreciation Expense		100	
	Accumulated Depreciation			100

- *Supplies Expense* is an **expense** account that is **increasing.**
- *Supplies* is an **asset** account that is **decreasing.**
- *Insurance Expense* is an **expense** account that is **increasing.**

- *Prepaid Insurance* is an **asset** account that is **decreasing.**
- *Rent Expense* is an **expense** account that is **increasing.**
- *Prepaid Rent* is an **asset** account that is **decreasing.**
- *Taxes Expense* is an **expense** account that is **increasing.**
- *Prepaid Taxes* is an **asset** account that is **decreasing.**
- *Depreciation Expense* is an **expense** account that is **increasing.**
- *Accumulated Depreciation* is a **contra asset** account that is **increasing.**

These will now each be explained in more detail.

SUPPLIES—DEFERRED EXPENSE

Supplies are relatively inexpensive operating items used to run your business. There are two ways to record the purchase of supplies.

Method #1: A company purchases $100 worth of supplies that will be used up within one month.

Date	Account		Debit	Credit
6/1	Supplies Expense		100	
	Cash			100

- *Supplies Expense* is an **expense** account that is **increasing.**
- *Cash* is an **asset** account that is **decreasing.**

NOTE: The word "expense" implies that the supplies will be used within the month. An expense is a cost of doing business, and it cost $100 in supplies this month to run the business.

Here is the Supplies Expense ledger where transaction above is posted. The $100 balance in the Supplies Expense account will appear on the income statement at the end of the month

Supplies Expense					
Date	**Item**	**Debit**	**Credit**	**Debit**	**Credit**
6/1		100		100	

OR

Method #2: A company purchases $1,000 worth of supplies that will NOT be used up within one month.

If you buy more supplies than you will use in a month (because it is convenient, because you get a good price, etc.), you record the purchase as an asset instead of an expense. New asset account: **Supplies**

Date	Account		Debit	Credit
6/1	Supplies		1,000	
	Cash			1,000

- Supplies is an **asset** account that is **increasing.**
- Cash is an **asset** account that is **decreasing.**

Here are the ledgers that relate to the purchase of supplies when the transaction above is posted.

Supplies					
Date	Item	Debit	Credit	Debit	Credit
6/1		1,000		1,000	

Supplies Expense					
Date	Item	Debit	Credit	Debit	Credit

During the month you will use some of these supplies, but you will wait until the end of the month to account for what you have used.

Let's assume you used $100 of the $1,000 of supplies you purchased on 6/1. If you DON'T "catch up" and adjust for the amount you used, you will show on your balance sheet that you have $1,000 worth of supplies at the end of the month when you actually have only $900 remaining. In addition, on your income statement you will show that you did not use ANY supplies to run the business during the month, when in fact you used $100 worth.

The adjusting entry for supplies updates the **Supplies** and **Supplies Expense** balances to reflect what you really have at the end of the month. The adjusting entry TRANSFERS $100 from **Supplies** to **Supplies Expense.** It is journalized and posted BEFORE financial statements are prepared so that the income statement and balance sheet show the correct, up-to-date amounts.

Date	Account		Debit	Credit
6/30	Supplies Expense		100	
	Supplies			100

- *Supplies Expense* is an **expense** account that is **increasing.**
- Supplies is an **asset** account that is **decreasing.**

NOTE: There are two ways this information can be worded, both resulting in the same adjusting entry above.

1. The company USED $100 of supplies this month. (So $900 worth remains.)
2. The company has $900 of supplies on hand at the end of the month. (So $100 worth was used.)

Here are the **Supplies** and **Supplies Expense** ledgers AFTER the adjusting entry has been posted.

Supplies					
Date	**Item**	**Debit**	**Credit**	**Debit**	**Credit**
6/1		1,000		1,000	
6/30			100	900	

Supplies Expense					
Date	**Item**	**Debit**	**Credit**	**Debit**	**Credit**
6/30		100		100	

The $100 balance in the **Supplies Expense** account will appear on the income statement at the end of the month. The remaining $900 in the **Supplies** account will appear on the balance sheet. This amount is still an asset to the company since it has not been used yet.

Summary

You had purchased supplies during the month and initially recorded them as an asset because they would last for more than one month. By the end of the month you used up some of these supplies, so you reduced the value of this asset to reflect what you actually had on hand at the end of the month ($900). What was used up ($100) became an expense, or cost of doing business, for the month. To transfer what was used, **Supplies Expense** was debited for the amount used and **Supplies** was credited to reduce the asset by the same amount. Any remaining balance in the **Supplies** account is what you have left to use in the future; it continues to be an asset since it is still available.

The adjusting entry ensures that the amount of supplies used appears as a business expense on the income statement, not as an asset on the balance sheet.

IMPORTANT: If this journal entry had been omitted, many errors on the financial statements would result.

1. The **Supplies Expense** amount on the income statement would have been too low ($0 instead of $100).
2. **Net income** on the income statement would have been too high **(Supplies Expense** should have been deducted from revenues but was not).

3. The **Supplies** amount on the balance sheet would have been too high ($1,000 instead of $900).
4. The **total assets** amount on the balance sheet would have been too high because **Supplies,** one asset, was too high.
5. The **total stockholders' equity** amount on the balance sheet would be too high because a **net income** amount that was too high would have been closed out to Retained Earnings.

PREPAID INSURANCE—DEFERRED EXPENSE

Insurance is protection from damages associated with the risks of running a business. There are two ways to record the purchase of insurance.

Method #1: A company purchases $100 worth of insurance that will be used up within one month.

Date	Account		Debit	Credit
6/1	Insurance Expense		100	
	Cash			100

- *Insurance Expense* is an **expense** account that is **increasing.**
- Cash is an **asset** account that is **decreasing.**

NOTE: The word "expense" implies that the insurance will expire, or be used up, within the month. An expense is a cost of doing business, and it cost $100 in insurance this month to run the business.

Here is the **Insurance Expense** ledger where transaction above is posted. The $100 balance in the **Insurance Expense** account will appear on the income statement at the end of the month.

Supplies Expense					
Date	**Item**	**Debit**	**Credit**	**Debit**	**Credit**
6/1		100		100	

OR

Method #2: A company purchases $1,200 worth of insurance that will apply toward the upcoming year (12 months).

If you buy more insurance than you will use in a month (because it is convenient, because you get a good price, etc.), you record the purchase as an asset. New asset account: **Prepaid Insurance**

Date	Account		Debit	Credit
6/1	Prepaid Insurance		1,200	
	Cash			1,200

- Prepaid Insurance is an **asset** account that 6/1 Prepaid Insurance 1,200 is **increasing.**
- *Cash* is an **asset** account that is **decreasing.**

Here are the ledgers that relate to the purchase of prepaid insurance when the transaction above is posted.

Prepaid Insurance					
Date	Item	Debit	Credit	Debit	Credit
6/1		1,200		1,200	

Insurance Expense					
Date	Item	Debit	Credit	Debit	Credit

During the month you will use some of this insurance, but you will wait until the end of the month to account for what has expired.

At the end of the month 1/12 of the prepaid insurance will be used up, and you must account for what has expired. After one month, $100 of the prepaid amount has expired, and you have only 11 months of prepaid insurance left. If you DON'T "catch up" and adjust for the amount you used, you will show on your balance sheet that you have $1,200 worth of prepaid insurance at the end of the month when you actually have only $1,100 remaining. In addition, on your income statement you will show that you did not use ANY insurance to run the business during the month, when in fact you used $100 worth.

The adjusting entry for insurance updates the **Prepaid Insurance** and **Insurance Expense** balances to reflect what you really have at the end of the month. The adjusting entry TRANSFERS $100 from **Prepaid Insurance** to **Insurance Expense.** It is journalized and posted BEFORE financial statements are prepared so that the income statement and balance sheet show the correct, up-to-date amounts

Date	Account		Debit	Credit
6/30	Insurance Expense		100	
	Prepaid Insurance			100

Insurance Expense is an **expense** account that is **increasing.**

Prepaid Insurance is an **asset** Prepaid Insurance 100 account that is **decreasing.**

NOTE: There are two ways this information can be worded, both resulting in the same adjusting entry above.

1. The amount of insurance expired (used) this month is $100. (So $1,100 worth remains.)
2. The amount of unexpired insurance is $1,100. (So $100 worth was used.)

Here are the **Prepaid Insurance** and **Insurance Expense** ledgers AFTER the adjusting entry has been posted.

Prepaid Insurance					
Date	Item	Debit	Credit	Debit	Credit
6/1		1,200		1,200	
6/30			100	1,100	

Insurance Expense					
Date	Item	Debit	Credit	Debit	Credit
6/30		100		100	

The $100 balance in the **Insurance Expense** account will appear on the income statement at the end of the month. The remaining $1,100 in the **Prepaid Insurance** account will appear on the balance sheet. This amount is still an asset to the company since it has not expired yet.

The same adjusting entry above will be made at the end of the month for 12 months to bring the **Prepaid Insurance** amount down by $100 each month. Here is an example of the **Prepaid Insurance** account balance at the end of October.

Prepaid Insurance					
Date	Item	Debit	Credit	Debit	Credit
6/1		1,200		1,200	
6/30			100	1,100	
7/31			100	1,000	
8/31			100	900	
9/30			100	800	
10/31			100	700	

After 12 full months, at the end of May in the year after the insurance was initially purchased, all of the prepaid insurance will have expired. If the company would still like to be covered by insurance, it will have to purchase more.

Summary

You prepaid a one-year insurance policy during the month and initially recorded it as an asset because it would last for more than one month. By the end of the month some of the insurance expired, so you reduced the value of this asset to reflect what you actually had on hand at the end of the month ($1,100). What was expired ($100) became an expense. To transfer what expired, **Insurance Expense** was debited for the amount *used* and *Prepaid Insurance* was credited to reduce the asset by the same amount. Any remaining balance in the **Prepaid Insurance** account is what you have left to use in the future; it continues to be an asset since it is still available.

The adjusting entry ensures that the amount of insurance expired appears as a business expense on the income statement, not as an asset on the balance sheet.

IMPORTANT: If this journal entry had been omitted, many errors on the financial statements would result.

1. The **Insurance Expense** amount on the income statement would have been too low ($0 instead of $100).
2. **Net income** on the income statement would have been too high **(Insurance Expense** should have been deducted from revenues but was not).
3. The **Prepaid Insurance** amount on the balance sheet would have been too high ($1,200 instead of $1,100).
4. The **total assets** amount on the balance sheet would have been too high because **Prepaid Insurance,** one asset, was too high.
5. The **total stockholders' equity** amount on the balance sheet would be too high because a **net income** amount that was too high would have been closed out to Retained Earnings.

PREPAID RENT—DEFERRED EXPENSE

Rent is the right to occupy the premises owned by another party. There are two ways to record the payment of rent.

Method #1: A company pays $1,000 worth of rent that will be used up within one month.

Date	Account		Debit	Credit
6/1	Rent Expense		1,000	
	Cash			1,000

- Rent **Expense** is an expense account that is **increasing.**
- Cash is an **asset** account that is **decreasing.**

NOTE: The word "expense" implies that the rent will expire, or be used up, within the month. An expense is a cost of doing business, and it cost $1,000 in rent this month to run the business.

Here is the **Rent Expense** ledger where transaction above is posted. The $1,000 balance in the **Rent Expense** account will appear on the income statement at the end of the month.

Rent Expense					
Date	Item	Debit	Credit	Debit	Credit
6/1		1,000		1,000	

OR

Method #2: A company prepays $12,000 worth of rent that will apply toward the upcoming year (12 months).

If you pay for more rent than you will use in a month (because it is convenient, because you get a good price, etc.), you record the payment as an asset New asset account: **Prepaid Rent**

Date	Account		Debit	Credit
6/1	Prepaid Rent		12,000	
	Cash			12,000

- *Prepaid Rent* is an **asset** account that is **increasing.**
- *Cash* is an **asset** account that is **decreasing.**

Here are the ledgers that relate to the purchase of prepaid rent when the transaction above is posted.

Prepaid Insurance					
Date	Item	Debit	Credit	Debit	Credit
6/1		12,000		12,000	

Insurance Expense					
Date	Item	Debit	Credit	Debit	Credit

During the month you will use some of this rent, but you will wait until the end of the month to account for what has expired.

At the end of the month 1/12 of the prepaid rent will be used up, and you must account for what has expired. After one month, $1,000 of the prepaid amount has expired, and you have only 11 months of prepaid rent left. If you DON'T "catch up" and adjust for the amount you used, you will show on your balance sheet that you have $12,000 worth of prepaid rent at the end of the month when you actually have only $11,000 remaining. In addition, on your income statement you will show that you did not use ANY rent to run the business during the month, when in fact you used $1,000 worth.

The adjusting entry for rent updates the **Prepaid Rent** and **Rent Expense** balances to reflect what you really have at the end of the month. The adjusting entry TRANSFERS $1,000 from **Prepaid Rent** to **Rent Expense.** It is journalized and posted BEFORE financial statements are prepared so that the income statement and balance sheet show the correct, up-to-date amounts.

ADJUSTING ENTRY				
Date	**Account**		**Debit**	**Credit**
6/30	Rent Expense		1,000	
	Prepaid Rent			1,000

- *Rent Expense* is an **expense** account that is **increasing.**
- *Prepaid Rent* is an **asset** account that is **decreasing.**

NOTE: There are two ways this information can be worded, both resulting in the same adjusting entry above.

1. The amount of rent expired (used) this month is $1,000. (So $11,000 worth remains.)
2. The amount of unexpired rent is $11,000. (So $1,000 worth was used.)

Here are the Prepaid Rent and Rent Expense ledgers AFTER the adjusting entry has been posted.

Prepaid Rent					
Date	**Item**	**Debit**	**Credit**	**Debit**	**Credit**
6/1		12,000		12,000	
6/30			1,000	11,000	

Rent Expense					
Date	**Item**	**Debit**	**Credit**	**Debit**	**Credit**
6/30		1,000		1,000	

The $1,000 balance in the **Rent Expense** account will appear on the income statement at the end of the month. The remaining $11,000 in the **Prepaid Rent** account will appear on the balance sheet. This amount is still an asset to the company since it has not expired yet.

The same adjusting entry above will be made at the end of the month for 12 months to bring the **Prepaid Rent** amount down by $1,000 each month. Here is an example of the **Prepaid Rent** account balance at the end of October.

Rent Expense					
Date	**Item**	**Debit**	**Credit**	**Debit**	**Credit**
6/1		12,000		12,000	
6/30			1,000	11,000	

Rent Expense					
Date	**Item**	**Debit**	**Credit**	**Debit**	**Credit**
7/31			1,000	10,000	
8/31			1,000	9,000	
9/30			1,000	8,000	
10/31			1,000	7,000	

After 12 full months, at the end of May in the year after the rent was initially purchased, all of the prepaid rent will have expired. If the company would like to continue to occupy the rental property, it will have to prepay again.

Summary

You prepaid a one-year rent policy during the month and initially recorded it as an asset because it would last for more than one month. By the end of the month some of the prepaid rent expired, so you reduced the value of this asset to reflect what you actually had on hand at the end of the month ($11,000). What was expired ($1,000) became an expense. To transfer what expired, **Rent Expense** was debited for the amount *used* and **Prepaid Rent** was credited to reduce the asset by the same amount. Any remaining balance in the **Prepaid Rent** account is what you have left to use in the future; it continues to be an asset since it is still available.

The adjusting entry ensures that the amount of rent expired appears as a business expense on the income statement, not as an asset on the balance sheet.

IMPORTANT: If this journal entry had been omitted, many errors on the financial statements would result.

1. The **Rent Expense** amount on the income statement would have been too low ($0 instead of $1,000).
2. **Net income** on the income statement would have been too high **(Rent Expense** should have been deducted from revenues but was not).
3. The **Prepaid Rent** amount on the balance sheet would have been too high ($12,000 instead of $11,000).
4. The **total assets** amount on the balance sheet would have been too high because **Prepaid Rent,** one asset, was too high.
5. The **total stockholders' equity** amount on the balance sheet would be too high because a net income amount that was too high would have been closed out to Retained Earnings.

BUSINESS LICENSE TAX—DEFERRED EXPENSE

A business license is a right to do business in a particular jurisdiction and is considered a tax. There are two ways to record the payment of this tax.

Method #1: The company is charged $100 per month by the county licensure department.

The word "expense" implies that the taxes will expire, or be used up, within the month. An expense is a cost of doing business, and it cost $100 in business license taxes this month to run the business.

Date	Account		Debit	Credit
6/1	Taxes Expense		100	
	Cash			100

- *Taxes Expense* is an **expense** account that is **increasing.**
- *Cash* is an **asset** account that is **decreasing.**

Here is the **Taxes Expense** ledger where transaction above is posted. The $100 balance in the **Taxes Expense** account will appear on the income statement at the end of the month.

Rent Expense					
Date	**Item**	**Debit**	**Credit**	**Debit**	**Credit**
6/1		100		100	

OR

Method #2: The company prepays $1,200 worth of taxes that will apply toward the upcoming year (12 months).

If prepay for your business license for the year, you record the payment as an asset. New asset account: **Prepaid Taxes**

Date	Account		Debit	Credit
6/1	Prepaid Taxes		1,200	
	Cash			1,200

- *Prepaid Taxes* is an **asset** account that is **increasing.**
- *Cash* is an **asset** account that is **decreasing.**

Here are the ledgers that relate to the purchase of prepaid taxes when the transaction above is posted.

Prepaid Taxes					
Date	Item	Debit	Credit	Debit	Credit
6/1		1,200		1,200	

Taxes Expense					
Date	Item	Debit	Credit	Debit	Credit

During the month you will use some of these taxes, but you will wait until the end of the month to account for what has expired.

At the end of the month 1/12 of the prepaid taxes will be used up, and you must account for what has expired. After one month, $100 of the prepaid amount has expired, and you have only 11 months of prepaid taxes left. If you DON'T "catch up" and adjust for the amount you used, you will show on your balance sheet that you have $1,200 worth of prepaid taxes at the end of the month when you actually have only $1,100 remaining. In addition, on your income statement you will show that you did not pay ANY taxes to run the business during the month, when in fact you paid $100.

The adjusting entry for taxes updates the **Prepaid Taxes** and **Taxes Expense** balances to reflect what you really have at the end of the month. The adjusting entry TRANSFERS $100 from **Prepaid Taxes** to **Taxes Expense.** It is journalized and posted BEFORE financial statements are prepared so that the income statement and balance sheet show the correct, up-to-date amounts.

Date	Account		Debit	Credit
6/30	Taxes Expense		100	
	Prepaid Taxes			100

- *Taxes Expense* is an **expense** account that is **increasing.**
- *Prepaid Taxes* is an **asset** account that is **decreasing.**
- NOTE: There are two ways this information can be worded, both resulting in the same adjusting entry above.

1. The amount of taxes expired (used) this month is $100. (So $1,100 worth remains.)
2. The amount of unexpired taxes is $1,100. (So $100 worth was used.)

Here are the **Prepaid Taxes** and **Taxes Expense** ledgers AFTER the adjusting entry has been posted.

Prepaid Taxes					
Date	**Item**	**Debit**	**Credit**	**Debit**	**Credit**
6/1		1,200		1,200	
6/30			100	1,100	

Taxes Expense					
Date	**Item**	**Debit**	**Credit**	**Debit**	**Credit**
6/30		100		100	

The $100 balance in the **Taxes Expense** account will appear on the income statement at the end of the month. The remaining $1,100 in the **Prepaid Taxes** account will appear on the balance sheet. This amount is still an asset to the company since it has not expired yet.

The same adjusting entry above will be made at the end of the month for 12 months to bring the **Prepaid Taxes** amount down by $100 each month. Here is an example of the **Prepaid Taxes** account balance at the end of October.

Prepaid Taxes					
Date	**Item**	**Debit**	**Credit**	**Debit**	**Credit**
6/1		1,200		1,200	
6/30			100	1,100	
7/31			100	1,000	
8/31			100	900	
9/30			100	800	
10/31			100	700	

After 12 full months, at the end of May in the year after the business license was initially purchased, all of the prepaid taxes will have expired. If the company would like to continue to do business in the upcoming year, it will have to prepay again.

Summary

You prepaid for a one-year business license during the month and initially recorded it as an asset because it would last for more than one month. By the end of the month some of the prepaid taxes expired, so you reduced the value of this asset to reflect what you actually had on hand at the end of the month ($1,100). What was expired ($100) became an expense. To transfer what expired, **Taxes Expense** was debited for the amount *used* and **Prepaid Taxes** was credited to reduce the asset by the same amount. Any remaining balance in the **Prepaid Taxes** account is what you have left to use in the future; it continues to be an asset since it is still available.

The adjusting entry ensures that the amount of taxes expired appears as a business expense on the income statement, not as an asset on the balance sheet.

IMPORTANT: If this journal entry had been omitted, many errors on the financial statements would result.

1. The **Taxes Expense** amount on the income statement would have been too low ($0 instead of $100).
2. **Net income** on the income statement would have been too high (Taxes Expense should have been deducted from revenues but was not).
3. **The Prepaid** Taxes amount on the balance sheet would have been too high ($1,200 instead of $1,100).
4. The **total assets** amount on the balance sheet would have been too high because **Prepaid Taxes,** one asset, was too high.
5. The **total stockholders' equity** amount on the balance sheet would be too high because a **net income** amount that was too high would have been closed out to Retained Earnings.

EXAMPLE

Prepayments are common in business. As a college student, you have likely been involved in making a prepayment for a service you will receive in the future. When you paid your tuition for the semester, you paid "up front" for about three months of service (the courses you are taking!) As each month you attend class passes, you have one fewer month to go in terms of what you paid for. If you want to attend school after the semester is over, you have to prepay again for the next semester.

The payment arrangement could be different. Your college could ask for four years' tuition before you take your first class. Can you see this would be unrealistic? Alternatively, the college could ask for no payment up front at all and just charge a $10 cover charge as students arrive each day, stationing a bouncer at each classroom door. Equally unreasonable? Finally, the college could wait until the semester is over and collect all the tuition at the end. Craziest plan of all?

The point is that a business has to select payment options that are reasonable and appropriate for their situations and circumstances and require payments in reasonable increments. What is suitable for one type of business may not work for another.

FIXED ASSETS—DEFERRED EXPENSE

A fixed asset is a tangible/physical item owned by a business that is relatively expensive and has a permanent or long life—more than one year. Examples are equipment, furnishings, vehicles, buildings, and land. Each of these is recorded as an asset at the time it is purchased. Its initial value, and the amount in the journal entry for the purchase, is what it costs.

Example Journal Entry: A company purchased equipment that cost $6,000, paying cash. It is expected to last five years—its useful life.

Date	Account		Debit	Credit
1/1	Equipment		6,000	
	Cash			6,000

- *Equipment* is an **asset** account that is **increasing.**
- *Cash* is an **asset** account that is **decreasing.**

Although fixed assets cost a company money, they are not initially recorded as expenses. (Notice in the journal entry above that the debit account is "Equipment," NOT "Equipment Expense"). Fixed assets are first recorded as assets that later are gradually "expensed off," or claimed as a business expense, over time.

The process of "expensing off" the cost of a fixed asset as it is "used up" over its estimated useful life is depreciation. (NOTE: Land is property that does not "get used up;" therefore it is not depreciated.)

Example

In this case, assume that the equipment depreciates at a rate of $100 per month, which is determined by dividing its cost of $6,000 by 60 months (five years). After one month, the equipment is no longer worth $6,000. It has lost $100 of its initial value, so it is now worth only $5,900. An adjusting entry must be made to recognize this loss of value.

Although supplies is not directly related to fixed assets, it may help to remember the adjusting entry for using up supplies in a month:

Date	Account		Debit	Credit
1/31	Supplies Expense		100	
	Supplies			100

- *Supplies Expense* is an **expense** account that is **increasing.**
- *Supplies* is an **asset** account that is **decreasing.**

If we "expensed" off equipment in a similar way, the journal entry would look like this:

Date	Account		Debit	Credit
1/31	Equipment Expense		100	
	Equipment			100

- *Equipment Expense* is an **expense** account that is **increasing.**
- *Equipment* is an **asset** account that is **decreasing.**

It makes sense since it follows the same pattern as supplies. In theory, it does do the job. **However, the items in red are considered incorrect.** There are two changes that will be made so that the journal entry is CORRECT for depreciation.

1. Equipment Expense may be a valid account, but it is not used for depreciation. It might instead be used for costs associated with owning and running the equipment, such as maintenance, oil, parts, etc. To recognize part of ANY fixed asset's cost as a business expense, use **Depreciation Expense** (not Equipment Expense).
2. In accounting, the **cost principle** requires that a fixed asset's ledger balance be the cost of the asset, or what was paid for it. In this example it means that we are not allowed to credit the **Equipment** account to reduce its balance from $6,000 to the updated $5,900. Its balance must stay at $6,000.
3. Therefore, we will credit a different account instead since we require a credit account to complete the entry. This account is Accumulated Depreciation. **Accumulated Depreciation is a contra asset** account that appears on the balance sheet with a credit balance under the particular asset it relates to (which has a debit balance). This account is used as a substitute for the fixed asset account, which cannot be credited for the depreciation amount since the asset's balance must always be its cost.

The following is the **CORRECT** monthly adjusting entry for the depreciation of a fixed asset:

ADJUSTING ENTRY				
Date	**Account**		**Debit**	**Credit**
1/31	Depreciation Expense		100	
	Accumulated Depreciation			100

- *Depreciation Expense* is an **expense** account that is **increasing.**
- *Acc. Depreciation* is a contra **asset** account that is **increasing.**

Notice that **Depreciation Expense** substitutes for Equipment Expense, and **Accumulated Depreciation** substitutes for Equipment.

Here are the **Equipment, Accumulated Depreciation,** and **Depreciation Expense** account ledgers AFTER the adjusting entry above has been posted.

Equipment					
Date	**Item**	**Debit**	**Credit**	**Debit**	**Credit**
1/1		6,000		6,000	

Accumulated Depreciation					
Date	Item	Debit	Credit	Debit	Credit
1/31	Adjusting		100		100

Depreciation Expense					
Date	Item	Debit	Credit	Debit	Credit
1/31	Adjusting	100		100	

Since the **Accumulated Depreciation** account was credited in the adjusting entry rather than the **Equipment** account directly, the **Equipment** account balance remains at $6,000, its cost. The adjusting entry above is made at the end of each month for 60 months.

Book Value is what a fixed asset is currently worth, calculated by subtracting an asset's **Accumulated Depreciation** balance from its cost. This calculation is reported on the balance sheet.

At the end of	Cost	-	Accumulated Depreciation	=	Book Value
1 month	$ 6,000		$ 100		$ 5,900
2 months	6,000		200		5,800
3 months	6,000		300		5,700
12 months	6,000		1,200		4,800
59 months	6,000		5,900		100
60 months	6,000		6,000		0
66 months	6,000		6,000		0

Accumulated Depreciation appears in the asset section of the balance sheet, so it is not closed out at the end of the month. Instead, its balance increases $100 each month. Here is its ledger after three months.

Accumulated Depreciation					
Date	Item	Debit	Credit	Debit	Credit
1/31			100		100
2/28			100		200
3/31			100		300

Here is the balance sheet presentation after three months:

Equipment	$ 6,000
Less: Accumulated depreciation	300
	$ 5,700

The adjusting entries split the cost of the equipment into two categories. The **Accumulated Depreciation** account balance is the amount of the asset that is "used up." The **book value** is the amount of value remaining on the asset. As each month passes, the **Accumulated Depreciation** account balance increases and, therefore, the book value decreases.

After 60 months, the balance in the **Accumulated Depreciation** account is $6,000 and therefore the equipment is fully depreciated and has no value. However, the business may continue to own and use the equipment. It just will not report any value for it on the balance sheet. After the asset is fully depreciated, no further adjusting entries are made for depreciation no matter how long the company owns the asset.

Here is calculation of the book value after 60 months:

Equipment	$ 6,000
Less: Accumulated depreciation	6,000
	$ 0

2.4 ADJUSTING ENTRIES—DEFERRALS

Deferrals are adjusting entries that update a previous transaction. The first journal entry is a general one; the journal entry that updates an account in this original transaction is an adjusting entry made before preparing financial statements. Deferrals are adjusting entries for items purchased in advance and used up in the future (deferred expenses) or when cash is received in advance and earned in the future (deferred revenue).

2.4.1 Deferred Revenue

Deferred revenues require adjusting entries. "Deferred" means "postponed into the future." In this case a customer has paid you in advance for a service you will perform in the future. (Think of a gift card you issue to a customer.) When you receive the cash, you debit the **Cash** account. However, you cannot credit your revenue, or **Fees Earned,** account at that point because you have not yet earned the money. Instead you credit **Unearned Fees,** which is a liability account, to recognize that you owe the customer a certain dollar amount of service.

At the end of the month, you make an adjusting entry for the part of that pre-payment that you did earn because you did do some of the work for the customer during the month. At this time you debit **Unearned Fees** for the amount of service provided, which reduces what you owe the customer. The credit part of the adjusting entry is the revenue account, whose value is increased by the amount earned. Any remaining balance in the liability account is what you still owe and have left to earn in the future.

These are the two adjusting entries for deferred revenue we will cover.

Date	Account		Debit	Credit
6/30	Unearned Fees		100	
	Fees Earned			100
6/30	Unearned Rent		100	
	Rent Revenue			100

- *Unearned Fees* is a **liability** account that is **decreasing.**
- *Fees Earned* is a **revenue** account that is **increasing.**
- *Unearned Rent* is a **liability** account that is **decreasing.**
- *Rent Revenue* is a **revenue** account that is **increasing.**

Both transactions above for deferred revenue are essentially the same, so the discussion will cover only the first one. The difference is that a landlord who deals in rent may prefer to name the accounts to better suit the rental income business.

EXAMPLE

Here is a simple example to understand deferred revenue. Assume you are a hair stylist.

Customer A comes in and you cut her hair. She pays you $30 cash. This is similar to the first example discussed.

Customer B comes in and buys a gift card for $100 to give to her mother as a birthday present. At this point you have the cash but have not given any service in return. You owe the mother $100 worth of hair styling.

Customer B's mother comes in at a later date and you cut and style her hair for $40. You don't collect any cash since she gives you the gift card. You reduce what you owe her by $40 for the work performed that day - you have now earned that $40. You still owe her service, but now you only owe $60 instead of $100. This is a form of deferred revenue.

UNEARNED FEES—DEFERRED REVENUE

When a customer pre-pays a company for a service that the company will perform in the future, the company experiences deferred revenue.

Fees are amounts that a company charges customers for performing services for them. A customer may pay the company immediately after the job is complete.

Method #1: A company completes a job for a customer and receives $600 cash.

The word "revenue" implies that the company has completed work for a customer. Fees Earned is an account that keeps track of sales to customers.

Date	Account		Debit	Credit
6/1	Cash		600	
	Fees Earned			600

- *Cash* is an asset account that is **increasing.**
- *Fees Earned* is a **revenue** account that is **increasing.**

Here is the **Fees Earned** ledger where transaction above is posted. The $600 balance in the **Fees Earned** account will appear on the income statement at the end of the month.

Fees Earned					
Date	Item	Debit	Credit	Debit	Credit
6/1			600		600

OR

Method #2: A customer prepays a company $1,000 for a job that the company will complete in the future.

If the customer pays in full before the company begins the job, the company records the receipt of cash as a liability since it now owes service in the future. The company cannot credit **Fees Earned** yet because it has not performed the work or earned the cash. New liability account: **Unearned Fees.**

Date	Account		Debit	Credit
6/1	Cash		1,000	
	Unearned Fees			1,000

- *Cash* is an **asset** account that is increasing.
- *Unearned Fees* is a **liability** account that is **increasing.**

Here are the ledgers that relate to a prepayment for a service when the transaction above is posted.

Unearned Fees					
Date	Item	Debit	Credit	Debit	Credit
6/1			1,000		1,000

Fees Earned					
Date	Item	Debit	Credit	Debit	Credit

During the month the company may earn some, but not all, of the cash that was prepaid if it performs some of the work for the customer but does not yet complete the job entirely. The company will wait until the end of the month to account for what it has earned. Let's assume it earned $600 of the $1,000 that was prepaid. If the company DOES NOT "catch up" and adjust for the amount it earned, it will show on the balance sheet that it has $1,000 of service still due to the customer at the end of the month when it actually has only $400 still owed. In addition, on the income statement it will show that it did not earn ANY of the prepaid amount when in fact the company earned $600 of it.

The adjusting entry for deferred revenue updates the **Unearned Fees** and **Fees Earned** balances so they are accurate at the end of the month. The adjusting entry is journalized and posted BEFORE financial statements are prepared so that the company's income statement and balance sheet show the correct, up-to- date amounts.

ADJUSTING ENTRY				
Date	Account		Debit	Credit
6/30	Unearned Fees		600	
	Fees Earned			600

- *Unearned Fees* is a **liability** account that is **decreasing.**
- *Fees Earned* is a **revenue** account that is **increasing.**

NOTE: There are two ways this information can be worded, both resulting in the same adjusting entry above.

1. The company earned $600 of the amount the customer prepaid. (So $400 of service is owed.)
2. The amount of unearned fees at the end of the month is $400. (So $600 worth was earned.)

Here are the ledgers that relate to a prepayment for a service when the transaction above is posted.

Unearned Fees					
Date	Item	Debit	Credit	Debit	Credit
6/1			1,000		1,000
6/30		600			400

Fees Earned					
Date	Item	Debit	Credit	Debit	Credit
6/30			600		600

The adjusting entry transfers $600 from the "unearned category" into the "earned category." The $600 will become part of the balance in the Fees Earned account on the income statement at the end of the month. The remaining $400 in the Unearned Fees account will appear on the balance sheet. This amount is still a liability to the company since it has not been earned yet.

Summary

You accepted cash in advance of doing a job during the month and initially recorded it as a liability. By the end of the month you earned some of this prepaid amount, so you reduced the value of this liability to reflect what you actually earned by the end of the month. What was earned became revenue. To do this, Unearned Fees was debited for the amount earned and Fees Earned was credited to increase revenue by the same amount. Any remaining balance in the Unearned Fees account is what you still owe in service in the future; it continues to be a liability until it is earned.

The adjusting entry ensures that the correct amount of revenue earned appears on the income statement, not as a liability on the balance sheet.

IMPORTANT: If this journal entry had been omitted, many errors on the financial statements would result.

1. The **Fees Earned** amount on the income statement would have been too low by $600.
2. Net Income on the income statement would have been too low (this revenue should have been included but was not).
3. The **Unearned Fees** amount on the balance sheet would have been too high ($1,000 instead of $400).
4. The total liabilities amount on the balance sheet would have been too high because **Unearned Fees,** one liability, was too high.
5. The **total stockholders' equity** amount on the balance sheet would be too low because a **net income** that was too low amount would have been closed out to Retained Earnings.

2.4.2 Summary of Revenues

There are three points in time: past, present, and future. There are also only possible debit accounts when **Fees Earned** is credited, reflecting these different points in time. All three are possible ways business can be conducted.

PAST – Cash was received before the services are provided.

Unearned Fees is debited when work is completed.

Date	Account		Debit	Credit
6/30	Unearned Fees		600	
	Fees Earned			600

- *Unearned Fees* is a **liability** account that is **decreasing.**
- *Fees Earned* is a **revenue** account that is **increasing.**

PRESENT – Cash is received when the services are provided.

Cash is debited when work is completed.

Date	Account		Debit	Credit
6/30	Cash		600	
	Fees Earned			600

- *Cash* is an **asset** account that is **increasing.**
- *Fees Earned* is a **revenue** account that is **increasing.**

FUTURE – Cash will be received after the services are provided.

Accounts Receivable is debited when work is completed.

Date	Account		Debit	Credit
6/30	Accounts Receivable		600	
	Fees Earned			600

- *Accounts Receivable* is an **asset** account that is **increasing.**
- *Fees Earned* is a **revenue** account that is **increasing.**

2.4.3 Adjusting Entries

There are two types of adjusting entries—deferrals and accruals. Deferrals may be either deferred expenses or deferred revenue. Accruals may be either accrued expenses or accrued revenue.

2.5 ADJUSTING ENTRIES—ACCRUALS

Accrue means "to grow over time" or "accumulate." Accruals are adjusting entries that record transactions in progress that otherwise would not be recorded because they are not yet complete. Because they are still in progress, but no journal entry has been made yet. Adjusting entries are made to ensure that the part that has occurred during a particular month appears on that same month's financial statements.

2.5.1 Accrued Expenses

Accrued expenses require adjusting entries. In this case someone is already performing a service for you but you have not paid them or recorded any journal entry yet. The transaction is in progress, and the expense is building up (like a "tab"), but nothing has been written down yet. This may occur with employee wages, property taxes, and interest—what you owe is growing over time, but you typically don't record a journal entry until you incur the full expense. However, if the end of an accounting period arrives before you record any of these growing expenses, you will make an adjusting entry to include the part of the expense that belongs in that period and on that period's financial statements. For the adjusting entry, you debit the appropriate expense account for the amount you owe through the end of the accounting period so this expense appears on your income statement. You credit an appropriate payable, or liability account, to indicate on your balance sheet that you owe this amount.

These are the three adjusting entries for accrued expenses we will cover.

Date	Account		Debit	Credit
6/30	Wages Expense		100	
	Wages Payable			100
6/30	Taxes Expense		100	
	Taxes Payable			100
6/30	Interest Expense		100	
	Interest Payable			100

- *Wages Expense* is an **expense** account that is **increasing.**
- *Wages Payable* is a **liability** account that is **increasing.**
- *Taxes Expense* is an **expense** account that is **increasing.**
- *Taxes Payable* is a **liability** account that is **increasing.**
- *Interest Expense* is an **expense** account that is **increasing.**
- *Interest Payable* is a **liability** account that is **increasing.**

WAGES—ACCRUED EXPENSE

Wages are payments to employees for work they perform on an hourly basis.

General journal entry: A company pays employees $1,000 every Friday for a five-day work week.

Date	Account		Debit	Credit
6/5	Wages Expense		1,000	
	Cash			1,000

- *Wages Expense* is an **expense** account that is **increasing.**
- *Cash* is an **asset** account that is **decreasing.**

Here is the **Wages Expense** ledger where transaction above is posted. Assume the transaction above was recorded four times for each Friday in June. The $4,000 balance in the **Wages Expense** account will appear on the income statement at the end of the month.

Wages Expense					
Date	**Item**	**Debit**	**Credit**	**Debit**	**Credit**
6/5		1,000		1,000	
6/12		1,000		2,000	
6/19		1,000		3,000	
6/26		1,000		4,000	

NOTE: An expense is a cost of doing business, and it cost $4,000 in wages this month to run the business.

Adjusting journal entry: Assume that June 30, the last day of the month, is a Tuesday. The Friday after, when the company will pay employees next, is July 3. Employees earn $1,000 per week, or $200 per day. Therefore, for this week, $400 of the $1,000 for the week should be a June expense and the other $600 should be a July expense.

An adjusting entry is required on June 30 so that the wages expense incurred on June 29 and June 30 appears on the June income statement. This entry splits the wages expense for that week: two days belong in June, and the other three days belong in July. Wages Expense is debited on 6/30, but Cash cannot be credited since 6/30 is a Tuesday and employees will not be paid until Friday. New liability account: **Wages Payable.**

ADJUSTING ENTRY				
Date	**Account**		**Debit**	**Credit**
6/30	Wages Expense		400	
	Wages Payable			400

- *Wages Expense* is an **expense** account that is **increasing.**
- *Wages Payable* is a **liability** account that is **increasing.**

Here are the **Wages Payable** and **Wages Expense** ledgers AFTER the adjusting entry has been posted.

Wages Payable					
Date	Item	Debit	Credit	Debit	Credit
6/30			400		400

Wages Expense					
Date	Item	Debit	Credit	Debit	Credit
6/5		1,000		1,000	
6/12		1,000		2,000	
6/19		1,000		3,000	
6/26		1,000		4,000	
6/30		400		4,400	

The adjusting entry for an accrued expense updates the **Wages Expense** and **Wages Payable** balances so they are accurate at the end of the month. The adjusting entry is journalized and posted BEFORE financial statements are prepared so that the company's income statement and balance sheet show the correct, up-to-date amounts.

Summary

The company had already accumulated $4,000 in **Wages Expense** during June -- $1,000 for each of four weeks. For the two additional work days in June, the 29th and 30th, the company accrued $400 additional in **Wages Expense.** To add this additional amount so it appears on the June income statement, **Wages Expense** was debited. **Wages Payable** was credited and will appear on the balance sheet to show that this $400 is owed to employees for unpaid work in June.

IMPORTANT: If this journal entry had been omitted, many errors on the financial statements would result.

1. The **Wages Expense** amount on the income statement would have been too low ($4,000 instead of $4,400).
2. **Net income** on the income statement would have been too high (An additional $400 of **Wages Expense** should have been deducted from revenues but was not).
3. The **Wages Payable** amount on the balance sheet would have been too low ($0 instead of $400).
4. The **total liabilities** amount on the balance sheet would have been too low because **Wages Payable,** one liability, was too low.
5. The **total stockholders' equity** amount on the balance sheet would be too high because a **net income** amount that was too high would have been closed out to Retained Earnings.

Although this is not an adjusting entry, it is important to know what the journal entry will be for wages on Friday, July 3rd—the next pay day.

Date	Account		Debit	Credit
7/3	Wages Expense		600	
	Wages Payable		400	
	Cash			1,000

- *Wages Expense* is an **expense** account that is **increasing.**
- *Wages Payable* is a **liability** account that is **decreasing.**
- *Cash* is an **asset** account that is **decreasing.**

Here are the **Wages Payable** and **Wages Expense** ledgers AFTER the closing entry (not shown) and the 7/3 entry have been posted.

Wages Payable					
Date	Item	Debit	Credit	Debit	Credit
6/30			400		400
7/3		400			0

Wages Expense					
Date	Item	Debit	Credit	Debit	Credit
6/5		1,000		1,000	
6/12		1,000		2,000	
6/19		1,000		3,000	
6/26		1,000		4,000	
6/30		400		4,400	
6/30			4,400	0	
7/3		600		600	

The $1,000 wages for the week beginning June 29th is split over two months in the **Wages Expense** accounts: $400 in June, and $600 in July.

Wages Payable has a zero balance on 7/3 since nothing is owed to employees for the week now that they have been paid the $1,000 in cash.

TAXES—ACCRUED EXPENSE

Property taxes are paid to the county in which a business operates and are levied on real estate and other assets a business owns. Typically the business operates for a year and pays its annual property taxes at the end of that year. At the beginning of the year, the company does have an estimate of what its total property tax bill will be at the end of the year.

Assume that a company's annual (January 1 to December 31) property taxes are estimated to be $6,000.

If the company prepares 12 monthly financial statements during the year, 1/12 of this estimate, or $500, should be included on each month's statements since this expense is accruing over time. New liability account: **Taxes Payable.**

No journal entry is made at the beginning of each month. At the end of each month, $500 of taxes expense has accumulated/accrued for the month. At the end of January, no property tax will be paid since payment for the entire year is due at the end of the year. However, $500 is now owed.

ADJUSTING ENTRY				
Date	Account		Debit	Credit
1/31	Taxes Expense		500	
	Taxes Payable			500

- *Taxes* Expense is an **expense** account that is **increasing.**
- *Taxes Payable* is a **liability** account that is **increasing.**

Here are the **Taxes Payable** and **Taxes Expense** ledgers AFTER the adjusting entry has been posted.

Taxes Payable					
Date	Item	Debit	Credit	Debit	Credit
1/31			500		500

Taxes Expense					
Date	Item	Debit	Credit	Debit	Credit
1/31		500		500	

This recognizes that 1/12 of the annual property tax amount is now owed at the end of January and includes 1/12 of this annual expense amount on January's income statement.

The same adjusting entry above will be made at the end of the month for 12 months to bring the Taxes Payable amount up by $500 each month. Here is an example of the Taxes Payable account balance at the end of December.

When the bill is paid on 12/31, Taxes Payable is debited and Cash is credited for $6,000. The Taxes Payable balance becomes zero since the annual taxes have been paid.

Taxes Payable					
Date	Item	Debit	Credit	Debit	Credit
1/31			500		500
2/28			500		1,000
3/31			500		1,500
4/30			500		2,000
5/31			500		2,500
6/30			500		3,000

Taxes Payable					
Date	**Item**	**Debit**	**Credit**	**Debit**	**Credit**
7/31			500		3,500
8/31			500		4,000
9/30			500		4,500
10/31			500		5,000
11/30			500		5,500
12/31			500		6,000
12/31		6,000			0

The adjusting entry for an accrued expense updates the **Taxes Expense** and **Taxes Payable** balances so they are accurate at the end of the month. The adjusting entry is journalized and posted BEFORE financial statements are prepared so that the company's income statement and balance sheet show the correct, up-to-date amounts.

Summary

Some expenses accrue over time and are paid at the end of a year. When this is the case, an estimated amount is applied to each month in the year so that each month reports a proportionate share of the annual cost.

IMPORTANT: If this journal entry had been omitted, many errors on the financial statements would result.

1. The **Taxes Expense** amount on the income statement would have been too low ($0 instead of $500).
2. **Net income** on the income statement would have been too high (**Taxes Expense** should have been deducted from revenues but was not).
3. The **Taxes Payable** amount on the balance sheet would have been too low ($0 instead of $500).
4. The **total liabilities** amount on the balance sheet would have been too low because **Taxes Payable,** one liability, was too low.
5. The **total stockholders' equity** amount on the balance sheet would be too high because a net income amount that was too high would have been closed out to Retained Earnings.

Accrued Revenue

Accrued revenues require adjusting entries. "Accrued" means "accumulated over time." In this case a customer will only pay you well after you complete a job that extends more than one accounting period. At the end of each accounting period, you record the part of the job that you did complete as a sale. This involves a debit to Accounts Receivable to acknowledge that the customer owes you for what you have completed and a credit to Fees Earned to record the revenue earned thus far.

FEES EARNED—ACCRUED REVENUE

Revenue is earned as a job is performed. Sometimes an entire job is not completed within the accounting period, and the company will not bill the customer until the job is completed. The earnings from the part of the job that has been completed must be reported on the month's income statement for this accrued revenue, and an adjusting entry is required.

Assume that a company begins a job for a customer on June 1. It will take two full months to complete the job. When it is complete, the company will then bill the customer for the full price of $4,000.

No journal entry is made at the beginning of June when the job is started. At the end of each month, the amount that has been earned during the month must be reported on the income statement. If the company earned $2,500 of the $4,000 in June, it must journalize this amount in an adjusting entry.

ADJUSTING ENTRY				
Date	Account		Debit	Credit
6/30	Accounts Receivable		2,500	
	Fees Earned			2,500

- *Accounts Receivable* is an **asset** account that is **increasing.**
- *Fees Earned* is a **revenue** account that is **increasing.**

Here are the **Accounts Receivable** and **Fees Earned** ledgers AFTER the adjusting entry has been posted.

Accounts Receivable					
Date	Item	Debit	Credit	Debit	Credit
6/1		500		500	
6/10		700		1,200	
6/15			500	700	
6/20		1,000		1,700	
6/25			700	1,000	
6/30		2,500		3,500	

Fees Earned					
Date	Item	Debit	Credit	Debit	Credit
6/1			500		500
6/10			700		1,200
6/15			800		2,000
6/20			1,000		3,000
6/25			600		3,600
6/30			2,500		6,100

Before the adjusting entry, **Accounts Receivable** had a debit balance of $1,000 and **Fees Earned** had a credit balance of $3,600. These balances were the result of other transactions during the month. When the accrued revenue from the additional unfinished job is added, Accounts Receivable has a debit balance of $3,500 and Fees Earned had a credit balance of $5,100 on 6/30. These final amounts are what appears on the financial statements.

The adjusting entry for accrued revenue updates the **Accounts Receivable** and **Fees Earned** balances so they are accurate at the end of the month. The adjusting entry is journalized and posted BEFORE financial statements are prepared so that the company's income statement and balance sheet show the correct, up-to-date amounts.

Summary

Some revenue accrues over time and is earned over more than one accounting period. When this is the case, the amount earned must be split over the months involved in completing the job based on when the work is done.

IMPORTANT: If this journal entry had been omitted, many errors on the financial statements would result.

1. The **Fees Earned** amount on the income statement would have been too low ($3,600 instead of $5,100).
2. **Net income** on the income statement would have been too low (The additional **Fees Earned** should have been included but was not).
3. The **Accounts Receivable** amount on the balance sheet would have been too low ($1,000 instead of $3,500).
4. The **total assets** amount on the balance sheet would have been too low because **Accounts Receivable,** one asset, was too low.
5. The **total stockholders' equity** amount on the balance sheet would be too low because a **net income** amount that was too low would have been closed out to Retained Earnings.

Accounts Summary Table - The following table summarizes the rules of debit and credit and other facts about all of the accounts that you know so far, including those needed for adjusting entries.

ACCOUNTS SUMMARY TABLE

ACCOUNT TYPE	ACCOUNTS	TO INCREASE	TO DECREASE	NORMAL BALANCE	FINANCIAL STATEMENT	CLOSE OUT?
Asset	Cash Accounts Receivable Supplies Prepaid Rent Prepaid Insurance Prepaid Taxes Land Truck Equipment Building Furnishings	debit	credit	debit	Balance Sheet	NO
Contra Asset	Accumulated Depreciation	credit	debit	credit	Balance Sheet	NO

ACCOUNT TYPE	ACCOUNTS	TO INCREASE	TO DECREASE	NORMAL BALANCE	FINANCIAL STATEMENT	CLOSE OUT?
Liability	Accounts Payable Note Payable Wages Payable Taxes Payable Interest Payable Unearned Fees Unearned Rent	credit	debit	credit	Balance Sheet	NO
Stockholders' Equity	Common Stock Retained Earnings	credit	debit	credit	Balance Sheet	YES
Revenue	Fees Earned Rent Revenue	debit	credit	debit	Income Statement	YES
Expense	Wages Expense Rent Expense Utilities Expense Supplies Expense Insurance Expense Advertising Expense Maintenance Expense Vehicle Expense Miscellaneous Expense Depreciation Expense Taxes Expense Interest Expense	debit	credit	debit	Income Statement	YES

ACCT 2101 Topics—Adjusting entries	Fact	Journal Entry	Calculate Amount	Format
Concept of adjusting entries	x			
Deferred expenses	x			
Journalize adjustment for prepaid supplies (deferred expense)		x	x	
Journalize adjustment for prepaid rent (deferred expense)		x	x	
Journalize adjustment for prepaid insurance (deferred expense)		x	x	
Journalize adjustment for prepaid taxes (deferred expense)		x	x	
Concept of depreciation	x			
Journalize adjustment for depreciation (deferred expense)		x	x	
Book value			x	
Deferred revenue	x			
Journalize adjustment for deferred revenue		x	x	
Accrued expenses	x			
Journalize adjustment for accrued wages (accrued expense)		x	x	
Journalize adjustment for accrued taxes (accrued expense)		x	x	
Journalize adjustment for accrued interest (accrued expense)		x	x	
Accrued revenue	x			
Journalize adjustment for accrued revenue		x	x	
Effect of omitting adjusting entries on the financial statements	x			
Financial statements	x			x
Journalize closing entries		x		
Post closing entries			x	

The accounts that are highlighted in bright yellow are the new accounts you just learned. Those highlighted in pale yellow are the ones you learned previously.

#1

Jonick Corporation
Income Statement
For the Month Ended June 30, 2014

Operating REVENUES:			
Fees Earned		$200,000	
Sales	$150,000		
Less: Sales returns	10,000		
Less: Sales discounts	5,000		
Net sales	135,000		
Cost of merchandise sold	55,000		
Gross profit		80,000	
Gross operating revenues			$280,000
Operating EXPENSES:			
Salaries expense		$25,000	
Wages expense		22,000	
Rent expense		20,000	
Insurance expense		19,000	
Supplies expense		18,000	
Advertising expense		17,000	
Maintenance expense		16,000	
Depreciation expense		15,000	
Taxes expense		14,000	
Utilities expense		13,000	
Payroll tax expense		12,000	
Bad debt expense		11,000	
Bank card expense		10,000	
Vehicle expense		9,000	
Delivery expense		8,000	
Amortization expense		7,000	
Miscellaneous expense		6,000	
Total operating expenses			242,000
Net income from operations			$38,000
Other revenue and expenses:			
Interest revenue		$5,000	
Interest expense		(4,000)	
Gain on sale of equipment		3,000	
Loss on redemption of bonds		(2,000)	2,000
Net income			$40,000

#3

Jonick Corporation
Balance Sheet
June 30, 2014

ASSETS			
Current assets:			
Cash		$40,000	
Accounts receivable	$28,000		
Less: Allowance for doubtful accounts	3,000	25,000	
Merchandise inventory		60,000	
Supplies		18,000	
Prepaid rent		12,000	
Prepaid insurance		6,000	
Prepaid taxes		4,000	
Note receivable		2,000	
Total current assets			$167,000
Fixed assets:			
Equipment	$16,000		
Less: Accumulated depreciation	2,000	14,000	
Van	30,000		
Less: Accumulated depreciation	5,000	25,000	
Building	200,000		
Less: Accumulated depreciation	70,000	130,000	
Land		110,000	
Total fixed assets			279,000
Intangible assets:			
Patents			14,000
Total assets			$460,000

LIABILITIES			
Current liabilities:			
Accounts payable	$14,000		
Unearned fees	13,000		
Wages payable	12,000		
Salaries payable	11,000		
Taxes payable	10,000		
Interest payable	9,000		
Notes payable	8,000		
Sales tax payable	7,000		
Social security tax payable	6,000		
Medicare tax payable	5,000		
Federal withholding tax payable	4,000		
State withholding tax payable	3,000		
Federal unemployment tax payable	2,000		
State unemployment tax payable	1,000		
Total current liabilities		$105,000	
Long-term liabilities:			
Mortgage note payable	$56,000		
Bonds payable	40,000		
Less: Discount on bonds payable	(6,000)		
Total long-term liabilities		90,000	
Total liabilities			$195,000
STOCKHOLDERS' EQUITY			
Common stock		$80,000	
Paid-in-capital in excess of par - common stock		34,000	
Preferred stock		50,000	
Paid-in-capital in excess of par - preferred stock		18,000	
Paid-in-capital from sale of treasury stock		13,000	
Retained earnings		90,000	
Treasury stock		(20,000)	
Total stockholders' equity			265,000
Total liabilities and stockholders' equity			$460,000

#2

Jonick Corporation
Retained Earnings Statement
For the Month Ended June 30, 2014

Retained earnings, June 1, 2014			$60,000
Net income		$40,000	
Less: Cash dividends	$6,000		
Stock dividends	4,000	10,000	
Increase in retained earnings			30,000
Retained earnings, June 30, 2014			$90,000

03 Accounting Cycle for a Merchandising Business

3.1 INTRODUCTION

So far our discussion has been limited to service businesses where companies sell expertise, knowledge, experiences, or the use of something to customers. In a service business, customers do not purchase or take ownership of a physical product. **Merchandising businesses** sell products. A merchandising business buys finished and packaged manufactured products, marks them up, and sells them to customers. A **merchandiser,** therefore, may be either the buyer or the seller in a given transaction, depending upon whether product is being purchased (and added to the stock of inventory), or sold (and removed from the stock of inventory.)

A **vendor** is a company or individual that a merchandiser purchases goods from. A **customer** is a company or individual that a merchandiser sells goods to. **Inventory** consists of items that are purchased for resale. Note that inventory is different from supplies. **Supplies** are items that are purchased to be used in the operation of the business, not to be sold to customers. For example, a merchandiser may have Windex glass cleaner on hand. It is considered inventory if it will be resold to customers and is considered a supply if it is used in running the business to keep the check-out counters clean. Similarly, inventory is also different from fixed assets such as **equipment**. For example, a merchandiser may have desktop computers on hand. They are considered inventory if they are to be resold to customers, such as in the case of Best Buy, Dell, or Apple. They would be classified as equipment if the merchandiser is using the computers to run its own business operations.

Sales is the new revenue account used to record income from selling products. This account replaces **Fees Earned,** the revenue account used for a service business.

The following are common sequences of events for merchandising businesses. When you are the **buyer,** you will (1) purchase product on account; (2) return product; and (3) pay for the product. When you are the **seller,** you will (1) sell product on account and reduce the inventory balance; (2) accept returns **and** increase the inventory balance; **and** (3) receive payment for sales.

ACCOUNT TYPE	ACCOUNTS	TO INCREASE	TO DECREASE	NORMAL BALANCE	FINANCIAL STATEMENT	CLOSE OUT?
Asset	**Merchandise Inventory** Account that keeps track of Items in stock for resale to customers	debit	credit	debi	Balance Sheet	No
Contra Asset	**Estimated Inventory Returns** Account that keeps track of the cost of the amount inventory that customers are expected to return	credit	debit	credit	Balance Sheet	No
Revenue	**Sales** Account that keeps track of the dollar amount of purchases made by customers	credit	debit	credit	Income statement	YES
Contra Revenue	**Sales Returns** Account that keeps track of the dollar amount of merchandise actually returned by customers **Allowance for Sales Returns** Account that keeps track of the dollar amount of merchandise esti- mated to be returned by customers **Sales Discounts** Account that keeps track of the dollar amount of discounts taken by customers under the gross method of recording sales **Sales Discounts Not Taken** Account that keeps track of the dollar amount of discounts not taken by customers under the net method of recording sales	debit	credit	debit	Imcome statement	YES
Expense	**Cost of Merchandise Sold** Account that keeps track of what a company paid for the inventory it has sold to customers **Delivery Expense** Account that keeps track of the transportation charges that a seller has absorbed as an expense	debit	credit	debit	Imcome statement	YRES

Most merchandising businesses use a **perpetual inventory system.** It is the process of keeping a current running total of inventory, both in number of units on hand and its dollar value, at all times. When product is purchased for resale, inventory immediately increases. When product is sold, the total value of the inventory on hand is immediately reduced.

This accounts summary table lists the new accounts used by merchandising businesses that use the perpetual inventory system for timing the recording of its changes in inventory value.

NOTE: When BUYING, the only new account above you may use is Merchandise Inventory. When SELLING, you may use any of the seven new accounts.

3.2 MERCHANDISING INCOME STATEMENT

The multi-step income statement is used to report revenue and expense activities for a merchandising business. It is an expanded, more detailed version of the single-step income statement.

The most significant cost that a merchandise business incurs is the cost of acquiring the inventory that is sold. It is important to match what was paid for an item to what it sells for. The multi-step income statement presents financial information so this relationship may easily be seen.

Here is a basic income statement for a merchandising business. Notice that Cost of Merchandise Sold, an expense account, is matched up with net sales at the top of the statement.

MERCHANDISING BUSINESS 1 Income Statement For the Month Ended June 30, 2013			
Sales		$1,000	Prices charged to customers on all inventory sold
Less: Sales returns	$40		Reduction in sales for items customers brought back
Sales Discounts	20	60	Amount of discounts taken by customers for early payment
Net Sales		940	Actual sales after return and discounts are removed
Cost of merchandise sold		340	What the company paid for the inventory that was sold
Gross profit		600	Mark-up, or the difference between selling price and cost
Operating expenses:			List of costs to the business unrelated to the cost of inventory
Wages expense	$150		
Supplies expense	30		
Depreciation expense	20	200	Total of costs unrelated to the cost of inventory
Net income		$400	Profit for the month

There are three calculated amounts on the multi-step income statement for a merchandiser - net sales, gross profit, and net income.

- Net Sales = Sales - Sales Returns - Sales Discounts
- Gross Profit = Net Sales - Cost of Merchandise Sold
- Net Income = Gross Profit - Operating Expenses

Net sales is the actual sales generated by a business. It represents everything that "went out the door" in sales minus all that came back in returns and in the form of sales discounts.

Gross profit is the same as "markup." It is the difference between what a company paid for a product and what it sells the product for to its customer.

Net income is the business's profit after all expenses have been deducted from the net sales amount.

A more complex manufacturing business may break out its operating expenses into two categories on the income statement: **selling expenses** and **administrative expenses.** Selling expenses are related to the people and efforts used to market and promote the product to customers. Administrative expenses relate to the general management of the business and may include costs such as the company president's office and the human resources and accounting departments. An example is shown below.

MERCHANDISING BUSINESS 2 Income Statement For the Month Ended June 30, 2013			
Sales		$1,000	Prices charged to customers on all inventory sold
Less: Sales returns	$40		Reduction in sales for items customers brought back
Sales Discounts	20	60	Amount of discounts taken by customers for early payment
Net Sales		940	Actual sales after return and discounts are removed
Cost of merchandise sold		340	What the company paid for the inventory that was sold
Gross profit		600	Mark-up, or the difference between selling price and cost
Selling expenses:			Costs related to marketing and selling products
Sales salaries expense	50		
Sales supplies expense	30		
Depreciation expense	10		
Administrative expenses:			Costs related to the general management of the business
Office salaries expense	$80		
Office supplies expense	20		
Depreciation expense	10		
Total selling and administrative expenses		200	Total of costs unrelated to the cost of inventory
Net income		$400	Profit for the month

3.3 BASIC MERCHANDISING TRANSACTIONS (PERPETUAL INVENTORY SYSTEM)

A merchandising business buys product from vendors, marks it up, and sells it to customers.

Transactions 1 through 3 are for **purchases** under the perpetual inventory system. The only new account used for purchases is **Merchandise Inventory.**

1. You purchase 50 items on account for $10 each.

Date	Account		Debit	Credit
1	Merchandise Inventory		500	
	Accounts Payable			500

- *Merchandise Inventory* is an **asset** account that is **increasing.**
- *Accounts Payable* is a **liability** account that is **increasing.**

2. You return 10 of the items to the vendor.

Date	Account		Debit	Credit
2	Accounts Payable		100	
	Merchandise Inventory			100

Just "flip" over the previous purchase transaction to undo it.

- *Accounts Payable* is a **liability** account that is **decreasing**
- *Merchandise Inventory* is an **asset** account that is **decreasing.**

3. You pay for the purchase, minus the return.

Date	Account		Debit	Credit
3	Accounts Payable		400	
	Cash			400

- *Accounts Payable* is a **liability** account that is **decreasing.**
- *Cash* is an **asset** account that is **decreasing.**

Transactions 4 through 8 are for **sales** under the perpetual inventory system. Any of the new accounts may be used for sales.

First, at the beginning of the accounting period (such as a year), a merchandising company estimates how much of its sales are likely to be returned during the year. On the first day of the year, the entire anticipated amount of sales returns is recorded in a journal entry. Under the perpetual system, a second entry simultaneously is recorded to estimate the cost of the merchandise returned. These entries attempt to match the sales for the year to the amount of sales returns in the same year. They do not represent an actual return, but instead an estimate of actual returns to come.

4a. You estimate sales returns for the year to be $450.

Date	Account		Debit	Credit
1/1	Sales Returns		450	
	Allowance for Sales Returns			450

- *Sales Returns* is a contra **revenue** account that is **increasing.**
- *Allowance for Sales Returns* is a contra account that is **increasing.**

4b. The cost of the estimated sales returns is $300.

Date	Account		Debit	Credit
1/1	Estimated Inventory Returns		300	
	Cost of Merchandise Sold			300

- *Estimated Inventory Returns* is an **asset** account that is **increasing.**
- *Cost of Merchandise Sold* is an **expense** account that is **decreasing.**

The following three transactions are used for sales, actual returns, and receipt of payments from customers.

5a. You sell 50 items on account for $15 each.

Date	Account		Debit	Credit
5a	Accounts Receivable		750	
	Sales			750

- *Accounts Receivable* is an **asset** account that is **increasing.**
- *Sales* is a **revenue** account that is **increasing.**

5b. You reduce inventory by cost of what was sold.

Date	Account		Debit	Credit
5b	Cost of Merchandise Sold		500	
	Merchandise Inventory			500

- *Cost of Merchandise Sold* is an **expense** account that is **increasing.**
- *Merchandise Inventory* is an **asset** account that is **decreasing.**

6a. Your customer returns 10 items to you.

Date	Account		Debit	Credit
6a	Allowance for Sales Returns		150	
	Accounts Receivable			150

The estimated account is reduced since some of the returns have occurred, so less is estimated to occur in the future.

- *Allowance for Sales Returns is* a contra account that is **decreasing.**
- *Accounts Receivable* is an **asset** account that is **decreasing.**

6b. You increase inventory by cost of returned items.

Date	Account		Debit	Credit
6b	Merchandise Inventory		100	
	Estimated Inventory Returns			100

- *Merchandise Inventory* is an **asset** account that is **increasing.**
- *Cost of Merchandise Sold* is an **expense** account that is **decreasing.**

7. You receive payment for the sale, minus the return.

Date	Account		Debit	Credit
7	Cash		600	
	Accounts Receivable			600

- *Cash* is an **asset** account that is **increasing.**
- *Accounts Receivable* is an **asset** account that is **decreasing.**

3.3.1 Merchandising Transactions (perpetual inventory system) with Discounts – The Buyer

Discounts are reductions in the purchase price of merchandise that a seller may offer to encourage the buyer to pay invoices off early. If the buyer pays within a designated time period, he/she will pay less than the full purchase price to satisfy the full invoice amount.

Only consider the discount when cash is actually paid by the purchaser. Before that, at the time of the purchase, neither party may be certain whether payment will be made within the discount period or not.

The amount of discount allowed is stated on the invoice using the following terminology:

- **Net 30** means the entire amount of the invoice is due in 30 days and no discount is allowed for early payment
- **2/10, net 30** means the purchaser may take a 2% discount on the cost of the merchandise if he pays within 10 days; otherwise, the entire amount of the invoice is due in 30 days. Other numbers may appear for the "2" and "10" to indicate a different percentage and/or a different number of days to qualify for the discount (such as **1/15** - 1% discount if paid within 15 days).

Transactions 8 and 9 are for purchases of product that will be resold. **Merchandise Inventory** is the account used to record the discount for the purchaser under the perpetual inventory system. It is credited to reduce the original debit by the amount of the discount, so ultimately the inventory is valued at the amount of cash paid for it.

8. You purchase 50 items on account for $10 each, 2/10 net 30.

Date	Account		Debit	Credit
8	Merchandise Inventory		500	
	Accounts Payable			500

- *Merchandise Inventory* is an **asset** account that is **increasing.**
- *Accounts Payable* is a **liability** account that is **increasing.**

9. You pay for the purchase, taking the discount.

Date	Account		Debit	Credit
9	Accounts Payable		500	
	Cash			490
	Merchandise Inventory			10

- *Accounts Payable* is a **liability** account that is **decreasing.**
- *Cash* is an **asset** account that is **decreasing.**
- *Merchandise Inventory* is an **asset** account that is **decreasing.**

When the inventory was purchased, it was recorded at full price of $500, without the discount. Later, at the time of payment, the buyer decided to take the $10 discount ($500 x 2%). The inventory account is reduced by $10 to recognize that the actual value of the inventory in the ledger is $490 – the amount of cash paid for it.

3.3.2 Merchandising Transactions (perpetual inventory system) with Discounts – The Seller

There are two methods for recording sales transactions when the seller offers its customer a discount to pay early. The choice depends on when the seller expects the buyer to pay. If the seller expects the buyer to pay the full amount after the discount period has expired, the gross method is typically used and the sale is recorded at the full amount. If the seller expects the buyer to pay the reduced amount within the discount period, the net method is usually selected and the sale is recorded at the selling price minus the discount amount. The goal is to best match revenue to the period in which it is earned.

In the examples that follow, the sale under the gross method is recorded at the full amount of $750. The sale under the net method is recorded at that amount minus the discount, or $735.

The amount for the entry to reduce the inventory and increase cost of goods sold is the samWe for both methods.

10a. You sell 50 items on account for $15 each, 2/10 net 30.		
GROSS METHOD		
Account	**Debit**	**Credit**
Accounts Receivable	750	500
Sales		750
Accounts Receivable is an **asset** account that is **increasing.**		
Sales is a **revenue** account that is **increasing.** 50 x $15 = 750		

10a. You sell 50 items on account for $15 each, 2/10 net 30.		
NET METHOD		
Account	**Debit**	**Credit**
Accounts Receivable	735	500
Sales		735
Accounts Receivable is an *asset* account that is **increasing.**		
Sales is a **revenue** account that is **increasing.** (50 x $15) – ((50 x $15) x .02) = 735		

10b. You reduce inventory by the cost of what was sold. Each item cost $10.		
Account	**Debit**	**Credit**
Cost of Merchandise Sold	500	
Merchandise Inventory		500
Cost of Merchandise Sold is an **expense** account that is **increasing.**		
Merchandise Inventory is an **asset** account that is **decreasing.**		

10b. You reduce inventory by the cost of what was sold. Each item cost $10.		
Account	**Debit**	**Credit**
Cost of Merchandise Sold	500	
Merchandise Inventory		500
Cost of Merchandise Sold is an **expense** account that is **increasing.**		
Merchandise Inventory is an **asset** account that is **decreasing.**		

11. You receive full payment for the sale AFTER the discount period, which is what you had anticipated.		
Account	**Debit**	**Credit**
Cash	750	
Accounts Receivable		750
Cash is an **asset** account that is **increasing.**		
Accounts Receivable is an **asset** account that is **decreasing.**		

11. You receive reduced payment for the sale WITHIN the discount period, which is what you had anticipated.		
Account	**Debit**	**Credit**
cash	735	
Accounts Receivable		735
Cash is an **asset** account that **is increasing.**		
Accounts Receivable is an **asset** account that is **decreasing.**		

Sales Discounts is a contra revenue account that may be used under the gross method when a customer pays within the discount period after the sale had been recorded at full price.

Sales Discounts Not Taken is a contra revenue account that may be used under the net method when a customer does not pay within the discount period after the sale had been recorded at the discounted price.

Both of these contra accounts substitute for the Sales revenue account.

If a return were involved, the customer would not take the discount on the amount that was returned under the gross method, but would under the net method.

OR, if payment is ultimately received at a time other than expected:

12. You receive payment for the sale WITHIN the discount period, although you had recorded the sale at the full amount.

Account	Debit	Credit
Cash	750	
Sales Discounts	15	
Accounts Receivable		750
Cash is an *asset* account that is **increasing.**		
Sales Discounts is a **contra revenue** account that is increasing.		
Accounts Receivable is an **asset** account that is **decreasing.**		

12. You receive payment for the sale AFTER the discount period, although you had recorded the sale at the discounted amount.

Account	Debit	Credit
Cash	750	
Sales Discounts Not Taken		50
Accounts Receivable		735
Cash is an asset account that is **increasing.**		
Sales Discounts Not Taken is **increasing.**		
Accounts Receivable is an asset account that is **decreasing.**		

3.4 TRANSPORTATION COSTS FOR MERCHANDISING TRANSACTIONS

Merchandise often must be delivered from the seller to the buyer. It is important to know which company - either the seller or the purchaser - owns the merchandise while it is in transit and in the hands of a third-party transportation company, such as UPS. The company that owns the merchandise must absorb the transportation cost as a business expense.

The shipping terms specify which company owns the merchandise while in transit. Terms may be **FOB destination** or **FOB shipping**. The acronym FOB stands for "Free On Board" and is a shipping term used in retail to indicate who is responsible for paying transportation charges. It is also the location where ownership of the merchandise transfers from seller to buyer.

If the shipping terms are **FOB destination**, ownership transfers at the destination, so the seller owns the merchandise all the while it in transit. Therefore, the seller absorbs the transportation cost and debits **Delivery Expense.** The buyer records nothing.

If the terms are **FOB shipping**, ownership transfers at the origin as it leaves the seller's facility, so the buyer owns the merchandise all the while it is in transit. The buyer therefore absorbs the transportation cost and debits Merchandise.

Inventory; the transportation charges just become part of the purchase price of the inventory. In the case of FOB shipping, the buyer may contract directly with the transportation company (and the seller records nothing) OR the seller may pre-pay the shipping costs and pass them along in the invoice to the buyer.

There are three possible scenarios regarding transportation, as follows:

1. Terms are FOB destination The seller calls UPS to pick up the shipment from his loading dock. The seller is billed by UPS and ultimately pays the bill and absorbs the expense.

11. Purchase 50 items on account for $10 each, terms **FOB destination.** Transportation charges are $20 on account.		
BUYER		
Account	**Debit**	**Credit**
Merchandise Inventory	750	500
Accounts Payable		500

11. Sell 50 items on account for $10 each, terms **FOB destination.** Each item cost $4. Transportation charges are $20 on account.		
SELLER		
Account	**Debit**	**Credit**
Accounts Receivable	500	
Sales		500

The purchaser does not record transportation charges at all since terms are FOB destination.

Date	Account		Debit	Credit
12	Cost of Merchandise Sold		200	
	Merchandise Inventory			200

Date	Account		Debit	Credit
12	Delivery Expense		20	
	Accounts Payable			20

The seller uses Delivery Expense to record transportation charges only when terms are FOB destination.

NOTE: If the information about the transportation says the seller is **billed** or **invoiced** by UPS, credit **Accounts Payable** (as shown above.) If the information says the buyer **paid** UPS, credit **Cash** instead.

11. You pay the amount invoiced at the time of the purchase.		
GROSS METHOD		
Account	**Debit**	**Credit**
Accounts Payable	500	
Cash		500

12. Your customer pays you the amount invoiced for the sale.		
NET METHOD		
Account	**Debit**	**Credit**
Cash	500	
Accounts Receivable		500

2. Terms are FOB shipping The purchaser calls UPS to pick up the shipment from the seller's loading dock. The purchaser is billed by UPS. Since the buyer is dealing with two different parties – the seller and the transportation company, the buyer records two journal entries.

13. Purchase 50 items on account for $10 each, terms FOB shipping. Transportation charges are $20 on account.					14. Sell 50 items on account for $10 each, terms FOB shipping. Each item cost $4. Transportation charges are $20 on account.				
BUYER					SELLER				
Date	Account		Debit	Credit	Date	Account		Debit	Credit
13	Merchandise Inventory		500		14	Accounts Receivable		500	
	Accounts Payable			500		Sales			500

Receive an invoice from UPS for the shipping.

Date	Account		Debit	Credit	Date	Account		Debit	Credit
13	Merchandise Inventory		20		14	Cost of Merchandise Sold		200	
	Accounts Payable			20		Merchandise Inventory			200

The purchaser uses Merchandise Inventory to record transportation charges when terms are FOB shipping. Shipping becomes part of the cost of the merchandise. The first Accounts Payable is to the seller; the second one is to the shipping company.

NOTE: If the information about the transportation says the buyer is **billed** or **invoiced** by UPS, credit **Accounts Payable** (as shown above.) If the information says the buyer **paid** UPS, credit **Cash** instead. The seller does not record transportation charges at all since terms are FOB shipping.

11. You pay the amount invoiced to the vendor. (You do not pay the UPS invoice yet.)				11. Your customer pays you the amount invoiced for the sale. Assume payment terms are 2/10, net 30 under the gross method.			
Account		Debit	Credit	Date Account		Debit	Credit
Accounts Payable		500		Cash		500	
Cash			490	Sales Discounts		10	
Merchandise Inventory			10	Accounts Receivable			500

3. Terms are FOB shipping As a courtesy and convenience, the seller calls UPS to pick up the shipment from his loading dock. The seller is billed by UPS and adds what UPS charges him to the purchaser's invoice. When the purchaser pays his bill, he pays for the product and reimburses the seller for prepaying the transportation for him.

15. Purchase 50 items on account for $10 each, terms **FOB shipping.** Transportation charges are $20 on account.

BUYER

Date	Account	Debit	Credit
15	Merchandise Inventory	520	
	Accounts Payable		520

The purchaser includes the shipping cost as part of the inventory cost and pays the seller not only the cost of the merchandise, but also reimbursement for the transportation charges.

16. Sell 50 items on account for $10 each, terms **FOB shipping.** Each item cost $4. Transportation charges are $20 on account.

SELLER

Date	Account	Debit	Credit
16	Accounts Receivable	520	
	Sales		500
	Accounts Payable		20

Date	Account	Debit	Credit
16	Cost of Merchandise Sold	200	
	Merchandise Inventory		200

The seller is owed the cost of the merchandise and the cost of the transportation. However, the seller owes those transportation charges of $20 to the shipping company.

Notice above that the buyer can combine the merchandise and transportation costs into one journal entry because the buyer is getting one invoice for both from the seller. Also notice that the seller can combine both the sale and the transportation added into one journal entry and send one invoice. Also notice that the transportation cost pre-paid by the seller does not become part of the Sales account.

The following transactions are **ALTERNATIVE** ways of presenting those above, splitting both the buyer's and the seller's transaction into two journal entries.

15. Purchase 50 items on account for $10 each, terms FOB shipping. Transportation charges are $20 on account.

BUYER

Date	Account	Debit	Credit
15	Merchandise Inventory	500	
	Accounts Payable		500

16. Sell 50 items on account for $10 each, terms FOB shipping. Transportation charges are $20 on account.

SELLER

Date	Account	Debit	Credit
16	Accounts Receivable	500	
	Sales		500

Date	Account		Debit	Credit
15	Merchandise Inventory		20	
	Accounts Payable			20

Date	Account		Debit	Credit
16	Accounts Receivable		500	
	Accounts Payable			20

The purchaser includes the shipping cost as part of the inventory cost and pays the seller not only the cost of the merchandise, but also reimbursement for the transportation charges. Date

Date	Account		Debit	Credit
16	Cost of Merchandise Sold		200	
	Merchandise Inventory			200

The seller is owed the cost of the merchandise and the cost of the transportation. However, the seller owes those transportation charges of $20 to the shipping company.

Regardless of which alternative was used to record the purchase and to record the sale, the following transactions record payment to the vendor when purchasing and payment by the customer when selling.

Account		Debit	Credit
Accounts Payable		520	
Cash			510
Merchandise Inventory			10
(500 – (500 x .02)) + 20 = 510			

Account		Debit	Credit
Cash		510	
Sales Discounts		10	
Accounts Receivable			510
(500 – (500 x .02)) + 20 = 510			

Important: When a purchases or sales discount is involved, be sure to only take the discount on the merchandise cost or sales price, respectively, and not on the transportation cost.

Accounts Summary Table - The following table defines and summarizes the new accounts for a merchandising business.

ACCOUNTS SUMMARY TABLE

ACCOUNT TYPE	ACCOUNTS	TO INCREASE	TO DECREASE	NORMAL BALANCE	FINANCIAL STATEMENT	CLOSE OUT?
	Merchandise Inventory Account that keeps track of Items in stock for resale to customers. Used only in closing en- tries under the periodic system.					
Asset (*temporary)						
	Purchases * Account that keeps track of the dollar amount of purchases of merchan- dise for sale made by a company **Freight-in *** Account that keeps track of the transportation charges that a buyer has incurred for the purchase of inventory **Purchases Returns *** Account that keeps track of the dollar amount of returns of merchandise previously purchased by a company	debit	credit	debit	Balance Sheet	NO
Contra Asset (*temporary)	Purchases Discounts * Account that keeps track of the dollar amount of discounts that the pur- chaser has claimed	credit	debit	credit	Balance Sheet	NO

3.5 BASIC MERCHANDISING TRANSACTIONS (PERIODIC INVENTORY SYSTEM)

A merchandising business buys product from vendors, marks it up, and sells it to customers.

Some companies do not keep an ongoing running inventory balance as was shown under the perpetual inventory system. Instead, these companies use the **periodic** inventory system and choose to wait until the end of the accounting period, just before financial statements are prepared, to conduct a physical inventory count to determine (1) how much ending inventory they still have in stock (counted) and (2) how much inventory they have sold during the period, which is their cost of merchandise sold (calculated).

Transactions 1 through 4 are for purchases under the periodic inventory system. Rather than using the *Merchandise Inventory* account to record purchases, returns, discounts, and transportation costs, four temporary accounts are used instead under the periodic system: Purchases, Purchases Returns, Purchases Discounts, and *Freight-in.* These accounts substitute for the Merchandise Inventory accounts during the accounting period and are closed into the Merchandise Inventory account at the end of the period.

1. You purchase 50 items on account for $10 each, terms 2/10, n/30.

Date	Account		Debit	Credit
1	Purchases		500	
	Accounts Payable			500

- *Purchases* is a temporary account (for an asset) that is **increasing.**
- *Accounts Payable* is a **liability** account that is **increasing.**

2. You pay transportation costs to UPS for merchandise purchases.

Date	Account		Debit	Credit
2	Purchases		500	
	Accounts Payable			500

- *Freight-in* is a temporary account (for an asset) that is **increasing.**
- *Accounts Payable* is a **liability** account that is **increasing.**

3. Return 10 of the items to the vendor.

Date	Account		Debit	Credit
3	Accounts Payable		100	
	Purchases Returns			100

"Flip" over the previous purchase transaction to undo it. Add the word "Returns" to the account name.

- *Accounts Payable* is a **liability** account that is **decreasing.**
- *Purchases Returns* is a temporary account (for an asset) that is decreasing.

4. Pay for the purchase (minus return/with the discount).

Date	Account		Debit	Credit
4	Accounts Payable		400	
	Cash			392
	Purchases Discounts			8

- *Accounts Payable* is a **liability** account that is **decreasing.**
- *Cash* is an **asset** account that is **decreasing.**
- *Purchases Discounts* is a temporary account (for an asset) that is *decreasing.*

Similar to the perpetual system, at the beginning of the accounting period (such as a year), a merchandising company under the periodic system estimates how much of its sales will be returned during the year. Assume that transaction has been recorded.

The following three transactions are used for sales, actual returns, and receipt of payments from customers under the periodic inventory system.

5a. Sell 50 items on account for $15 each, n/30.

Date	Account		Debit	Credit
5a	Accounts Receivable		750	
	Sales			750
	Purchases Discounts			8

- *Accounts Receivable* is an **asset** account that is **increasing.**
- *Sales* is a **revenue** account that is **increasing.**

6a. Customer returns 10 items.

Date	Account		Debit	Credit
6a	Allowance for Sales Returns		150	
	Accounts Receivable			150

The estimate account is reduced since some of the returns actually occurred, so less is estimated to occur in the future.

- *Allowance for Sales Returns* is a contra account that is **decreasing.**
- *Accounts Receivable* is an **asset** account that is **decreasing.**

7. Receive payment for the sale (minus the return).

Date	Account		Debit	Credit
7	Cash		600	
	Accounts Receivable			600

- *Cash* is an **asset** account that is **increasing.**
- *Accounts Receivable* is an **asset** account that is **decreasing.**

Notice that under the periodic system there is no corresponding adjustment for the amount of inventory at the time of a sale or a return. That is what makes this system different from the perpetual system. *Running balances for the Cost of Merchandise Sold and Merchandising Inventory* accounts are not maintained on an ongoing basis during the accounting period.

Therefore, at the end of the year, an entry must be made to record the total amount of cost of merchandise sold for the year and to adjust the Merchandising Inventory account to its current ending balance. This is done by deducting the ending inventory balance, which includes items that were not yet sold, from the total cost of goods available for sale during the year.

As an example, assume the following about a company's inventory for the year.

Beginning inventory on January 1	$ 10,000
Purchases	30,000
Freight-in	5,000
Purchases Discounts	(1,000)
Purchases Returns	(2,000)
Ending inventory balance on December 31	8,000

Total cost of goods available for sale during the year is $42,000, determined by adding the first five amounts above. Of that $42,000 available for sale, only $8,000 remains in inventory at the end of the year based on a physical inventory count. That means that $34,000 of what was available must have been sold.

The $34,000 is the cost of goods sold amount for the year, and that amount must be journalized so that it ultimately appears on the company's end-of-year income statement. In the same journal entry, the four temporary accounts used in the periodic inventory system – *Purchases, Freight-in, Purchases Discounts, and Purchases Returns* – are closed to their related permanent account, *Merchandise Inventory.* Using the previous data, the journal entry would be as follows:

Account	Debit	Credit	
Cost of Merchandise Sold	34,000		*Cost of Merchandise Sold* is an **expense** account **increasing.**

Account	Debit	Credit	
Merchandise Inventory	8,000		**Merchandise Inventory** is an **asset** account that is **decreasing.**
Purchases Discounts	1,000		*Purchases Discounts* is a temporary account **decreasing.**
Purchases Returns	2,000		***Purchases*** Returns is a temporary account that is **decreasing.**
Purchases		30,000	*Purchases* is a temporary account that is **decreasing.**
Freight-in		5,000	*Freight-in* is a temporary account that is **decreasing.**
Merchandise Inventory		10,000	*Merchandise Inventory* is an **asset** account that is **increasing.**

3.5.1 Inventory Shrinkage

Under the perpetual inventory system, a business keeps a running total of its inventory balance at all times by debiting (adding to) Merchandise Inventory when items are purchased and crediting (subtracting from) Merchandise Inventory when items are sold. With each transaction, the debit balance is updated. Occasionally businesses will take a physical inventory count to determine if it actually has all items it thinks it has per its accounting records. Inventory shrinkage is the difference that results when the amount of actual inventory physically counted is less than the amount of inventory listed in the accounting records. Any shrinkage amount may be due to previous miscounts, loss, or theft.

When a shortage is discovered as a result of a physical inventory count, the following entry would be made to adjust the accounting records:

17. Discover an inventory shortage of $300.

Date	Account		Debit	Credit
17	Cost of Merchandise Sold		300	
	Merchandise Inventory			300

- *Cost of Merchandise Sold* is an **expense** account that is **increasing.**
- *Merchandise Inventory* is an **asset** account that is **decreasing.**

This is the same as the entry made when there is a sale; however, this transaction does not "match up" with any particular sale. Further investigation would take place if the amount of the shortage was significant.

3.6 CLOSING ENTRIES FOR MERCHANDISING ACCOUNTS

Six of the seven new accounts appear on the income statement and therefore are closed to Retained Earnings at the end of the accounting period.

The following June income statement shows these six accounts.

MERCHANDISING BUSINESS 3 Income Statement For the Month Ended June 30, 2013		
Sales		$1,000
Less: Sales returns		$40
Sales Discounts	20	60
Net Sales		**940**
Cost of merchandise sold		340
Gross profit		**$600**
Operating expenses:		
Delivery expense		140
Bank card expense	60	200
Net income		$400

The closing entries at the end of June would be as follows:

Date	Account		Debit	Credit
6/30	Sales		1,000	
	Retained Earnings			1,000
6/30	Retained Earnings		40	
	Sales Returns			40
6/30	Retained Earnings		20	
	Sales Discounts			20
6/30	Retained Earnings		340	
	Cost of Merchandise Sold			340
6/30	Retained Earnings		140	
	Delivery Expense			140

- *Sales* is a **revenue** account that is **decreasing.**
- *Retained Earnings* is an **equity** account that is **increasing.**
- *Retained Earnings* is an **equity** account that is **decreasing.**
- *Sales Returns* is a contra **revenue** account that is **decreasing.**
- *Retained Earnings* is an **equity** account that is **decreasing.**
- *Sales Discounts* is a contra **revenue** account that is **decreasing.**
- *Retained Earnings* is an **equity** account that is **decreasing.**
- *Cost of Merchandise Sold* is an **expense** account that is **decreasing.**
- *Retained Earnings* is an **equity** account that is **decreasing.**
- *Delivery Expense* is an **expense** account that is **decreasing.**

Key questions to ask when dealing with merchandising transactions:

1. Are you the buyer or the seller?
2. Are there any returns?
3. What is the form of payment (cash or on account)?
4. Does the discount apply?
5. Who is to absorb the transportation cost?
6. If the buyer is to absorb the freight cost, did the seller prepay it?

ACCT 2101 Topics—Adjusting entries	Fact	Journal Entry	Calculate Amount	Format
Concept of a merchandising business	x			
Concept of a perpetual inventory system	x			
Merchandising income statement: net sales, gross profit, and net income			x	x
Journalize purchase of inventory on account		x	x	
Journalize purchaser's return of inventory on account		x	x	
Journalize payment on account		x	x	
Journalize payment on account with a discount		x	x	
Journalize purchaser's payment of transportation charges terms FOB shipping		x	x	
Journalize sale of merchandise on account under perpetual system		x	x	
Journalize return of merchandise on account/for cash under perpetual system		x	x	
Journalize receipt of payment on account		x	x	
Journalize receipt of payment on account with a discount		x	x	

ACCT 2101 Topics—Adjusting entries	Fact	Journal Entry	Calculate Amount	Format
Journalize seller's payment of transportation charges terms FOB destination		x	x	
Journalize seller's payment of transportation charges terms FOB shipping		x	x	
Journalize bank charges		x	x	
Financial statements	x			x
Journalize closing entries		x		
Post closing entries to ledgers			x	

The accounts that are highlighted in yellow are the new accounts you just learned. Those in pale yellow are the ones you learned previously.

#1

Jonick Corporation
Income Statement
For the Month Ended June 30, 2014

Operating REVENUES:			
Fees Earned		$200,000	
Sales	$150,000		
Less: Sales returns	10,000		
Less: Sales discounts	5,000		
Net sales	135,000		
Cost of merchandise sold	55,000		
Gross profit		80,000	
Gross operating revenues			$280,000
Operating EXPENSES:			
Salaries expense		$25,000	
Wages expense		22,000	
Rent expense		20,000	
Insurance expense		19,000	
Supplies expense		18,000	
Advertising expense		17,000	
Maintenance expense		16,000	
Depreciation expense		15,000	
Taxes expense		14,000	
Utilities expense		13,000	
Payroll tax expense		12,000	
Bad debt expense		11,000	
Bank card expense		10,000	
Vehicle expense		9,000	
Delivery expense		8,000	
Amortization expense		7,000	
Miscellaneous expense		6,000	
Total operating expenses			242,000
Net income from operations			$38,000
Other revenue and expenses:			
Interest revenue		$5,000	
Interest expense		(4,000)	
Gain on sale of equipment		3,000	
Loss on redemption of bonds		(2,000)	2,000
Net income			$40,000

#3

Jonick Corporation
Balance Sheet
June 30, 2014

ASSETS			
Current assets:			
Cash		$40,000	
Accounts receivable	$28,000		
Less: Allowance for doubtful accounts	3,000	25,000	
Merchandise inventory		60,000	
Supplies		18,000	
Prepaid rent		12,000	
Prepaid insurance		6,000	
Prepaid taxes		4,000	
Note receivable		2,000	
Total current assets			$167,000
Fixed assets:			
Equipment	$16,000		
Less: Accumulated depreciation	2,000	14,000	
Van	30,000		
Less: Accumulated depreciation	5,000	25,000	
Building	200,000		
Less: Accumulated depreciation	70,000	130,000	
Land		110,000	
Total fixed assets			279,000
Intangible assets:			
Patents			14,000
Total assets			$460,000

LIABILITIES			
Current liabilities:			
Accounts payable	$14,000		
Unearned fees	13,000		
Wages payable	12,000		
Salaries payable	11,000		
Taxes payable	10,000		
Interest payable	9,000		
Notes payable	8,000		
Sales tax payable	7,000		
Social security tax payable	6,000		
Medicare tax payable	5,000		
Federal withholding tax payable	4,000		
State withholding tax payable	3,000		
Federal unemployment tax payable	2,000		
State unemployment tax payable	1,000		
Total current liabilities		$105,000	
Long-term liabilities:			
Mortgage note payable	$56,000		
Bonds payable	40,000		
Less: Discount on bonds payable	(6,000)		
Total long-term liabilities		90,000	
Total liabilities			$195,000
STOCKHOLDERS' EQUITY			
Common stock		$80,000	
Paid-in-capital in excess of par - common stock		34,000	
Preferred stock		50,000	
Paid-in-capital in excess of par - preferred stock		18,000	
Paid-in-capital from sale of treasury stock		13,000	
Retained earnings		90,000	
Treasury stock		(20,000)	
Total stockholders' equity			265,000
Total liabilities and stockholders' equity			$460,000

#2

Jonick Corporation
Retained Earnings Statement
For the Month Ended June 30, 2014

Retained earnings, June 1, 2014			$60,000
Net income		$40,000	
Less: Cash dividends	$6,000		
Stock dividends	4,000	10,000	
Increase in retained earnings			30,000
Retained earnings, June 30, 2014			$90,000

04 Assets in More Detail

4.1 INVENTORY

A merchandising business manufactures products, marks them up, and sells them to customers. A merchandiser may therefore be either the buyer or the seller in a given transaction.

Inventory is items that are purchased for resale. The process of inventory valuation involves determining the quantities and dollar value of the inventory that a company owns.

The **perpetual inventory system** is the process of keeping a current running total of inventory, both in number of units on hand and its dollar value, at all times. When product is purchased for resale, inventory immediately increases. When inventory is sold, its total value is immediately reduced.

Items in inventory are not always purchased at the same price; the same items may cost different amounts at different times. Therefore, a business needs a system of deciding which cost to select as its expense amount for **Cost of Merchandise Sold** when it sells an item.

As a simple example, let's say a company has purchased 30 identical items for resale to customers. It bought 10 items on 2/2 for $1 each, 10 items on 2/3 for $2 each, and 10 items on 2/4 for $3 each. The total cost of the 30 units in inventory is $60.

Date	Purchases		
2/2	10	$1	$10
2/3	10	$2	$20
2/4	10	$3	$30
TOTAL	30		$60

The issue is this: If the company sells ONE item to a customer for $10, the cost of that one item needs to be determined.

Date	Account		Debit	Credit
2/12	Accounts Receivable		10	
	Sales			10

- *Accounts Receivable* is an **asset** account that is **increasing.**
- Sales is a **revenue** account that is **increasing.**

Date	Account		Debit	Credit
2/12	Cost of Merchandise Sold		???	
	Merchandise Inventory			???

- *Cost of Merchandise Sold* is an **expense** account that is **increasing.**
- *Merchandise Inventory* is an **asset** account that is **decreasing.**

The company will select an accepted method of valuing withdrawals from inventory. Three common methods are the following:

FIFO (First-In, First-Out) method withdraws inventory beginning with those units purchased earliest. In the example above, the **Cost of Merchandise Sold** would be $1, one of the items purchased on 2/2. As a result, the gross profit on the sale would be $9 ($10 - $1).

LIFO (Last-In, First-Out) method withdraws inventory beginning with those units purchased most recently. In the example above, the **Cost of Merchandise Sold** would be $3, one of the items purchased on 2/4. As a result, the gross profit on the sale would be $7 ($10 - $3).

Average Cost Method uses an average of the cost of all items currently in stock. In the example above, the average is $60/30 units, so the **Cost of Merchandise Sold** would be $2 per unit. As a result, the gross profit on the sale would be $8 ($10 - $2).

We will be answering the following four questions about inventory for an accounting period:

1. What is total sales?
2. What is total cost of merchandise sold?
3. What is gross profit?
4. What is the ending inventory balance?

4.1.1 Perpetual Inventory System

INVENTORY GRIDS

By entering transactions into a cost grid, you can organize your data to easily determine Cost of Merchandise Sold amounts and Merchandise Inventory balances after every purchase and sale. The grids show increases in Merchandise Inventory due to purchases, decreases in Merchandise Inventory due to sales, and the running Merchandise Inventory balance.

The following grid organizes the purchases and sales of a merchandiser for one of its products. It is essentially an expanded Merchandise Inventory account ledger. Not only does it show the dollar amount for each transaction and the updated running balance in dollars, but it also keeps track of the number of items bought, sold, and currently in inventory.

Date	Purchases			Cost of Merchandise Sold			Inventory Balance		
	Units	Cost	Total	Units	Cost	Total	Units	Cost	Total
6/1							10	$4	$40
6/5				1	$4	$4	9	$4	$36
6/10	10	$5	$50				9	$4	$36
							10	$5	$50

The **Purchases** columns show the details about items that were bought on different dates for resale to customers. Entries in the Purchases columns are the same regardless of the inventory valuation method selected. For a purchase, there is a debit to **Merchandise Inventory** and total inventory increases.

The **Cost of Merchandise Sold** columns show the detail about the order in which items are withdrawn from inventory for each sale. The amounts in these columns will vary based on whether the method is FIFO, LIFO, or average cost. For a sale, there is a debit to **Cost of Merchandise Sold** and total inventory decreases.

The **Inventory Balance** columns keep a running total of the number of items and their costs on each date. Each purchase is added to any inventory balance that already appears there. With a purchase, it is a good practice to first copy down what was in stock on the previous date in the Inventory Balance columns and add the new purchase below that. This clearly shows what is in stock on any given date. Each sale reduces the inventory balance by the cost of merchandise sold amount.

NOTE: Only costs are entered into the grid; not the price that you sell the merchandise for to customers. If you are given the selling price, you can also determine the amount of sales and gross profit amounts outside of the grid.

There is a journal entry that corresponds to each purchase and sale. One key reason for the grid is that it enables you to determine the amounts for the cost of merchandise sold for each sale.

FIFO under the perpetual inventory system—FIFO (first-In, first-out) is a method of inventory valuation where the cost of the items purchased earliest is used in Cost of Merchandise Sold when one item is resold. The balance in Merchandise Inventory, which includes those items still available for sale, is comprised of the costs of those items purchased most recently.

Date	Account	Debit	Credit
6/5	Accounts Receivable	10	
	Sales		10
6/5	Cost of Merchandise Sold	4	
	Merchandise Inventory		4

Date	Account	Debit	Credit
6/10	Merchandise Inventory	50	
	Accounts Payable		50

Date	Account	Debit	Credit
6/16	Accounts Receivable	120	
	Sales		120
6/16	Cost of Merchandise Sold	51	
	Merchandise Inventory		51

Date	Account	Debit	Credit
6/22	Merchandise Inventory	60	
	Accounts Payable		60

Date	Account	Debit	Credit
6/30	Accounts Receivable	60	
	Sales		60
6/30	Cost of Merchandise Sold	30	
	Merchandise Inventory		30

The following are sample transactions for a single product for a merchandising company in June:

6/1	Beginning inventory	10 units @ $ 4	6/16	Sale	12 units @ $10
6/5	Sale	1 unit @ $10	6/22	Purchase	10 units @ $ 6
6/10	Purchase	10 units @ $ 5	6/30	Sale	6 units @ $10

This FIFO inventory cost grid summarizes the transactions above.

Date	Purchases			Cost of Merchandise Sold			Inventory Balance		
	Units	Cost	Total	Units	Cost	Total	Units	Cost	Total
6/1							10	$4	$40
6/5				1	$4	$4	9	$4	$36
6/10	10	$5	$50				9	$4	$36
						$51	10	$5	$50
6/16				9	$4	$36			
				3	$5	$15	7	$5	$35
6/22	10	$6	$60				7	$5	$35
							10	$6	$60
6/30				6	$5	$30	1	$5	$ 5
							10	$6	$60
6/30 Balances						$85	11		$65

$86

$95

$65

Ending inventory

Total cost of merchandise sold

6/1 The inventory balance that is given is entered. This is carried over from the previous month.

6/5 One unit is sold. Since all 10 units in stock cost $4, the only choice is a $4 cost for that item in the Cost of Merchandise Sold columns. This is deducted from the inventory balance.

6/10 Purchases are entered in the Purchases columns and added to the inventory balance.

6/16 Now it is important to know you are using FIFO. The customer ordered 12 items. You have 19 in stock at two different costs. Under FIFO you use the "oldest" ones first – the $4 items. You sell all 9 of those and then need 3 items that cost $5 to complete the order. You use two lines in the Cost of Merchandise Sold columns – one for each unit cost. This is deducted from the inventory balance.

6/22 Purchases are entered in the Purchases columns and added to the inventory balance.

6/30 The customer ordered 6 items. You have 17 in stock at two different costs. Under FIFO you use the "oldest" ones first – the $5 items. You sell 6 of those and enter this in the Cost of Merchandise Sold. This is deducted from the inventory balance.

Four inventory questions under FIFO:

1. **What is total sales?** 19 units, $190 (1 + 12 + 6) = 19 units sold x $10 per unit
2. **What is total cost of merchandise sold?** $85 ($4 + $36 + $15 + $30) from cost of merchandise sold column
3. **What is gross profit?** $105 Sales – cost of merchandise sold is $190 - $85
4. **What is the ending inventory balance?** 11 units, $65 6/30 inventory balance amounts in cost grid

LIFO under the perpetual inventory system—LIFO (last-in, first-out) is a method of inventory valuation where the cost of the item purchased most recently is used in Cost of Merchandise Sold when one item is resold. The balance in Merchandise Inventory, which includes those items still available for sale, is comprised of the costs of those items purchased earliest.

Date	Account	Debit	Credit
6/5	Accounts Receivable	10	
	Sales		10
6/5	Cost of Merchandise Sold	4	
	Merchandise Inventory		4

Date	Account	Debit	Credit
6/10	Merchandise Inventory	50	
	Accounts Payable		50

Date	Account	Debit	Credit
616	Accounts Receivable	120	
	Sales		120
6/16	Cost of Merchandise Sold	58	
	Merchandise Inventory		58

Date	Account	Debit	Credit
6/22	Merchandise Inventory	60	
	Accounts Payable		60

Date	Account	Debit	Credit
6/30	Accounts Receivable	60	
	Sales		60
6/30	Cost of Merchandise Sold	36	
	Merchandise Inventory		36

The following are sample transactions for a single product for a merchandising company in June:

6/1	Beginning inventory	10 units @ $ 4	6/16	Sale	12 units @ $10
6/5	Sale	1 unit @ $10	6/22	Purchase	10 units @ $ 6
6/10	Purchase	10 units @ $ 5	6/30	Sale	6 units @ $10

This LIFO inventory cost grid summarizes the transactions above.

Date	Purchases			Cost of Merchandise Sold			Inventory Balance		
	Units	Cost	Total	Units	Cost	Total	Units	Cost	Total
6/1							10	$4	$40
6/5				1	$4	$4	9	$4	$36
6/10	10	$5	$50				9	$4	$36
							10	$5	$50
6/16				10	$5	$50			
				2	$4	$ 8	7	$4	$28
6/22	10	$6	$60				7	$4	$28
							10	$6	$60
6/30				6	$6	$36	7	$4	$28
							4	$6	$24
6/30 Balances						$98	11		$52

Annotations: $86; $58; $88; $52; Total cost of merchandise sold ($98); Ending inventory ($52)

6/1 The inventory balance that is given is entered. This is carried over from the previous month.

6/5 One unit is sold. Since all 10 units in stock cost $4, the only choice is a $4 cost for that item in the Cost of Merchandise Sold columns. This is deducted from the inventory balance.

6/10 Purchases are entered in the Purchases columns and added to the inventory balance.

6/16 Now it is important to know you are using LIFO. The customer ordered 12 items. You have 19 in stock at two different costs. Under LIFO you use the "newest" ones first – the $5 items. You sell all 10 of those and then need 2 items that cost $4 to complete the order. You use two lines in the Cost of Merchandise Sold columns – one for each unit cost. This is deducted from the inventory balance.

6/22 Purchases are entered in the Purchases columns and added to the inventory balance.

6/30 The customer ordered 6 items. You have 17 in stock at two different costs. Under LIFO you use the "newest" ones first - the $6 items. You sell 6 of those and enter this in the Cost of Merchandise Sold. This is deducted from the inventory balance.

Four inventory questions under LIFO:

1. **What is total sales?** 19 units, $190 (1 + 12 + 6) = 19 units sold x $10 per unit
2. **What is total cost of merchandise sold?** $98 ($4 + $50 + $8 + $36) from cost of merchandise sold column
3. **What is gross profit?** $92 Sales – cost of merchandise sold is $190 - $98
4. **What is the ending inventory balance?** 11 units, $52 6/30 inventory balance amounts in cost grid

Average cost under the perpetual inventory system—Average cost is a method of inventory valuation where each time there is a purchase or sale, the dollar value of the remaining inventory on hand is divided by the number of units in stock to arrive at an average cost per unit. Likewise, the cost of merchandise sold is determined by using an average cost per unit.

Date	Account	Debit	Credit
6/5	Accounts Receivable	10.00	
	Sales		10.00
6/5	Cost of Merchandise Sold	4.00	
	Merchandise Inventory		4.00

Date	Account	Debit	Credit
6/10	Merchandise Inventory	50.00	
	Accounts Payable		50.00

Date	Account	Debit	Credit
616	Accounts Receivable	120.00	
	Sales		120.00
6/16	Cost of Merchandise Sold	54.36	
	Merchandise Inventory		54.36

Date	Account	Debit	Credit
6/22	Merchandise Inventory	60.00	
	Accounts Payable		60.00

Date	Account	Debit	Credit
6/30	Accounts Receivable	60.00	
	Sales		60.00
6/30	Cost of Merchandise Sold	32.34	
	Merchandise Inventory		32.34

The following are sample transactions for a single product for a merchandising company in June:

6/1	Beginning inventory	10 units @ $ 4	6/16	Sale	12 units @ $10
6/5	Sale	1 unit @ $10	6/22	Purchase	10 units @ $ 6
6/10	Purchase	10 units @ $ 5	6/30	Sale	6 units @ $10

This LIFO inventory cost grid summarizes the transactions above.

Date	Purchases			Cost of Merchandise Sold			Inventory Balance		
	Units	Cost	Total	Units	Cost	Total	Units	Cost	Total
6/1							10	$4.00	$40.00
6/5				1	$4.00	$4.00	9	$4.00	$36.00
6/10	10	$5.00	$50.00				19	$4.53	$86.07
Calculation for inventory balance above: (50.00 + 36.00) / 19 units = $4.53 (rounded)									
6/16				12	$4.53	$54.36	7	$4.53	$31.71
6/22	10	$6.00	$60.00				17	$5.39	$91.63
Calculation for inventory balance above: (60.00 + 31.71) / 17 units = $5.39 (rounded)									
6/30				6	$5.39	$32.34	11	$5.39	$58.74
6/30 Balances					Total cost of merchandise sold	$90.70	11		$58.74 Ending inventory

6/1 The inventory balance that is given is entered. This is carried over from the previous month.

6/5 One unit is sold. Since all 10 units in stock cost $4, the only choice is a $4 cost for that item in the Cost of Merchandise Sold columns. This is deducted from the inventory balance.

6/10 Purchases are entered in the Purchases columns and added to the inventory balance.

6/16 Now it is important to know you are using the average cost method. The customer ordered 12 items. You have 19 in stock at an average cost of $4.53 per unit. The amount of 12 x $4.53 is deducted from the inventory balance.

6/22 Purchases are entered in the Purchases columns and added to the inventory balance.

6/30 The customer ordered 6 items. You have 17 in stock at an average cost of $5.39 per unit. The amount of 6 x $5.39 is deducted from the inventory balance.

Four inventory questions under LIFO:

1. **What is total sales?** 19 units, $190.00 (1 + 12 + 6) = 19 units sold x $10 per unit
2. **What is total cost of merchandise sold?** $90.70 ($4 + $54.36 + $32.34) from cost of merchandise sold column
3. **What is gross profit?** $99.30 Sales – cost of merchandise sold is $190.00 - $90.70
4. **What is the ending inventory balance?** 11 units, $58.74 6/30 inventory balance amounts in cost grid

The results of the preceding example for both FIFO and LIFO under the perpetual inventory system can be summarized in four questions.

Four inventory questions	FIFO	LIFO	Average cost
1. What is total sales? (19 units)	$190.00	$190.00	$190.00
2. What is total cost of merchandise sold?	85.00	98.00	90.70
3. What is gross profit?	105.00	92.00	99.30
4. What is the ending inventory balance? (11 units)	65.00	52.00	58.74

Under all three methods, 19 units were sold and total sales were $190. Notice, however, that under FIFO the 19 units COST $85, under LIFO these same 19 units COST $98, and under average cost these same 19 units COST $90.70. This is a $13 difference between the highest and lowest costing method.

Gross profit is also different among the three methods. Because less cost is deducted from sales under the FIFO method, gross profit is $13 higher under FIFO than it is for LIFO.

That $13 difference also appears in the ending inventory balances. Since the cost of merchandise sold was lower under FIFO than it was under LIFO and average cost, the ending inventory balance under FIFO is higher that with the other two methods.

To summarize, there is a $13 difference between FIFO and LIFO in the cost of goods sold and ending inventory amounts. FIFO includes that $13 as part of ending inventory; LIFO considers that $13 to be part of cost of merchandise sold.

NOTE: The pattern above will result when costs are rising over time. In this example, they increased from $4 to $5 to $6. If costs decrease over time, the results will be the opposite: LIFO would include the difference as part of ending inventory and FIFO would consider the difference to be part of cost of merchandise sold. The results for the average cost method typically fall between those for LIFO and FIFO.

4.1.2 Periodic Inventory System

As was mentioned in the merchandising discussion, some companies do not keep an ongoing running inventory balance as was shown under the perpetual inventory system. Instead, these companies choose to wait until the end of the accounting period, just before financial statements are prepared, to conduct a physical inventory count to determine (1) how much ending inventory they still have in stock (counted) and (2) how much inventory they have sold during the period, which is their cost of merchandise sold (calculated).

Cost of merchandise sold is determined by first calculating cost of merchandise available for sale, which is the beginning inventory value plus purchases during the period.

The following is sample information for a single product for a merchandising company that uses the periodic inventory system in June:			
6/1	Beginning inventory	10 units @ $ 4 =	$ 40
6/10	Purchase	10 units @ $ 5 =	50
6/22	Purchase	10 units @ $ 6 =	60
Cost of goods available for sale: 30 units at a total cost of $150			
6/5	Sale	1 units @ $ 10	
6/16	Sale	12 units @ $ 10	
6/30	Sale	6 units @ $ 10	
Total units sold 19 units			
Ending inventory 11 units (30 units available – 19 units sold from above)			

The same three flow methods of withdrawing inventory from stock—FIFO, LIFO, and average cost—are used under the periodic system. The periodic system disregards the dates of the purchases and sales and just looks at the totals of each collectively.

FIFO UNDER THE PERIODIC INVENTORY SYSTEM

Under FIFO, the **19 units sold** are drawn from earliest inventory in stock to determine cost of goods sold. The first 10 units are from the beginning inventory and the remaining 8 units are from the 6/10 purchase.

Cost of merchandise sold = (10 x $4) + (9 x $5) = $40 + $45 = $85

The **11 units in ending inventory** include the remaining 1 unit from the 6/10 purchase and all 10 units from the 6/22 purchase.

Ending inventory = (1 x $5) + (10 x $6) = $5 + $60 = $65

The total cost of goods available for sale during the period, which was **30 units at a total cost of $150**, is split between cost of merchandise sold and ending inventory.

LIFO UNDER THE PERIODIC INVENTORY SYSTEM

Under LIFO, the **18 units sold** are drawn from latest inventory in stock to determine cost of goods sold. The first 10 units are from the 6/22 purchase and the remaining 8 units are from the 6/10 purchase.

Cost of merchandise sold = (10 x $6) + (9 x $5) = $60 + $45 = $105

The **12 units in ending inventory** include the remaining 2 units from the 6/10 purchase and all 10 units from beginning inventory.

Ending inventory = (1 x $5) + (10 x $4) = $5 + $40 = $45

The total cost of goods available for sale during the period, which was **30 units at a total cost of $150,** is split between cost of merchandise sold and ending inventory.

AVERAGE COST UNDER THE PERIODIC INVENTORY SYSTEM

Under average cost, the 30 units available for sale are divided into their total cost, as follows:

$150 / 30 = $5 per unit

The 19 units sold are all costed at $5. Cost of merchandise sold = 19 x $5 = **$95.** The 11 units in ending inventory are all costed at $5. Ending inventory = 11 x $5 = **$55.**

The total cost of goods available for sale during the period, which was 30 units at a total cost of $150, is split between cost of merchandise sold and ending inventory.

The results of the preceding example for both FIFO and LIFO under the periodic inventory system can be summarized in four questions.

Four inventory questions	FIFO	LIFO	Average cost
1. What is total sales? (19 units)	$190	$190	$190.00
2. What is total cost of merchandise sold?	85	105	95
3. What is gross profit?	105	85	95
4. What is the ending inventory balance? (11 units)	65	45	55

Under all three methods, 19 units were sold and total sales were $190. Notice, however, that under FIFO the 19 units COST $85, under LIFO these same 19 units COST $105, and under average cost these same 19 units COST $95. This is a $30 difference between the highest and lowest costing method.

Gross profit is also different among the three methods. Because less cost is deducted from sales under the FIFO method, gross profit is $30 higher under FIFO that it is for LIFO.

That $30 difference also appears in the ending inventory balances. Since the cost of merchandise sold was lower under FIFO than it was under LIFO and average cost, the ending inventory balance under FIFO is higher that with the other two methods.

To summarize, there is a $30 difference between FIFO and LIFO in the cost of goods sold and ending inventory amounts. FIFO includes that $30 as part of ending inventory; LIFO considers that $30 to be part of cost of merchandise sold.

NOTE: The pattern above will result when costs are rising over time. In this example, they increased from $4 to $5 to $6. If costs decrease over time, the results will be the opposite: LIFO would include the difference as part of ending inventory and FIFO would consider the difference to be part of cost of merchandise sold.

The results for the average cost method typically fall between those for LIFO and FIFO. Also note that the results for FIFO are the same under the periodic and perpetual inventory systems.

4.1.3 Lower-of-Cost-or-Market Inventory Valuation

A company should follow the principle of conservatism, which means that if there is more than one way to report its financial information, the approach that shows the results in the least favorable light should be presented. In this way, readers of the financial information see the "worst-case scenario" and are not misled into believing the results are more positive than they really are.

The value of a company's inventory is one of the amounts where this principle should apply. Therefore, after a company has valued its ending inventory by the FIFO, LIFO, or average cost method, it may take an additional step to ensure that the value of the inventory that is reported is not misinterpreted or overstated. Lower-of-cost-or-market is an additional calculation that is used to value inventory if the cost of a product (or products) declines after the item(s) has been purchased for inventory. "Market" can be interpreted as replacement cost, or what the item is selling for today. The company lists all the products it sells and for each product compares the price paid (cost) to the current market value. The lower of the two numbers is used to report the value of a product's inventory on the balance sheet.

Notice how Merchandise Inventory is presented on the balance sheet when lower-of-cost-or-market is used.

Balance Sheet
June 30, 2013

ASSETS			
Current assets:			
Cash		$40,000	
Accounts receivable		28,000	
Merchandise inventory - at lower of cost		32,000	
(first-in, first out) or market			
Supplies		6,000	

LIABILITIES			
Current liabilities:			
Accounts payable	$14,000		
Unearned fees	13,000		
Wages payable	12,000		
Salaries payable	11,000		
Notes payable	8,000		

The following example presents inventory data for July 31 for a business that uses the lower-of-cost-or-market basis of inventory valuation. The information in the white cells is given. The gray boxes are the cells that need to be calculated.

Commodity	Quantity	Unit Cost	Unit Market Price	Total Cost	Total Market	Lower of Cost or Market
A	10	$ 6	$ 5	$ 60	$ 50	$ 50
B	20	10	11	200	220	200
C	30	9	8	270	240	240
D	40	3	4	120	160	120
Totals				$650		$610

1. Multiply the inventory quantity by the unit cost price to get total cost.
2. Multiply the inventory quantity by the unit market price to get total market value.
3. For lower of cost or market, take the lower of the two results in each row.

The total purchase price of all of the merchandise combined is $650. The total lower-of-cost-or-market amount for all of the merchandise as of July 31 is $610. The inventory lost $40 of value due to market decline/prices dropping.

KEEPING UP WITH THE TIMES

A business has two models of cell phones in stock to sell to customers.

It has 200 units of Model #1. Each of those cost the company $100. If the company were to buy these phones today, each unit would cost $110.

It also has 200 units of Model #2, which were purchased two years ago for

$100 per unit. The market price for these is currently $60 per unit. It has dropped because these units are somewhat out of date.

If lower-of-cost-or-market is NOT used, the total inventory is valued at $40,000.

Model #1:	200 x $100 = $20,000	(number of units x cost per unit)
Model #2:	200 x $100 = 20,000	(number of units x cost per unit)
Total	$40,000	

If lower-of-cost-or-market is used, the total inventory is valued at $32,000.

Model #1:	**200 x $100 = $20,000**	(number of units x cost per unit)
Model #2:	200 x $ 60 = 12,000	(number of units x market price per unit since it is lower)
Total	$32,000	

The inventory should be reported at $32,000 on the balance sheet even though it was purchased for $40,000. This gives the reader a clearer picture of what the inventory is actually worth.

4.1.4 Physical Inventory Count

Companies using a perpetual inventory system keep a running total of the inventory they have on hand in their record books. At times, a physical inventory count is done to verify that a company actually has the amount of inventory that is indicated in its records.

The company will count/include the items **that it owns** that are on hand on its premises. Items may be on the company's premises that it does **not** own, and these should not be included in the physical inventory count. These may include:

a. Items on consignment from someone else (the company has agreed to sell someone else's product for them)

b. Items in for warranty repair (the company does not re-possess these)

c. Items held aside for customers that have been paid for already (ownership has been transferred)

The following items would be owned by the company and should be included:

a. Items returned by customers (the company re-possesses these)

b. Items held aside for customers that have not been paid for yet (ownership has not yet been transferred)

The company must also count/include items that it owns that are off premise at other locations. These may include:

a. Items on consignment to someone else (the other party has agreed to sell the company's items for them)

b. Items out for warranty repair with another company (the other party does not re-possess these)

c. Items that the company has **purchased** that are in transit (i.e., on the UPS truck) if the shipping terms are **FOB shipping**

d. Items that the company has **sold** that are in transit (i.e., on the UPS truck) if the shipping terms are **FOB destination**

NOTE: Whoever is responsible for absorbing the transportation cost (buyer or seller) also owns the merchandise while it is in transit.

EFFECT OF ERRORS IN PHYSICAL INVENTORY COUNT

To see the effect of an error in the physical inventory count on the financial statements, let's assume that a business reports what it counts as its **Merchandise Inventory** amount on the balance sheet.

In the example below, assume that the correct amount of merchandise inventory on hand is $20,000. The amounts in yellow in the excerpts of the following financial statements are correct.

Income Statement
For the Month Ended June 30, 2013

Sales		$200,000	
Cost of merchandise sold		80,000	
Gross profit			$120,000
Operating expenses:			
Salaries expense		$24,000	
Rent expense		10,000	
Insurance expense		6,000	
Total operating expenses			40,000
Net income from operations			$80,000

Balance Sheet
June 30, 2013

ASSETS			
Current assets:			
Cash		$40,000	
Accounts receivable		30,000	
Merchandise inventory		20,000	
Supplies		15,000	
Prepaid rent		9,000	
Prepaid insurance		6,000	
Total current assets			$120,000

Understating Merchandise Inventory (reporting an amount that is too low) The financial statements that follow show the effect of understating Merchandise Inventory, where something was missed in the physical inventory count. Only $19,500 rather than $20,000 is reported on the balance sheet.

As a result of this error, (1) Merchandise Inventory is understated, (2) Total assets are understated, (3) Cost of merchandise sold is overstated, (4) Net income is understated, and (5) Retained earnings and total stockholders' equity (not shown) are understated.

Income Statement
For the Month Ended June 30, 2013

Sales		$200,000	
Cost of merchandise sold		80,500	
Gross profit			$119,500
Operating expenses:			
Salaries expense		$24,000	
Rent expense		10,000	
Insurance expense		6,000	
Total operating expenses			40,000
Net income from operations			$79,500

Balance Sheet
June 30, 2013

ASSETS			
Current assets:			
Cash		$40,000	
Accounts receivable		30,000	
Merchandise inventory		19,500	
Supplies		15,000	
Prepaid rent		9,000	
Prepaid insurance		6,000	
Total current assets			$119,500

Overstating Merchandise Inventory (reporting an amount that is too high) The financial statements that follow show the effect of overstating Merchandise

Inventory, where something in the physical inventory count was included that should not have been. Instead of $20,000, $20,500 is reported on the balance sheet.

As a result of this error, (1) Merchandise Inventory is overstated, (2) Total assets are overstated, (3) Cost of merchandise sold is understated, (4) Net income is overstated, and (5) Retained earnings and total stockholders' equity (not shown) are overstated.

Income Statement
For the Month Ended June 30, 2013

Sales		$200,000	
Cost of merchandise sold		79,500	
Gross profit			$120,500
Operating expenses:			
Salaries expense		$24,000	
Rent expense		10,000	
Insurance expense		6,000	
Total operating expenses			40,000
Net income from operations			$80,500

Balance Sheet
June 30, 2013

ASSETS			
Current assets:			
Cash		$40,000	
Accounts receivable		30,000	
Merchandise inventory		20,500	
Supplies		15,000	
Prepaid rent		9,000	
Prepaid insurance		6,000	
Total current assets			$120,500

ACCT 2101 Topics—Inventory Valuation	Fact	Journal Entry	Calculate Amount	Format
Concept of inventory valuation methods	x			
Calculate cost of merchandise sold under FIFO			x	
Calculate ending inventory under FIFO			x	
Calculate cost of merchandise sold under LIFO			x	
Calculate ending inventory under LIFO			x	
Calculate cost of merchandise sold under average cost method			x	
Calculate ending inventory under average cost method			x	
Journalize purchase of merchandise on account under perpetual system		x	x	
Journalize sale of merchandise on account under perpetual system		x	x	
Calculate gross profit			x	
Calculate lower-of-cost-or-market amounts			x	
Financial statements			x	x
Physical inventory counts	x		x	

4.2 CASH

A company journalizes many transactions that involve cash and maintains a Cash ledger to track inflows and outflows and the running cash balance after each entry. A sample ledger for a new business that began on June 1 is shown below.

Cash							
Date	**Item**	**Debit**	**Credit**	**Debit**			
6/1	Deposit cash	12,000		12,000		✓	
6/2	Check #1111 payment		3,000	9,000		✓	
6/3	Check #1112 payment		500	8,500		✓	
6/4	Check #4689 deposit	450		8,950		✓	
6/5	Electronic transfer out		50	8,900		✓	
6/6	Check #326 deposit	500		9,400		✓	
6/7	Check #1113 payment		150	9,250			2
6/8	Check #3810 deposit	300		9,550		✓	
6/9	Electronic transfer out		1,200	8,350		✓	
6/11	Check #9100 deposit	900		9,250		✓	
6/12	Check #1114 payment		75	9,175		✓	
6/18	Check #1115 payment		80	9,095	800	x	6
6/20	Check #669 deposit	700		9,795		✓	
6/22	Electronic credit card payment #7994		250	9,545		✓	
6/24	Check #1116 payment		450	9,095			2
6/28	Check #761 deposit	600		9,695			3
6/29	Check #1117 payment		140	9,555			2
6/30	Electronic transfer out		1,100	8,455		✓	1

Almost all companies open a checking account at a bank to safeguard their cash as well as to be able to accept and write checks, transfer funds electronically, and make and receive loan payments.

The bank provides an independent record of the account holder's cash transactions up to the current date on bank statements, which are available online. Each monthly bank statement typically lists a beginning balance, deposits, withdrawals, and an ending balance related to that time period.

The following sample online bank statement lists transactions that a business may typically expect to see each month:

Account Activity My Statements Find Transactions

Download Print

Go to: July 2011 Newest · Next · Previous · Oldest Quick Find Find

Date	Description	Amount	Balance	
6/30/2011	Commons Electric: Payment ID 0008457050	-1,100	9,375	✓ 7
6/30/2011	Monthly Service Charge	-50	10,475	5c
6/27/2011	Ace Pest Control: Scheduled Payment ID 0004938567	-150	10,525	5a
6/24/2011	Online Banking payment to CRD 7927 ID 2739861441	-250	10,675	✓
6/23/2011	NSF Check ID 000593802	-900	10,925	5b
6/22/2011	Deposit	700	11,825	✓
6/22/2011	Check #1115: Edit Details	-800	11,125	✓
6/21/2011	Hammond Co.: Direct Deposit ID 0004867032	2,500	11,925	4a
6/13/2011	Check #1114: Edit Details	-75	9,425	✓
6/13/2011	Deposit: Note Receivable Collection Arctic Co.	100	9,500	4b
6/12/2011	Deposit	900	9,400	✓
6/9/2011	Commons Electric: Payment ID 0008473012	-1,200	8,500	✓
6/8/2011	Check #1112: Edit Details	-500	9,700	✓
6/8/2011	Deposit	300	10,200	✓
6/7/2011	Deposit	500	9,900	✓
6/6/2011	Cannon Supply: Payment ID 0004938567	-50	9,400	✓
6/6/2011	Deposit	450	9,450	✓
6/3/2011	Check #1111: Edit Details	-3,000	9,000	✓
6/2/2011	Deposit	12,000	12,000	✓

4.2.1 Bank Reconciliation

Since cash is susceptible to theft, fraud, and loss, it is important to continuously verify that the amount shown in the ledger balance is what the business actually has. A bank reconciliation helps do this. A bank reconciliation compares the company's record of cash on hand to the bank statement, adjusts for missing or incorrect entries, and is complete when the result equals the ending balance on the bank statement. A bank reconciliation should be completed at least once a month but can be done more frequently using online statements that provide up- to-date information.

One key purpose of the bank reconciliation is to notify the account holder of transactions that the bank has processed on the company's behalf so the company can record them and update its cash balance accordingly.

Begin the reconciliation process by comparing the company's cash ledger to the bank statement. First, check off all transactions that match in both the ledger and on the bank statement to indicate that both the company and the bank have recorded these items. This is shown as red checkmarks on the right side in both the sample cash ledger and the sample bank statement on the previous page.

The bank reconciliation is a two-fold process. Essentially what it accomplishes is to update the company's balance and update the bank balance for items each party did not yet know about and therefore had not recorded at the end of the month.

Secondly, update the company's Cash ledger balance to include amounts from the bank statement that are not yet listed in the ledger AND adjust for any errors in the ledger. The numbers in blue below correspond to amounts on the previous page in either the Cash ledger account or on the bank statement.

1. Note the end-of-month balance in the company's Cash ledger.	$ 8,455
Add deposits that appear on the bank statement but not in the ledger. 4a. Electronic transfer in/payment from a customer 4b. Collection of a note receivable 4c. Interest earned on the company's account	+2,500 +100
Deduct withdrawals that appear on the bank statement but not in the ledger. 5a. Electronic transfer out/auto payment to a vendor 5b. Customer check returned for not sufficient funds 5c. Bank service charge	-150 -900 -50
6. Adjust for any errors in the amounts in the ledger. Since a deduction for check #1115 was entered as $80 rather than $800 in the ledger, the remaining $720 must be deducted.	-720
Adjusted result	$9,235
7. Note the end-of-month balance on the company's bank statement.	$9,375
3. Add deposits in the ledger that are not yet listed on the bank statement.	+600

2. Subtract deductions for checks and withdrawals in the ledger that are not yet listed on the bank statement.	-150 -450 -140
Adjust for any errors in the amounts on the bank statement. There are none in this example.	
Adjusted result	$9,235

Next, update the bank statement balance to include amounts in the Cash ledger that do not appear on the bank statement AND adjust for any errors on the bank statement. The numbers in blue below correspond to amounts on the previous page in either the Cash ledger account or on the bank statement.

Then compare the two results to verify that they are equal. They are: both results are $9,235.

The bank reconciliation may be summarized as follows:

Adjustments to the Cash Ledger Account	
Description	Amount
Cash ledger balance per company records as per books	$8,455
Note receivable plus interest collected by the bank	100
Electronic transfer from a customer's account	2,500
Bank charges	(50)
Electronic transfer to a vendor's account	(150)
Returned check due to insufficient funds	(900)
Check recording error in the ledger	(720)
Adjusted result	$9,235

Adjustments to the Bank Statement Ending Balance	
Description	Amount
Bank balance per the bank statement	$9,375
Deposits in transit	600
Outstanding checks	(740)
Adjusted result	$9,235

Finally, the company's Cash ledger must be updated to reflect transactions it has learned about from the bank statement as well as any changes that must be made to correct errors in the company's books. The notation in blue for each transaction relates back to the instruction numbers on the previous pages.

Electronic payment from customer Hammond Co. on the bank statement

Date	Account		Debit	Credit
(4a)	Cash		2,500	
	Accounts Receivable			2,500

- *Cash* is an **asset** account that is **increasing.**
- *Accounts Receivable* is an asset account that is decreasing.

Note Receivable collection from Arctic Co. per bank statement

Date	Account		Debit	Credit
(4b)	Cash		100	
	Note Receivable			98
	Interest Revenue			98

- *Cash* is an **asset** account that is **increasing.**
- *Notes Receivable* is an **asset** account that is **decreasing.**
- *Interest Revenue* is a **revenue** account that is **increasing.**

Scheduled payment to a vendor – Ace Pest Control – per bank statement

Date	Account		Debit	Credit
(5a)	Maintenance Expense		150	
	Cash			150

- *Maintenance Expense* is an **expense** account that is **increasing.**
- *Cash* is an **asset** account that is **decreasing.**

NSF returned check per bank statement

Date	Account		Debit	Credit
(5b)	Accounts Receivable		900	
	Cash			900

- *Accounts Receivable* is an **asset** account that is **increasing.**
- *Cash* is an **asset** account that is **decreasing.**

Monthly bank charge per bank statement

Date	Account		Debit	Credit
(5c)	Bank Card Expense		50	
	Cash			50

- *Bank Card Expense* is an **expense** account that is **increasing.**
- *Cash* is an **asset** account that is **decreasing.**

Error correction in company's records – check #1115 should be $800 rather than $80

Date	Account		Debit	Credit
(6)	Rent Expense		720	
	Cash			720

- *Rent Expense* is an **expense** account that is **increasing.**
- *Cash* is an **asset** account that is **decreasing.**

The Cash ledger below has been updated to include the six transactions above.

Cash							
Date	**Item**	**Debit**	**Credit**	**Debit**			
6/1	Deposit cash	12,000		12,000		✓	
6/2	Check #1111 payment		3,000	9,000		✓	
6/3	Check #1112 payment		500	8,500		✓	
6/4	Check #4689 deposit	450		8,950		✓	
6/5	Electronic transfer out		50	8,900		✓	
6/6	Check #326 deposit	500		9,400		✓	
6/7	Check #1113 payment		150	9,250			2
6/8	Check #3810 deposit	300		9,550		✓	
6/9	Electronic transfer out		1,200	8,350		✓	
6/11	Check #9100 deposit	900		9,250		✓	
6/12	Check #1114 payment		75	9,175		✓	
6/18	Check #1115 payment		80	9,095	800	x	6
6/20	Check #669 deposit	700		9,795		✓	
6/22	Electronic credit card payment #7994		250	9,545		✓	
6/24	Check #1116 payment		450	9,095			2
6/28	Check #761 deposit	600		9,695			3
6/29	Check #1117 payment		140	9,555			2
6/30	Electronic transfer out		1,100	8,455		✓	1
6/30	Electronic transfer in from customer	2,500		10,955			
6/30	Note receivable collection	100		11,055			
6/30	Electronic transfer out to vendor		150	10,905			
6/30	Returned check not sufficient funds		900	10,005			
6/30	Bank charge		50	9,955			
6/30	Error correction Check #115 amount		720	9,235			

4.2.2 Bank Card Expense

Businesses that accept credit and debit cards typically pay processing fees to a company that handles the electronic transactions for them. The charges may be flat fees, per transaction fees, or various combinations. The processing company automatically withdraws these fees from the business's bank account.

On a monthly basis, the processing company sends the business a statement of fees. At that time the business makes the following journal entry to record this cost of accepting credit/debit cards.

18. Paid card processing fees of $300.

Date	Account		Debit	Credit
(5c)	Bank Card Expense		50	
	Cash			50

- *Bank Card Expense* is an **expense** account that is **increasing.**
- *Cash* is an **asset** account that is **decreasing.**

Bank Card Expense is an account that keeps track of costs related to accepting credit and debit cards

ACCOUNTS SUMMARY TABLE

ACCOUNT TYPE	ACCOUNTS	TO INCREASE	TO DECREASE	NORMAL BALANCE	FINANCIAL STATEMENT	CLOSE OUT?
Expense	Bank Card Expense	debit	credit	debit	Income Statement	YES

4.3 NOTE RECEIVABLE

A business may lend money to an individual or to a customer. These loans are typically short term, due to be repaid to the business within one year. In this case, the current asset account Note Receivable is used to keep track of amounts that are owed to the business.

A note receivable is a loan contract that specifies the principal (amount of the loan), the interest rate stated as an annual percentage, and the terms stated in number of days or months.

4.3.1 Issue Date

There are two situations where a company may receive a short-term note.

1. A direct short-term loan for cash when an employee or other individual asks to borrow money and the company agrees and distributes cash.

In the following example, a company received a 60-day, 12% note for $1,000 from one of its executives on January 1.

Date	Account		Debit	Credit
1/1	Note Receivable		1,000	
	Cash			1,000

- *Note Receivable* is an **asset** account that is **increasing.**
- *Cash* is an **asset** account that is **decreasing.**

2. The transfer of what a customer already owes the company for services or products it had previously purchased on account. The following would be a sample sequence of events.

   a. A company sells merchandise to a customer on account and gives the customer 30 days to pay.

Date	Account		Debit	Credit
1/1	Accounts Receivable		1,000	
	Sales			1,000

- *Accounts Receivable* is an **asset** account that is **increasing.**
- *Sales* is a **revenue** account that is **increasing.**

   c. After 30 days the customer's **accounts receivable** amount of $1,000 is due, but the customer is unable to pay. If both parties agree, the customer's Accounts Receivable account balance can be transferred to the **Note Receivable** account on that date. This gives the customer an extension of time in which to pay, but from this point on an interest charge will be imposed.

Interest is essentially the cost of renting money from its owner, similar to the cost of renting an apartment from a landlord. The borrower is paying to use someone else's money. There is no need, however, to include the interest amount on the issue date—wait until the note comes due.

On the issue date, debit **Note Receivable** to increase it; credit **Accounts Receivable** to decrease it.

In the following example, a company received a 60-day, 12% note for $1,000 from a customer on account on January 1.

Date	Account		Debit	Credit
1/1	Note Receivable		1,000	
	Accounts Receivable			1,000

- *Note Receivable* is an **asset** account that is **increasing.**
- *Accounts Receivable* is an **asset** account that is **decreasing.**

This journal entry causes the balance in Accounts Receivable to decrease and the balance in Note Receivable to increase. The same $1,000 that the customer owes is now classified as an interest-bearing loan rather than just an interest-free amount owed on an invoice.

4.3.2 Maturity (Due) Date

At the end of the term of the loan, on the maturity date, the note is void. At that time the **Note Receivable** account must be credited for the principle amount. In addition, the amount of interest earned must be recorded in the journal entry as **Interest Revenue.** The amount of interest is calculated using the following equation:

Principal x Rate x Time = Interest Earned

To simplify the math, we will assume every month has 30 days and each year has 360 days.

For a 12% interest rate on a 60-day note, the interest on a $1,000 note would be $20, calculated as follows:

$1,000 x 12% x 60/360 = $20

Note that since the 12% is an annual rate (for 12 months), it must be pro-rated for the number of months or days (60/360 days or 2/12 months) in the term of the loan.

On the maturity date, both the **Note Receivable** and **Interest Revenue** accounts are credited. **Note Receivable** is credited because it is no longer valid and its balance must be set back to zero. **Interest Revenue** is credited because it is now earned, regardless of whether the company receives the cash.

Date	Account		Debit	Credit
2/28	????		1,020	
	Note Receivable			1,000
	Interest Revenue			20

- One of three **asset** accounts will be **increasing.**
- **Note Receivable** is an **asset** account that is **decreasing.**
- *Interest Revenue* is a **revenue** account that is **increasing.**

The asset that the lender debits after 60 days depends on what the customer does on the maturity date of the note. There are the three possibilities:

1. **Cash** – customer pays what is owed
2. **Note Receivable** – customer issues a new note to replace the first note for another extension
3. **Accounts Receivable** – customer does not pay or make arrangements for an extension of time

Situation 1 – The customer pays off the note with cash.

Date	Account		Debit	Credit
2/28	Cash		1,020	
	Note Receivable			1,000
	Interest Revenue			20

- *Cash* is an **asset** account that is **increasing.**
- *Note Receivable* is an **asset** account that is **decreasing.**
- *Interest Revenue* is a **revenue** account that is **increasing.**

Situation 2a – The company receives another note from the customer for the principal of the first note plus the interest. Assume the new note is for another 60 days at 10%.

Date	Account		Debit	Credit
2/28	Note Receivable		1,020	
	Note Receivable			1,000
	Interest Revenue			20

- *Note Receivable* is an **asset** account that is **increasing.**
- *Note Receivable* is an **asset** account that is **decreasing.**
- *Interest Revenue* is a **revenue** account that is **increasing.**

Situation 2b – The company receives another note from the customer for the principal and receives cash for the interest only. Assume the new note is for another 60 days at 10%.

Date	Account		Debit	Credit
2/28	Cash		20	
	Note Receivable		1,000	
	Note Receivable			1,000
	Interest Revenue			20

- *Cash* is an **asset** account that is **increasing.**
- *Note Receivable* is an **asset** account that is **increasing.**
- *Note Receivable* is an **asset** account that is **decreasing.**
- *Interest Revenue* is a **revenue** account that is **increasing.**

Situation 3 - The customer dishonors the note and does not pay on the due date.

Date	Account		Debit	Credit
2/28	Accounts Receivable		1,020	
	Note Receivable			1,000
	Interest Revenue			20

- *Accounts Receivable* is an **asset** account that is **increasing.**
- *Note Receivable* is an *asset* account that is **decreasing.**
- *Interest Revenue* is a **revenue** account that is increasing.

Since the note is void but the customer did not pay or make arrangements for a new note, the only account remaining to record what is owed is Accounts Receivable. This will immediately indicate that the customer's account is overdue.

Situation 2a – wrapping it up

This was the journal entry in Situation 2a above.

Date	Account		Debit	Credit
2/28	Note Receivable		1,020	
	Note Receivable			1,000
	Interest Revenue			20

- *Note Receivable* is an **asset** account that is **increasing.**
- *Note Receivable* is an **asset** account that is **decreasing.**
- *Interest Revenue* is a **revenue** account that is **increasing.**

Now let's look at what happens when the customer in Situation 2a above finally pays the company back after the period. The new note was for another 60 days at 10%. Additional interest revenue earned on this second notes is $1,020 x 10% x 60/360, or $17.

Date	Account		Debit	Credit
4/30	Cash		1,037	
	Note Receivable			1,020
	Interest Revenue			17

- *Cash* is an **asset** account that is **increasing.**
- *Note Receivable* is an **asset** account that is **decreasing.**
- *Interest Revenue* is a *revenue* account that is **increasing.**

Situation 3 – wrapping it up

This was the journal entry in Situation 3 above.

Date	Account		Debit	Credit
2/28	Accounts Receivable		1,020	
	Note Receivable			1,000
	Interest Revenue			20

- *Accounts Receivable* is an **asset** account that is **increasing.**
- *Note Receivable* is an **asset** account that is **decreasing.**
- *Interest Revenue* is a **revenue** account that is **increasing.**

Assume two more months pass. Two possible things can happen now.

Possibility 1 - The customer finally pays on 4/30, two months after the original due date. The company charges a 10% penalty on the outstanding balance, which is $17 (1,020 x 10% x 60/360). A penalty is recorded as interest revenue

Date	Account		Debit	Credit
4/30	Cash		1,037	
	Note Receivable			1,020
	Interest Revenue			17

- *Cash* is an **asset** account that is **increasing.**
- *Note Receivable* is an **asset** account that is **decreasing.**
- *Interest Revenue* is a **revenue** account that is **increasing.**

Possibility 2 - The company realizes the customer will NEVER be able to pay and writes him off.

Date	Account		Debit	Credit
4/30	Allowance Doubtful Accounts		1,037	
	Accounts Receivable			1,020

- *Allow Doubt Accts* is a contra **asset** account that is **decreasing.**
- *Accounts Receivable* is an **asset** account that is **decreasing.**

This will be covered in the next section.

4.4 .UNCOLLECTIBLE ACCOUNTS

When a company extends credit to its customers, it invoices customers and gives them time (usually 30 days) to pay.

SALE ON ACCOUNT: The company debits **Accounts Receivable** rather than **Cash** when it sells on account.

Date	Account		Debit	Credit
4/1	Accounts Receivable		3,000	
	Sales			3,000

- *Accounts Receivable* is an **asset** account that is **increasing**.
- *Sales* is a **revenue** account that is **increasing.**

RECEIPT OF PAYMENT: When customers pay off their account within the time allowed, Cash is debited and Accounts Receivable is credited.

Date	Account		Debit	Credit
4/30	Cash		3,000	
	Accounts Receivable			3,000

- *Cash* is an **asset** account that is **increasing.**
- *Accounts Receivable* is an **asset** account that is **decreasing.**

The customer has paid the entire amount owed on account and now owes nothing.

However, there may be cases when customers default on their accounts and can or will never pay. If the company is certain that it will never be paid, it can write off the customer's account and claim the non-payment as a business expense. A write-off is forgiveness of a customer's debt. This is done only when a company is absolutely certain that a customer can never pay (due to death, bankruptcy, his own admission, etc.)

There are two methods for recording bad debt.

1. Direct write-off method—for companies that rarely have bad debt
2. Allowance method—for companies that consistently have bad debt

The method a company selects depends on how frequently it anticipates it will experience bad debt. A business such as a movie theater, which primarily accepts cash from customers rather than invoicing them, would not write off bad debt often, if ever. Conversely, a utility company that provides electricity to homeowners constantly must write off bad debt as customers cannot pay or move and do not pay their last bill. The movie theater would select the direct method; the utility company would employ the allowance method.

4.4.1 Direct Write-off Method

The direct write-off method is used by companies that rarely experience any bad debt. A new account—Bad Debt Expense—is an expense account that absorbs this non-payment when the account receivable is closed out. The ONLY account that is written off is Accounts Receivable—it is credited to remove the customer's balance.

SALE ON ACCOUNT: The company debits Accounts Receivable rather than **Cash** when it sells on account.

Date	Account		Debit	Credit
4/1	Accounts Receivable		3,000	
	Sales			3,000

- *Accounts Receivable* is an **asset** account that is **increasing.**

- *Sales* is a **revenue** account that is **increasing.**

WRITE-OFF OF ALL OF AN ACCOUNTS RECEIVABLE: If none of what the customer owes will ever be received, Bad Debt Expense is debited instead of Cash to close out the account.

Date	Account		Debit	Credit
4/30	Bad Debt Expense		3,000	
	Accounts Receivable			3,000

- *Bad Debt Expense* is an **expense** account that is **increasing.**
- *Accounts Receivable* is an **asset** account that is **decreasing.**

WRITE-OFF OF PART OF AN ACCOUNTS RECEIVABLE: If the customer pays some of what he owes but will never be able to pay the rest, the company records the receipt of cash and also writes off the remaining amount that it will never receive. In this case the customer pays $1,000 and the company writes off the remaining $2,000.

Date	Account		Debit	Credit
4/30	Cash		1,000	
	Bad Debt Expense		2,000	
	Accounts Receivable			3,000

- *Cash* is an **asset** account that is **increasing.**
- *Bad Debt Expense* is an **expense** account that is **increasing.**
- *Accounts Receivable* is an **asset** account that is **decreasing.**

REINSTATEMENT OF FULL AMOUNT: If, for some reason, the customer returns to pay his entire bill AFTER the write-off, just “flip over” the previous transaction to void it. This is called reinstating. Then make the journal entry to collect the cash. Note that there are two journal entries for a reinstatement.

Date	Account		Debit	Credit
6/17	Accounts Receivable		3,000	
	Bad Debt Expense			3,000
	Cash		3,000	
	Accounts Receivable			3,000

- *Accounts Receivable* is an **asset** account that is **increasing.**
- *Bad Debt Expense* is an **expense** account that is **decreasing.**
- *Cash* is an **asset** account that is **increasing.**
- *Accounts Receivable* is an **asset** account that is **decreasing.**

REINSTATEMENT OF PARTIAL AMOUNT: If, for some reason, the customer returns to pay only part of what he owed AFTER the write-off (for example, $1,000), just "flip over" the previous transaction to void it. This is called reinstating. Then make the journal entry to collect the cash. Only include the amount the customer repays, not the entire amount that was written off

Date	Account		Debit	Credit
6/17	Accounts Receivable		1,000	
	Bad Debt Expense			1,000
	Cash		1,000	
	Accounts Receivable			1,000

- *Accounts Receivable* is an **asset** account that is **increasing.**
- *Bad Debt Expense* is an **expense** account that is **decreasing.**
- *Cash* is an **asset** account that is **increasing.**
- *Accounts Receivable* is an **asset** account that is **decreasing.**

4.4.2 Allowance Method

The **allowance method** is used by companies that frequently experience bad debt. A new account—**Allowance for Doubtful Accounts**—is a contra asset account that absorbs this non-payment when the account receivable is closed out. An allowance is an estimate. Companies that have continuous bad debt make an adjusting entry at the beginning of the year to estimate how much of its **Accounts Receivable** it believes it will never collect due to non-payment. This is recorded before any customer's account actually defaults during the year.

ADJUSTING ENTRY TO SET UP BAD DEBT ESTIMATE of $15,000 FOR THE YEAR: A credit to Allowance for Doubtful Accounts increases it, since it is a contra asset. NOTE: The only time **Bad Debt Expense** is used under the allowance method is in the annual adjusting entry. There are two ways of estimating the amount of bad debt for the upcoming year; these will be discussed shortly.

Date	Account		Debit	Credit
1/1	Bad Debt Expense		15,000	
	Allowance for Doubtful Accounts			15,000

- *Bad Debt Expense* is an *expense* account that is **increasing.**
- *Allow Doubt Accts* is a contra **asset** account that is **increasing.**

SALE ON ACCOUNT: The company debits Accounts Receivable rather than Cash when it sells on account.

Date	Account		Debit	Credit
4/1	Accounts Receivable		3,000	
	Sales			3,000

- *Accounts Receivable* is an **asset** account that is **increasing.**
- *Sales* is a **revenue** account that is **increasing.**

WRITE-OFF OF ALL OF AN ACCOUNTS RECEIVABLE: If none of what the customer owes will ever be received, Allowance for Doubtful Accounts is debited instead of Cash to close out the account.

Date	Account		Debit	Credit
4/30	Allowance Doubtful Accounts		3,000	
	Accounts Receivable			3,000

- *Allow Doubt Accts* is a contra **asset** account that is **decreasing.**
- *Accounts Receivable* is an **asset** account that is **decreasing.**

WRITE-OFF OF PART OF AN ACCOUNTS RECEIVABLE: If the customer pays] some of what he owes but will never be able to pay the rest, the company records the receipt of cash and also writes off the remaining amount that it will never receive. In this case the customer pays $1,000 and the company writes off the remaining $2,000.

Date	Account		Debit	Credit
4/30	Cash		1,000	
	Allowance Doubtful Accounts		2,000	
	Accounts Receivable			3,000

- *Cash* is an **asset** account that is **increasing.**
- *Allow Doubt Accts* is a contra **asset** account that is **decreasing.**
- *Accounts Receivable* is an **asset** account that is **decreasing.**

REINSTATEMENT OF FULL AMOUNT: If, for some reason, the customer returns to pay his entire bill AFTER the write-off, just "flip over" the previous transaction to void it. This is called reinstating. Then make the journal entry to collect the cash. Note that there are two journal entries for a reinstatement.

Date	Account		Debit	Credit
6/17	Accounts Receivable		3,000	
	Allowance for Doubtful Accounts			3,000
	Cash		3,000	
	Accounts Receivable			3,000

- *Accounts Receivable* is an **asset** account that is **increasing.**
- *Allow Doubt Accts* is a contra **asset** account that is **increasing.**
- *Cash* is an **asset** account that is **increasing.**
- *Accounts Receivable* is an **asset** account that is **decreasing.**

REINSTATEMENT OF PARTIAL AMOUNT: If, for some reason, the customer returns to pay only part of what he owed AFTER the write-off (for example, $1,000), just "flip over" the previous transaction to void it. This is called reinstating. Then make the journal entry to collect the cash. Only include the amount the customer repays, not the entire amount that was written off.

Date	Account		Debit	Credit
6/17	Accounts Receivable		1,000	
	Allowance for Doubtful Accounts			1,000
	Cash		1,000	
	Accounts Receivable			1,000

- *Accounts Receivable* is an *asset* account that is **increasing.**
- *Allow Doubt Accts* is a contra *asset* account that is **increasing.**
- *Cash* is an **asset** account that is **increasing.**
- *Accounts Receivable* is an **asset** account that is **decreasing.**

Net Realizable Value is the amount of a company's total Accounts Receivable that it expects to collect. It is calculated and appears on the Balance Sheet as follows:

Net Realizable Value is the amount of a company's total Accounts Receivable that it expects to collect. It is calculated and appears on the Balance Sheet as follows:

	Accounts Receivable	$97,000 (amount owed to a company)
Less:	Allowance for Doubtful Accounts	12,000 (amount the company expects will "go bad")
	Net Realizable Value	$85,000

In fairness to the readers of the balance sheet, the company admits on the balance sheet that even though it is owed $97,000 from customers (an asset), it does not expect to ever receive $12,000 of it. The **Accounts Receivable** and Allowance for **Doubtful Accounts amounts** on the balance sheet are the current ledger balances.

ALLOWANCE METHOD—ANALYSIS OF RECEIVABLES

The **allowance method** is used by companies that frequently experience bad debt. An allowance is an estimate. Companies that have continuous bad debt make an adjusting entry at the beginning of the year to estimate how much of its Accounts Receivable it believes it will never collect due to non-payment. The question now is this: How is the amount of the adjusting entry determined?

Sample: ADJUSTING ENTRY TO SET UP BAD DEBT ESTIMATE FOR THE YEAR

Date	Account		Debit	Credit
1/1	Bad Debt Expense		?????	
	Allowance for Doubtful Accounts			?????

- *Bad Debt Expense* is an **expense** account that is **increasing.**
- *Allow Doubt Accts* is a **contra** *asset* account that is **increasing.**

There are two ways to arrive at the estimate for the upcoming year (the amount of the adjusting entry) under the allowance method. These are **analysis of receivables and percent of sales.**

1. **Analysis of receivables** involves analyzing and/or contacting all customers, determining who is likely to default and adding the amounts for all customers who are likely to become bad debt. **The adjusting entry should include the amount necessary to bring the Allowance for Doubtful Accounts ledger balance up to this number.**

In the three examples that follow, assume that after analyzing receivables on 1/1, it is estimated that there will be $8,000 of bad debt during the upcoming year.

Example 1 – Analysis of Receivables: No balance in the Allowance for Doubtful Accounts ledger.

Date	Item	Debit	Credit	Debit	Credit
1/1	Balance			?????	

Since there is no balance in the account "left over" from last year, it will take a credit of $8,000 to bring the year's beginning balance up to $8,000.

Date	Account		Debit	Credit
1/1	Bad Debt Expense		8,000	
	Allowance for Doubtful Accounts			8,000

- *Bad Debt Expense* is an **expense** account that is **increasing.**
- *Allow Doubt* Accts is a *contra* asset account that is *increasing.*

Allowance for Doubtful Accounts					
Date	Item	Debit	Credit	Debit	Credit
1/1			8,000		8,000

The adjusting entry for the estimate brings the

Accumulated Depreciation credit balance to $8,000

Example 2– Analysis of Receivables: A $600 credit balance in the Allowance for Doubtful Accounts ledger.

This means that the company overestimated its Bad Debt Expense last year—it had less bad debt than it had estimated it would have.

Allowance for Doubtful Accounts					
Date	**Item**	**Debit**	**Credit**	**Debit**	**Credit**
1/1	Balance				6,00

Since there is already a $600 credit balance in the account "left over" from last year, it will only take an additional credit of $7,400 to bring the year's beginning balance up to $8,000.

Date	Account		Debit	Credit
1/1	Bad Debt Expense		7,400	
	Allowance for Doubtful Accounts			7,400

- *Bad Debt Expense* is an **expense** account that is **increasing.**
- *Allow Doubt Accts* is a contra **asset** account that is **increasing.**

Allowance for Doubtful Accounts					
Date	**Item**	**Debit**	**Credit**	**Debit**	**Credit**
1/1	Balance				600
1/1			7,400		8,000

The adjusting entry for the estimate brings the **Accumulated Depreciation** credit balance to $8,000.

Example 3– Analysis of Receivables: A $600 debit balance in the Allowance for Doubtful Accounts ledger.

This means that the company underestimated its Bad Debt Expense last year—it had more bad debt than it had estimated it would have.

Allowance for Doubtful Accounts					
Date	**Item**	**Debit**	**Credit**	**Debit**	**Credit**
1/1	Balance			600	

Since there is already a $600 debit balance in the account "left over" from last year, it will take an additional credit of $8,600 to bring the year's beginning balance up to $8,000.

Date	Account		Debit	Credit
1/1	Bad Debt Expense		8,600	
	Allowance for Doubtful Accounts			8,600

- *Bad Debt Expense* is an **expense** account that is **increasing.**
- *Allow Doubt Accts* is a contra **asset** account that is **increasing.**

Allowance for Doubtful Accounts					
Date	**Item**	**Debit**	**Credit**	**Debit**	**Credit**
1/1	Balance			600	
1/1			8,600		8,000

The adjusting entry for the estimate brings the **Accumulated Depreciation** credit balance to $8,000.

ALLOWANCE METHOD – PERCENT OF SALES

2. **Percent of Sales** involves a simple calculation: Sales on account in previous year times the historical percent of sales that default. **The adjusting entry should include the result of the calculation; the credit to Allowance for Doubtful Accounts increases the account's ledger balance.**

In the three examples below assume that sales on account for the previous year were $400,000 and an estimated 2% of those sales will have to be written off. The amount of $8,000, which his $400,000 x 2%, is the amount that will be entered in the adjusting entry for the estimate.

Example 1 – Percent of Sales: No balance in the **Allowance for Doubtful Accounts** ledger.

Allowance for Doubtful Accounts					
Date	**Item**	**Debit**	**Credit**	**Debit**	**Credit**
1/1	Balance				

There is no balance in the account "left over" from last year.

Date	Account		Debit	Credit
1/1	Bad Debt Expense		8,000	
	Allowance for Doubtful Accounts			8,000

$400,000 x 2% = $8,000

- *Bad Debt Expense* is an **expense** account that is **increasing.**
- *Allow Doubt Accts* is a contra **asset** account that is **increasing.**

Allowance for Doubtful Accounts					
Date	**Item**	**Debit**	**Credit**	**Debit**	**Credit**
1/1			8,000		8,000

The adjusting entry for the estimate brings the Allowance for Doubtful Accounts credit balance to $8,000.

Example 2– Percent of Sales: A $600 credit balance in the Allowance for Doubtful Accounts ledger.

This means that the company overestimated its Bad Debt Expense last year—it had less bad debt than it had estimated it would have.

Allowance for Doubtful Accounts					
Date	**Item**	**Debit**	**Credit**	**Debit**	**Credit**
1/1	Balance				600

There is a $600 credit balance in the account "left over" from last year.

Date	Account		Debit	Credit
1/1	Bad Debt Expense		8,000	
	Allowance for Doubtful Accounts			8,000

$400,000 x 2% = $8,000

- *Bad Debt Expense* is an **expense** account that is **increasing.**
- *Allow Doubt Accts* is a contra **asset** account that is **increasing.**

Allowance for Doubtful Accounts					
Date	**Item**	**Debit**	**Credit**	**Debit**	**Credit**
1/1	Balance				600
1/1			8,000		8,600

The adjusting entry for the estimate adds the additional $8,000 to the previous credit balance.

Example 3– Percent of Sales: A $600 debit balance in the Allowance for Doubtful Accounts ledger.

This means that the company underestimated its Bad Debt Expense last year—it had more bad debt than it had estimated it would have.

Allowance for Doubtful Accounts					
Date	Item	Debit	Credit	Debit	Credit
1/1	Balance			600	

There is a $600 debit balance in the account "left over" from last year.

Date	Account		Debit	Credit
1/1	Bad Debt Expense		8,000	
	Allowance for Doubtful Accounts			8,000

$400,000 x 2% = $8,000

- *Bad Debt Expense* is an **expense** account that is **increasing.**
- *Allow Doubt Accts* is a contra **asset** account that is **increasing.**

Allowance for Doubtful Accounts					
Date	Item	Debit	Credit	Debit	Credit
1/1	Balance			600	
1/1			8,000		7,400

The adjusting entry for the estimate adds the additional $8,000 to the previous debit balance.

The following table summaries the new asset accounts.

ACCOUNTS SUMMARY TABLE

ACCOUNT TYPE	ACCOUNTS	TO INCREASE	TO DECREASE	NORMAL BALANCE	FINANCIAL STATEMENT	CLOSE OUT?
Asset	Accounts Receivable Notes Receivable	debit	credit	debit	Balance Sheet	NO
Contra Asset	Allowance for Doubtful Accounts	credit	debit	credit	Balance Sheet	NO
Revenue	Interest Revenue	credit	debit	credit	Income Statement	YES
Expense	Bad Debt Expense	debit	credit	debit	Income Statement	YES

ACCT 2101 Topics—Inventory Valuation	Fact	Journal Entry	Calculate Amount	Format
Concept of short-term loans	x			
Review sales transactions on account	x			
Journalize the receipt of a note receivable for cash		x	x	
Journalize the receipt of a note receivable on account		x	x	
Journalize the receipt of payment for a note due		x	r	
Journalize the receipt of a new note for a note due		x	x	
Journalize a dishonored note		x	x	
Journalize the receipt of payment on a dishonored note		x	x	
Concept of bad debt and write-offs	x			
Journalize a full write-off under the direct write-off method		x	x	
Journalize a partial write-off under the direct write-off method		x	x	
Journalize a full reinstatement under the direct write-off method		x	x	
Journalize a partial reinstatement under the direct write-off method		x	x	
Journalize bad debt estimates using an analysis of receivables		x	x	
Journalize a full write-off under the allowance method		x	x	
Journalize a partial write-off under the allowance method		x	x	
Journalize a full reinstatement under the allowance method		x	x	
Journalize a partial reinstatement under the allowance method		x	x	
Journalize bad debt estimates using percent of sales		x	x	
Financial statements			x	x
Journalize closing entries		x		
Post closing entries to ledgers			x	

The accounts that are highlighted in bright yellow are the new accounts you just learned. Those highlighted in light yellow are the ones you learned previously.

#1

Jonick Corporation
Income Statement
For the Month Ended June 30, 2014

Operating REVENUES:			
Fees Earned		$200,000	
Sales	$150,000		
Less: Sales returns	10,000		
Less: Sales discounts	5,000		
Net sales	135,000		
Cost of merchandise sold	55,000		
Gross profit		80,000	
Gross operating revenues			$280,000
Operating EXPENSES:			
Salaries expense		$25,000	
Wages expense		22,000	
Rent expense		20,000	
Insurance expense		19,000	
Supplies expense		18,000	
Advertising expense		17,000	
Maintenance expense		16,000	
Depreciation expense		15,000	
Taxes expense		14,000	
Utilities expense		13,000	
Payroll tax expense		12,000	
Bad debt expense		11,000	
Bank card expense		10,000	
Vehicle expense		9,000	
Delivery expense		8,000	
Amortization expense		7,000	
Miscellaneous expense		6,000	
Total operating expenses			242,000
Net income from operations			$38,000
Other revenue and expenses:			
Interest revenue		$5,000	
Interest expense		(4,000)	
Gain on sale of equipment		3,000	
Loss on redemption of bonds		(2,000)	2,000
Net income			$40,000

#3

Jonick Corporation
Balance Sheet
June 30, 2014

ASSETS			
Current assets:			
Cash		$40,000	
Accounts receivable	$28,000		
Less: Allowance for doubtful accounts	3,000	25,000	
Merchandise inventory		60,000	
Supplies		18,000	
Prepaid rent		12,000	
Prepaid insurance		6,000	
Prepaid taxes		4,000	
Note receivable		2,000	
Total current assets			$167,000
Fixed assets:			
Equipment	$16,000		
Less: Accumulated depreciation	2,000	14,000	
Van	30,000		
Less: Accumulated depreciation	5,000	25,000	
Building	200,000		
Less: Accumulated depreciation	70,000	130,000	
Land		110,000	
Total fixed assets			279,000
Intangible assets:			
Patents			14,000
Total assets			$460,000

LIABILITIES			
Current liabilities:			
Accounts payable	$14,000		
Unearned fees	13,000		
Wages payable	12,000		
Salaries payable	11,000		
Taxes payable	10,000		
Interest payable	9,000		
Notes payable	8,000		
Sales tax payable	7,000		
Social security tax payable	6,000		
Medicare tax payable	5,000		
Federal withholding tax payable	4,000		
State withholding tax payable	3,000		
Federal unemployment tax payable	2,000		
State unemployment tax payable	1,000		
Total current liabilities		$105,000	
Long-term liabilities:			
Mortgage note payable	$56,000		
Bonds payable	40,000		
Less: Discount on bonds payable	(6,000)		
Total long-term liabilities		90,000	
Total liabilities			$195,000
STOCKHOLDERS' EQUITY			
Common stock		$80,000	
Paid-in-capital in excess of par - common stock		34,000	
Preferred stock		50,000	
Paid-in-capital in excess of par - preferred stock		18,000	
Paid-in-capital from sale of treasury stock		13,000	
Retained earnings		90,000	
Treasury stock		(20,000)	
Total stockholders' equity			265,000
Total liabilities and stockholders' equity			$460,000

#2

Jonick Corporation
Retained Earnings Statement
For the Month Ended June 30, 2014

Retained earnings, June 1, 2014			$60,000
Net income		$40,000	
Less: Cash dividends	$6,000		
Stock dividends	4,000	10,000	
Increase in retained earnings			30,000
Retained earnings, June 30, 2014			$90,000

4.5 FIXED AND INTANGIBLE ASSETS

Fixed assets are relatively expensive physical items such as equipment, furnishings, vehicles, buildings, and land that typically last for several years. Fixed assets are also called Property, Plant and Equipment.

Equipment and other fixed assets are definitely costs of running a business. However, the company does not debit an expense account such as Equipment Expense for its cost at the time of purchase. If this were done, the income statement for the year of the purchase would have this large expense that reduces net income. The other years' income statements would show no expense for this equipment, even though the equipment is used during this time. Instead of an expense account, the company records the purchase of a fixed asset by debiting an asset account for its cost. For equipment, the Equipment account is debited.

The following journal entry records the purchase of equipment for $27,900 cash.

Date	Account		Debit	Credit
1/1	Equipment		27,900	
	Cash			27,900

- *Equipment* is an **asset** account that is **increasing.**
- *Cash* is an *asset* account that is **decreasing.**

Depreciation is the periodic expiration of a fixed asset, which means its cost is gradually claimed as an expense over its useful life rather than all at once at the time it is purchased. The company recognizes that a portion of the asset is "used up" as time passes or as the asset is used. The value that a fixed asset loses each year becomes an expense.

All fixed assets except Land are depreciated. Land is considered to be permanent property that is not "used up;" therefore it is not depreciated.

4.5.1 Depreciation Terms

Cost is the amount a company pays or the value it exchanges to acquire a fixed asset. The cost includes the price of the asset plus everything it takes to get the asset to the company and up and running, such as transportation, sales tax, insurance in transit, professional fees of attorneys or engineers, site preparation, and installation. The cost of the asset does not include damage or vandalism during shipment or installation.

EXAMPLE				
Equipment +	transportation +	sales tax +	installation cost =	depreciable cost of the asset
$9,000 +	$350	+ $450	+ $200	= $10,000 depreciable cost of the equipment

Some fixed assets have a residual value. This is a minimal guaranteed amount that someone will pay at any time, even if the asset no longer is functional, to purchase it from the owner. For example, the manufacturer of a piece of equipment may pay a company a minimal amount and haul away an old piece of equipment that it may then disassemble for spare parts or scrap metal.

EXAMPLE

Years ago, my dad worked in an area where nice cars tended to disappear from their parking spaces. He chose to drive old "clunkers" that did not appeal to car thieves. Each "clunker" would ultimately die in front of our nice suburban home, and my mother would soon be after him to remove it from the premises. Dad would call his "junk dealer," a man with a tow truck who would pay my father $50 and haul the wreck off. No matter how bad the condition one of those vehicles was in, it was always worth at least the $50 the "junk dealer" was willing to pay for it. Its residual value was $50.

The useful life is the length of time or amount of activity that a fixed asset is expected to last or have value to a company. It is often measured in years of service, but may also be stated in terms of usage, such as miles, hours, or units of output.

EXAMPLE

Two people may buy the identical cars for the same price on the same day. If depreciation is measured in years, both cars may be expected to last for eight years. However, if one driver is a salesman who is always on the road traveling long distances and the other is a retiree who drives locally and only occasionally, it is likely that the salesman's car will last fewer years than the retiree's. It may be more meaningful to state the useful life in miles, such as 150,000 miles, to better track the usage of the vehicles. In fact, automobile warranties are often stated in dual ways, such as "five years or 60,000 miles, whichever comes first." Similarly, rather than years, the useful life of a light bulb might be number of hours and a photocopy machine might be number of copies.

Depreciation Expense is an expense account on the income statement that is closed at the end of each accounting period. Debit **Depreciation Expense** rather than *Equipment Expense, Building Expense, Truck Expense,* etc. for the amount of a fixed asset that has been "used up" during the accounting period.

Although the value of a fixed asset decreases over time or with usage, the **cost principle** requires that a fixed asset's ledger balance be the cost of the asset, or what was paid for it. We cannot credit the asset's debit balance to show that it is losing value—its debit balance in the ledger must always be what it cost. In the previous equipment example it means that we are not allowed to credit the Equipment account to reduce its balance from $27,900. Its balance must stay at $27,900 as long as the company owns it.

Accumulated Depreciation substitutes for the fixed asset account and is credited to complete the entry. **Accumulated Depreciation is a contra asset** account that appears in the Asset section on the balance sheet just under the particular asset it relates to. It is not closed at the end of the accounting period. Instead, its credit balance increases each year as a fixed asset loses more and more value.

Each fixed asset account has its own **Accumulated Depreciation account.** The fixed asset account has a debit balance for the cost of the asset. The **Accumulated Depreciation** has a credit balance that indicates how much value the fixed asset has lost.

The adjusting entry for depreciation is as follows:

Date	Account		Debit	Credit
1/31	Depreciation Expense		8,700	
	Accumulated Depreciation			8,700

- *Depreciation Expense* is an **expense** account that is **increasing.**
- *Acc. Depreciation* is a contra **asset** account that is **increasing.**

Equipment	$27,900
Less: Accumulated depreciation	8,700
	$19,200

The book value of a fixed asset is what it is currently worth. The cost of a fixed asset is what was originally paid to acquire it. The credit balance in Accumulated Depreciation indicates how much of the asset's cost has been "used up." Book value is calculated by subtracting an asset's **Accumulated Depreciation** credit balance from its cost. This calculation is reported on the balance sheet.

Book value = Cost - Accumulated Depreciation

The following is the book value of equipment that cost $27,900 at the end of each year in its useful life, assuming it depreciates at a rate of $8,700 per year. This is shown on the balance sheet as follows:

	2012	2013	2014
Equipment	$27,900	$27,900	$27,900
Less: Accumulated depreciation	8,700	147,400	26.1000
Book Value	$19,200	$10,500	$1,800

Accumulated Depreciation increases over time. Book value decreases over time by the same amount.

The adjusting entries for depreciation split the cost of the equipment into two categories. The **Accumulated Depreciation** account balance is the amount of the asset that is "used up". The book value is the amount of value remaining on the asset.

It is important monitor the book value of fixed assets since the book value cannot be lower than the residual value. A company must stop depreciating any further once the book value equals the residual value since the asset will always be worth at least what someone will pay to purchase it from the owner, regardless of its condition. However, even there is no longer any remaining value to depreciate, a company may still continue to use a fixed asset.

4.5.2. Depreciation Methods

We will look at three methods of calculating the amount of depreciation on a fixed asset that should be recorded in the adjusting entry at the end of the accounting period. A company will select one method for each of its assets and use that method throughout the useful life of the asset. Each method requires that you know the cost of the asset, any residual value, and its useful life.

Regardless of the method used, the adjusting entry is a debit to Depreciation Expense and a credit to Accumulated Depreciation.

Date	Account		Debit	Credit
1/31	Depreciation Expense		XXX	
	Accumulated Depreciation			XXX

- *Depreciation Expense* is an **expense** account that is **increasing.**
- *Acc. Depreciation* is a contra **asset** account that is **increasing.**

STRAIGHT-LINE METHOD

Full-year straight-line depreciation

The straight-line method of depreciation is the simplest and most commonly used. It takes the depreciable base (cost minus residual amount) of the asset and expenses it off evenly over the useful life of the asset.

The annual depreciation amount is calculated as follows using straight-line:

$$\frac{\text{Cost - Residual value}}{\text{Useful life in years}}$$

The asset is fully depreciated when the years in its useful life have passed. At that point the book value equals the residual value.

EXAMPLE

On January 1, 2012, a company purchases equipment that costs $27,000. It has a residual value of $900, and has a three-year useful life. The company prepares its financial statements once a year on December 31.

$$\frac{\$27{,}000 - \$900}{3} = \$8{,}700 \text{ per full year}$$

The company purchased the equipment on January 1, 2012, so it can depreciate the asset for the full calendar year.

12/31/12 adjusting entry for depreciation:

Date	Account		Debit	Credit
12/31	Depreciation Expense		8,700	
	Accumulated Depreciation			8,700

After the 12/31/13 adjusting entry:

Cost	$27,000
Accumulated depreciation	8,700
Book value	$18,300

12/31/13 adjusting entry for depreciation:

Date	Account		Debit	Credit
12/31	Depreciation Expense		8,700	
	Accumulated Depreciation			8,700

After the 12/31/12 adjusting entry:

Cost	$27,000
Accumulated depreciation	17,400
Book value	$9,600

12/31/14 adjusting entry for depreciation:

Date	Account		Debit	Credit
12/31	Depreciation Expense		8,700	
	Accumulated Depreciation			8,700

After the 12/31/14 adjusting entry:

Cost	$27,000
Accumulated depreciation	26,100
Book value	$900

Partial-year straight-line depreciation

Fixed assets may be purchased throughout the calendar year, not only on January 1. They may only be depreciated for the amount of time during the year that a company owns them. For a partial year, the amount of annual depreciation on December 31 must be pro-rated by the number of months the asset was owned during the year. The following ratios may be used to pro-rate annual depreciation amounts to account for partial-year ownership:

Purchase date	Months owned as of 12/31	Fraction used to pro-rate annual amount
January	12	12/12
February	11	11/12
March 1	10	10/12

Purchase date	Months owned as of 12/31	Fraction used to pro-rate annual amount
April 1	9	9/12
May 1	8	8/12
June 1	7	7/12
July 1	6	6/12
August 1	5	5/12
September 1	4	4/12
October 1	3	3/12
November 1	2	2/12
December 1	1	1/12

EXAMPLE

On April 1, 2012, a company purchases equipment that costs $27,000. It has a residual value of $900, and has a three-year useful life. The company prepares its financial statements once a year on December 31.

$$\frac{\$27{,}000 - \$900}{3} = \$8{,}700 \text{ per full year for years 2 and 3}$$

$$\$8{,}700 \text{ per full year} \times 9/12 = \frac{\$6{,}525 \text{ for year 1}}{\text{(April through December, inclusive = 9 months)}}$$

$$\$8{,}700 \text{ per full year} \times 3/12 = \frac{\$2{,}175 \text{ for year 4}}{\text{(January through March, inclusive = 3 months)}}$$

12/31/12 adjusting entry for depreciation:

Date	Account		Debit	Credit
12/31	Depreciation Expense		6,525	
	Accumulated Depreciation			6,525

After the 12/31/12 adjusting entry:

Cost	$27,000
Accumulated depreciation	6,525
Book value	$20,475

After the 12/31/12 adjusting entry:

Date	Account		Debit	Credit
12/31	Depreciation Expense		8,700	
	Accumulated Depreciation			8,700

After the 12/31/13 adjusting entry:

Cost	$27,000
Accumulated depreciation	15,225
Book value	$11,775

12/31/14 adjusting entry for depreciation:

Date	Account		Debit	Credit
12/31	Depreciation Expense		8,700	
	Accumulated Depreciation			8,700

After the 12/31/14 adjusting entry:

Cost	$27,000
Accumulated depreciation	23,925
Book value	$3,075

12/31/15 adjusting entry for depreciation:

Date	Account		Debit	Credit
12/31	Depreciation Expense		2,175	
	Accumulated Depreciation			2,175

After the 12/31/15 adjusting entry:

Cost	$27,000
Accumulated depreciation	26,100
Book value	$900

Although the useful life of the equipment is three years, there will be four end-of-year adjusting entries because the three years of ownership do not correspond with calendar years (which are January through December). The adjusting entry amount in year 1 is for nine months ($8,700 x 9/12). In years 2 and 3 the amount is for a full year's depreciation. In year 4 the adjusting entry amount is for the remaining three months that make up the 36-month, or three-year, useful life ($8,700 x 3/12).

UNITS OF PRODUCTION METHOD

The units of production method of depreciation is similar to straight-line except that it uses a rate of usage—such as miles, hours, or units of output—rather than years as the basis for determining the amount of depreciation expense. This method takes the depreciable base (cost minus residual amount) of the asset and expenses it off based on usage during the calendar year.

Assume that the unit of usage is machine hours. The depreciation amount per unit of usage is calculated as follows using units of production:

$$\frac{\text{Cost - Residual value}}{\text{Useful life in machine hours}}$$

The asset is fully depreciated when the machine has been used the number of hours in its useful life. At that point the book value equals the residual value.

EXAMPLE

On January 1, 2012, a company purchases equipment that costs $27,000. It has a residual value of $900, and has an 8,700-hour useful life. The company prepares its financial statements once a year on December 31

$$\frac{\$27{,}000 - \$900}{8{,}700} = \$3.00 \text{ per machine hour}$$

The company used the equipment as follows: 2,100 hours in 2012; 2,300 hours in 2013; 2,600 hours in 2014; and 2,400 hours in 2015.

12/31/12 adjusting entry for depreciation: 2,100 x $3.00 = $6,300 Total of 2,100 hours used

Date	Account		Debit	Credit
12/31	Depreciation Expense		6,300	
	Accumulated Depreciation			6,300

After the 12/31/12 adjusting entry:

Cost	$27,000
Accumulated depreciation	6,300
Book value	$20,700

12/31/13 adjusting entry for depreciation: 2,300 x $3.00 = $6,900 Total of 4,400 hours used

Date	Account		Debit	Credit
12/31	Depreciation Expense		6,900	
	Accumulated Depreciation			6,900

After the 12/31/13 adjusting entry:

Cost	$27,000
Accumulated depreciation	13,200
Book value	$13,800

12/31/14 adjusting entry for depreciation: 2,600 x $3.00 = $6,300 Total of 7,000 hours used

Date	Account		Debit	Credit
12/31	Depreciation Expense		7,800	
	Accumulated Depreciation			7,800

After the 12/31/14 adjusting entry:

Cost	$27,000
Accumulated depreciation	21,000
Book value	$6,000

12/31/15 adjusting entry for depreciation: 1,700 x $3.00 = $5,100 Total of 8,700 hours used*

Date	Account		Debit	Credit
12/31	Depreciation Expense		5,100	
	Accumulated Depreciation			5,100

After the 12/31/15 adjusting entry:

Cost	$27,000
Accumulated depreciation	26,100
Book value	$900

*Although the equipment was used for 2,400 hours in 2015, only 1,700 of those hours may be depreciated. That brings the total number of hours depreciated to 8,700, which is the useful life of the equipment. Be sure not to depreciate more than 8,700 hours.

This same process is followed whether the equipment is owned for a full or partial year. In a partial year, the number of hours used will be proportionately fewer to reflect the reduced amount of time available.

DECLINING BALANCE METHOD

Full-year declining balance depreciation

Declining balance is an accelerated method of depreciation that allows businesses to take more depreciation expense in earlier years and less in later years of the asset's useful life.

The annual depreciation amount using declining balance is calculated by multiplying the asset's book value at the beginning of the year by a fraction, which is always "2" divided by the number of years in the useful life. This is done for all years except the last year. In the last year, the depreciation amount is the difference between the current book value minus the residual value. This ensures that in the last year you do not depreciate below the residual value.

The asset is fully depreciated when the years in its useful life have passed. At that point the book value equals the residual value. Do not subtract out residual value in the first year (which you do for straight-line.) It is subtracted out instead in the last year.

EXAMPLE

On January 1, 2012, a company purchases equipment that costs $27,000. It has a residual value of $900, and has a three-year useful life. The company prepares its financial statements once a year on December 31.

	Book Value	x	Rate	=	Amount of Depreciation Expense
Year 1	27,000	x	2/3	=	18,000
	- 18,000				
Year 2	9,000	x	2/3	=	6,000
	- 6,000				
Year 3	3,000	-	900	=	2,100

The company purchased the equipment on January 1, 2012, so it can depreciate the asset for the full calendar year.

12/31/12 adjusting entry for depreciation:

Date	Account		Debit	Credit
12/31	Depreciation Expense		18,000	
	Accumulated Depreciation			18,000

After the 12/31/12 adjusting entry:

Cost	$27,000
Accumulated depreciation	18,000
Book value	$9,000

12/31/13 adjusting entry for depreciation:

Date	Account		Debit	Credit
12/31	Depreciation Expense		6,000	
	Accumulated Depreciation			6,000

After the 12/31/12 adjusting entry:

Cost	$27,000
Accumulated depreciation	24,000
Book value	$3,000

12/31/14 adjusting entry for depreciation:

Date	Account		Debit	Credit
12/31	Depreciation Expense		2,100	
	Accumulated Depreciation			2,100

After the 12/31/12 adjusting entry:

Cost	$27,000
Accumulated depreciation	26,100
Book value	$900

Partial-year declining balance depreciation

Fixed assets may be purchased throughout the calendar year, not only on January 1. They may only be depreciated for the amount of time during the year that a company owns them. For a partial year, the amount of annual depreciation on December 31 must be pro-rated by the number of months the asset was owned during the year. The same ratios provided for straight-line partial-year depreciation should be used for declining balance.

EXAMPLE

On April 1, 2012, a company purchases equipment that costs $27,000. It has a residual value of $600 and a three-year useful life. The company prepares its financial statements once a year on December 31.

Since the company purchased the equipment on April 1, 2012, it can only depreciate the asset for nine months in year 1.

	Book Value	x	Rate	=	Amount of Depreciation Expense
Year 1	27,000	x	2/3	=	18,000 x 9/12 = 13,500
	- 13,500				
Year 2	13,500	x	2/3	=	9,000
	- 9,000				
Year 3	4,500	x	2/3	=	3,000
	- 3,000				
Year 4	1,500	-	900		600

12/31/12 adjusting entry for depreciation:

Date	Account		Debit	Credit
12/31	Depreciation Expense		13,500	
	Accumulated Depreciation			13,500

After the 12/31/12 adjusting entry:

Cost	$27,000
Accumulated depreciation	13,500
Book value	13,500

12/31/13 adjusting entry for depreciation:

Date	Account		Debit	Credit
12/31	Depreciation Expense		13,500	
	Accumulated Depreciation			13,500

After the 12/31/13 adjusting entry:

Cost	$27,000
Accumulated depreciation	22,500
Book value	$4,500

12/31/14 adjusting entry for depreciation:

Date	Account		Debit	Credit
12/31	Depreciation Expense		13,500	
	Accumulated Depreciation			13,500

After the 12/31/14 adjusting entry:

Cost	$27,000
Accumulated depreciation	24,500
Book value	$1,500

12/31/15 adjusting entry for depreciation:

Date	Account		Debit	Credit
12/31	Depreciation Expense		900	
	Accumulated Depreciation			900

After the 12/31/15 adjusting entry:

Cost	$27,000
Accumulated depreciation	26,400
Book value	$600

4.6 SUMMARY

An asset costs $27,000, has a residual value of $900, and has a three-year or 8,700-hour useful life. The company used the asset as follows: 2,200 hours in 2012; 2,500 hours in 2013; 2,700 hours in 2014; and 2,400 hours in 2015.

Method	Process	Comments	Example (below)
Straight-Line	$\frac{\text{Cost - Residual value}}{\text{Useful life in years}}$	Asset is fully depreciated once it has been used the number of years in its useful life.	$\frac{27{,}000-900}{3}$ 8,700 per year
Units of Production	$\frac{\text{Cost - Residual value}}{\text{Useful life in hours}}$	Multiply hourly rate times number of hours used in the year. Asset is fully depreciated once it has been used the number of hours in its useful life.	$\frac{27{,}000-600}{8{,}700}$ \$3 per hours 2,100 in year 1 (\$3 x 2200 hours) 2,300 in year 2 (\$3 x 2500 hours) 2,600 in year 3 (\$3 x 2700 hours) 1,700 in year 4 (\$3 x 2400 hours)
Declining Balance ("Twice the straight-line rate" just means to divide 2 by the number of years)	Multiply the book value at the beginning of each year by 2/ number of years to determine the amount for the adjusting entry.	Do not subtract out residual value at the beginning (which you did for straight-line.) In the last year, the depreciation amount is the difference between whatever the current book value is minus the residual value - do not depreciate lower than the residual value in the last year.	**BV x Rate = Amt. Dep.** Year 1 2700 x 2/3 = 18,000 Year 2 -18,000 / 900 x 2/3 = 6,000 Year 3 -6,000 / 3,000 - 900 = 2,100

4.7 GAINS AND LOSSES ON DISPOSAL OF ASSETS

A company may no longer need a fixed asset that it owns, or an asset may have become obsolete or inefficient. In this case, the company may dispose of the asset. Prior to discussing disposals, the concepts of gain and loss need to be clarified.

A gain results when an asset is disposed of in exchange for something of greater value.

Gains are increases in the business's wealth resulting from peripheral activities unrelated to its main operations. Recall that revenue is earnings a business generates by selling products and/or services to customers in the course of normal business operations. That is, earnings result from the business doing what it was set up to do operationally, such as a dry cleaning business cleaning customers' clothes. A gain is different in that it results from a transaction outside of the business's normal operations. Although in terms of debits and credits a gain account is treated similarly to a revenue account, it is maintained in a separate account from revenue. In that way the results of gains are not mixed with operations revenues, which would make it difficult for companies to track operation profits and losses—a key element of gauging a company's success.

Similarly, losses are decreases in a business's wealth due to non-operational transactions. Recall that expenses are the costs associated with earning revenues, which is not the case for losses. Although in terms of debits and credits a loss account is treated similarly to an expense account, it is maintained in a separate account so as not to impact the net income amount from operations.

Both gains and losses do appear on the income statement, but they are listed under a category called "other revenue and expenses" or similar heading. This category appears below the net income from operations line so it is clear that these gains and losses are non-operational results.

4.7.1 Disposal of Fixed Assets

There are three ways to dispose of a fixed asset: discard it, sell it, or trade it in.

1. Discard - receive nothing for it
2. Sale - receive cash for it
3. Exchange (trade-in) - receive a similar asset for the original one

The first step is to determine the book value, or worth, of the asset on the date of the disposal. Book value is determined by subtracting the asset's Accumulated Depreciation credit balance from its cost, which is the debit balance of the asset.

Next, compare its book value to the value of what you get for in return for the asset to determine if you breakeven, have a gain, or have a loss.

The company breaks even on the disposal of a fixed asset if the cash or trade-in allowance received is equal to the book value. It also breaks even of an asset with no remaining book value is discarded and nothing is received in return.

The company recognizes a gain if the cash or trade-in allowance received is greater than the book value of the asset.

A loss results from the disposal of a fixed asset if the cash or trade-in allowance received is less than the book value of the asset. The company also experiences a loss if a fixed asset that still has a book value is discarded and nothing is received in return.

Start the journal entry by crediting the asset for its current debit balance to zero it out. Then debit its accumulated depreciation credit balance set that account balance to zero as well. Build the rest of the journal entry around this beginning. Debit Cash or the new asset if either is received in exchange for the one disposed of, if applicable. Finally, debit any loss or credit any gain that results from a difference between book value and asset received.

PARTIAL-YEAR DEPRECIATION

Recall that when a company purchases a fixed asset during a calendar year, it must pro-rate the first year's 12/31 adjusting entry amount for depreciation by the number of months it actually owned the asset.

A similar situation arises when a company disposes of a fixed asset during a calendar year. The adjusting entry for depreciation is normally made on 12/31 of each calendar year. If a fixed asset is disposed of during the year, an additional adjusting entry for depreciation on the date of disposal must be journalized to bring the accumulated depreciation balance and book value up to date.

EXAMPLE

Equipment that cost $6,000 depreciates $1,200 on 12/31 of each year. Accumulated depreciation on the equipment at the end of the third year is $3,600, and the book value at the end of the third year is $2,400 ($6,000 - $3,600).

Scenario #1

The equipment will be disposed of (discarded, sold, or traded in) on 4/1 in the fourth year, which is three months after the last annual adjusting entry was journalized. The first step is to journalize an additional adjusting entry on 4/1 to capture the additional three months' depreciation. This ensures that the book value on 4/1 is current. Since the annual depreciation amount is $1,200, the asset depreciates at a rate of $100 a month, for a total of $300.

Date	Account		Debit	Credit
4/1	Depreciation Expense		300	
	Accumulated Depreciation			300

- *Depreciation Expense* is an **expense** account that is **increasing.**
- *Accumulated Dep.* is a contra ***asset*** account that is **increasing.**

The asset's book value on 4/1 of the fourth year is $2,100 ($6,000 - $3,900).

Scenario #2

The equipment will be disposed of (discarded, sold, or traded in) on 10/1 in the fourth year, which is nine months after the last annual adjusting entry was journalized. The first step is to journalize an additional adjusting entry on 10/1 to capture the additional nine months' depreciation. This ensures that the book value on 10/1 is current.

Date	Account		Debit	Credit
10/1	Depreciation Expense		900	
	Accumulated Depreciation			900

- *Depreciation Expense* is an **expense** account that is **increasing.**
- *Accumulated Dep.* is a contra ***asset*** account that is **increasing.**
- The asset's book value on 10/1 of the fourth year is $1,500 ($6,000 - $4,500).

EXAMPLE

A company buys equipment that costs $6,000 on May 1, 2011. The equipment depreciates $1,200 per calendar year, or $100 per month. The company disposes of the equipment on November 1, 2014. How much depreciation expense is incurred in 2011, 2012, 2013, and 2014? What is the Accumulated Depreciation credit balance on November 1, 2014? What is the book value of the equipment on November 1, 2014?

2011	$800	May 1 through December 31 – 8 months	(Year of purchase)
2012	$1,200	January 1 through December 31 – 12 months	
2013	$1,200	January 1 through December 31 – 12 months	
2014	$1,000	January 1 through November 1 – 10 months	(Year of disposal)

Accumulated Depreciation balance on November 1, 2014: $4,200 ($800 + $1,200 + $1,200 + $1,000)

Book value of the equipment on November 1, 2014: $1,800 ($6,000 - $4,200)

DISCARDING A FIXED ASSET (BREAKEVEN)

When a fixed asset that does not have a residual value is fully depreciated, its cost equals its Accumulated Depreciation balance and its book value is zero.

EXAMPLE

The ledgers below show that a truck cost $35,000. It is fully depreciated after five years of ownership since its Accumulated Depreciation credit balance is also $35,000. The book value of the truck is zero (35,000 – 35,000).

Truck					
Date	Item	Debit	Credit	Debit	Credit
1/1		35,000		35,000	

Fees Earned					
Date	Item	Debit	Credit	Debit	Credit
12/31			7,000		7,000
12/31			7,000		14,000
12/31			7,000		21,000
12/31			7,000		28,000
12/31			7,000		35,000

Compare the book value to what was received for the asset. The truck is not worth anything, and nothing is received for it when it is discarded. If the truck is discarded at this point, there is no gain or loss. Both account balances above must be set to zero to reflect the fact that the company no longer owns the truck.

To record the transaction, debit Accumulated Depreciation for its $35,000 credit balance and credit Truck for its $35,000 debit balance.

Date	Account		Debit	Credit
12/31	Accumulated Depreciation		35,000	
	Truck			35,000

- *Accumulated Dep.* is a contra **asset** account that is **decreasing.**
- *Truck* is an **asset** account that is **decreasing.**

As a result of this journal entry, both account balances related to the discarded truck are now zero.

Truck					
Date	Item	Debit	Credit	Debit	Credit
1/1		35,000		35,000	
12/31			35,000	0	

Accumulated Depreciation					
Date	Item	Debit	Credit	Debit	Credit
12/31			7,000		7,000
12/31			7,000		14,000
12/31			7,000		21,000
12/31			7,000		28,000
12/31			7,000		35,000
12/31		35,000			0

When a fixed asset that does not have a residual value is not fully depreciated, it does have a book value.

EXAMPLE

The ledgers below show that a truck cost $35,000. Its Accumulated Depreciation credit balance is $28,000. The book value of the truck is $7,000.

Truck					
Date	Item	Debit	Credit	Debit	Credit
1/1		35,000		35,000	

Accumulated Depreciation					
Date	Item	Debit	Credit	Debit	Credit
12/31			7,000		7,000
12/31			7,000		14,000
12/31			7,000		21,000
12/31			7,000		28,000

DISCARDING A FIXED ASSET (LOSS)

Compare the book value to what was received for the asset. The truck's book value is $7,000, but nothing is received for it if it is discarded. If truck is discarded at this point there is a $7,000 loss. Both account balances above must be set to zero to reflect the fact that the company no longer owns the truck. In addition, the loss must be recorded.

To record the transaction, debit **Accumulated Depreciation** for its $28,000 credit balance and credit Truck for its $35,000 debit balance. Debit **Loss on Disposal of Truck** for the difference.

Date	Account		Debit	Credit
12/31	Loss on Disposal of Truck		7,000	
	Accumulated Depreciation		28,000	
	Truck			35,000

- *Loss* is an **expense** account that is **increasing.**
- *Accumulated Dep.* is a contra **asset** account that is **decreasing.**
- *Truck* is an **asset** account that is **decreasing.**

SELLING A FIXED ASSET

A company receives cash when it sells a fixed asset. Take the following steps for the sale of a fixed asset:

1. Make any necessary adjusting entry to update the Accumulated Depreciation balance so it is current as of the date of the disposal.
2. Calculate the asset's book value.

3. Compare the book value to the amount of cash received. Decide if there is a gain, loss, or if you break even.
4. Zero out the fixed asset account by crediting it for its current debit balance.
5. Zero out the Accumulated Depreciation account by debiting it for its current credit balance.
6. Debit Cash for the amount received.
7. Debit **Loss on Sale of Asset** or credit **Gain on Sale of Asset**, if necessary.

SELLING A FIXED ASSET (BREAKEVEN) EXAMPLE

A truck that was purchased on 1/1/2010 at a cost of $35,000 has a $28,000 credit balance in Accumulated Depreciation as of 12/31/2013. The truck is sold on 12/31/2013, four years after it was purchased, for $7,000 cash.

Solution Facts

- No additional adjusting entry is necessary since the truck was sold after a full year of depreciation
- Book value is $7,000
- Cash received is $7,000
- Break even – no gain or loss since book value equals the amount of cash received

Date	Account		Debit	Credit
12/31	Cash		7,000	
	Accumulated Depreciation		28,000	
	Truck			35,000

- *Cash* is an **asset** account that is **increasing.**
- *Accumulated Dep.* is a contra **asset** account that is **decreasing.**
- *Truck* is an **asset** account that is **decreasing.**

SELLING A FIXED ASSET (LOSS)

EXAMPLE

A truck that was purchased on 1/1/2010 at a cost of $35,000 has a $28,000 credit balance in **Accumulated Depreciation** as of 12/31/2013. The truck is sold on 12/31/2013, four years after it was purchased, for $5,000 cash.

Solution Facts

- No additional adjusting entry is necessary since the truck was sold after a full year of depreciation
- Book value is $7,000

- Cash received is $5,000
- Loss of $2,000 since book value is more than the amount of cash received

Date	Account		Debit	Credit
12/31	Loss on Sale of Truck		2,000	
	Cash		5,000	
	Accumulated Depreciation		28,000	
	Truck			35,000

- *Loss* is an **expense** account that is **increasing.**
- *Cash* is an **asset** account that is **increasing.**
- *Accumulated Dep.* is a contra *asset* account that is **decreasing.**
- *Truck* is an **asset** account that is **decreasing.**

SELLING A FIXED ASSET (GAIN) EXAMPLE

A truck that was purchased on 1/1/2010 at a cost of $35,000 has a $28,000 credit balance in Accumulated Depreciation as of 12/31/2013. The truck is sold on 12/31/2013, four years after it was purchased, for $10,000 cash.

Solution Facts

- No additional adjusting entry is necessary since the truck was sold after a full year of depreciation
- Book value is $7,000
- Cash received is $10,000
- Gain of $3,000 since the amount of cash received is more than the book value

Date	Account		Debit	Credit
12/31	Cash		10,000	
	Accumulated Depreciation		28,000	
	Truck			35,000
	Gain on Sale of Truck			3,000

- *Cash* is an **asset** account that is **increasing.**
- *Accumulated Dep.* is a contra **asset** account that is **decreasing.**
- *Truck* is an **asset** account that is **decreasing.**
- *Gain* is a **revenue** account that is **increasing.**

SELLING A FIXED ASSET (PARTIAL YEAR) EXAMPLE

A truck that was purchased on 1/1/2010 at a cost of $35,000. The truck depreciates at a rate of $7,000 per year and has a $28,000 credit balance in **Accumulated**

Depreciation as of 12/31/2013. The truck is sold on 4/1/2014, four years and three months after it was purchased, for $5,000 cash.

The following adjusting entry updates the **Accumulated Depreciation** account to its current balance as of 4/1/2014, the date of the sale. Normally the adjusting entry is made only on 12/31 for the full year, but this is an exception since the asset is being sold. It is necessary to know the exact book value as of 4/1/2014, and the accumulated depreciation credit amount is part of the book value calculation.

Journalize the adjusting entry for the additional three months' depreciation since the last 12/31 adjusting entry. Pro-rate the annual amount by the number of months owned in the year. The amount is $7,000 x 3/12 = $1,750.

Date	Account		Debit	Credit
4/1	Depreciation Expense		1,750	
	Accumulated Depreciation			1,750

- *Depreciation Expense* is an **expense** account that is **increasing.**
- *Accumulated Dep.* is a contra **asset** account that is **increasing.**

Accumulated depreciation as of 2/31/2013:

Accumulated Depreciation					
Date	**Item**	**Debit**	**Credit**	**Debit**	**Credit**
12/31			7,000		7,000
12/31			7,000		14,000
12/31			7,000		21,000
12/31			7,000		28,000

Accumulated depreciation as of /1/2014:

Accumulated Depreciation					
Date	**Item**	**Debit**	**Credit**	**Debit**	**Credit**
12/31			7,000		7,000
12/31			7,000		14,000
12/31			7,000		21,000
12/31			7,000		28,000
4/1			1,750		29,750

Solution Facts

- Journalize the adjusting entry for the additional three months' depreciation since the last 12/31 adjusting entry. The amount is $7,000 x 3/12 = $1,750.
- Book value is $5,250 ($35,000 – $29,750)
- Cash received is $5,000
- Loss of $250 since book value is more than the amount of cash received

Date	Account		Debit	Credit
12/31	Loss on Sale of Truck		250	
	Cash		5,000	
	Accumulated Depreciation		29,750	
	Truck			35,000

- *Loss* is an **expense** account that is **increasing.**
- *Cash* is an **asset** account that is **increasing.**
- *Accumulated Dep.* is a contra **asset** account that is **decreasing.**
- *Truck* is an **asset** account that is **decreasing.**

Partial-year depreciation to update the truck's book value at the time of sale could also result in a gain or break even situation.

EXCHANGING/TRADING IN A FIXED ASSET

A company may dispose of a fixed asset by trading it in for a similar asset. This must be supplemented by a cash payment and possibly by a loan. The company receives a trade-in allowance for the old asset that may be applied toward the purchase of the new asset.

The new asset must be paid for. Its cost can be covered by several forms of payment combined, such as a trade-in allowance + cash + a note payable.

Take the following steps for the exchange of a fixed asset:

1. Make any necessary adjusting entry to update the **Accumulated Depreciation** balance so it is current as of the date of the disposal.
2. Calculate the asset's book value.
3. Compare the book value to the amount of trade-in allowance received on the old asset. Determine if there is a gain, loss, or if you break even.
4. Zero out the fixed asset account by crediting it for its current debit balance.
5. Zero out the **Accumulated Depreciation** account by debiting it for its current credit balance.
6. Debit the account for the new fixed asset for its cost.
7. Debit **Loss on Exchange of Asset** or credit **Gain on Exchange of Asset,** if necessary.

EXCHANGING A FIXED ASSET (BREAKEVEN) EXAMPLE

A truck that was purchased on 1/1/2010 at a cost of $35,000 has a $28,000 credit balance in **Accumulated Depreciation** as of 12/31/2013. The truck is traded in on 12/31/2013, four years after it was purchased, for a new truck that costs $40,000. The company receives a $7,000 trade-in allowance for the old truck. The company pays cash for the remainder.

Solution Facts

- No additional adjusting entry is necessary since the truck was traded in after a full year of depreciation
- Book value is $7,000
- Trade-in allowance is $7,000
- Break even – no gain or loss since book value equals the trade-in allowance
- Cost of the new truck is $40,000. The trade-in allowance of $7,000. The company must pay $33,000 to cover the $40,000 cost.

Date	Account		Debit	Credit
12/31	Truck (new)		40,000	
	Accumulated Depreciation		28,000	
	Truck (old)			35,000
	Cash			35,000

- *Truck* is an **asset** account that is **increasing.**
- **Accumulated Dep.** is a contra **asset** account that is **decreasing.**
- *Truck* is an **asset** account that is **decreasing.**
- *Cash* is an **asset** account that is **decreasing.**

EXCHANGING A FIXED ASSET (BREAK EVEN WITH A LOAN) EXAMPLE

A truck that was purchased on 1/1/2010 at a cost of $35,000 has a $28,000 credit balance in Accumulated Depreciation as of 12/31/2013. The truck is traded in on 12/31/2013, four years after it was purchased, for a new truck that costs $40,000. The company receives a $7,000 trade-in allowance for the old truck. The company pays $20,000 in cash and takes out a loan for the remainder.

Solution Facts

- No additional adjusting entry is necessary since the truck was traded in after a full year of depreciation
- Book value is $7,000
- Trade-in allowance is $7,000
- Break even – no gain or loss since book value equals the trade-in allowance
- Cost of the new truck is $40,000. The trade-in allowance of $7,000 plus the cash payment of $20,000 covers $27,000 of the cost. The company must take out a loan for $13,000 to cover the $40,000 cost.

Date	Account		Debit	Credit
12/31	Truck (new)		40,000	
	Accumulated Depreciation		28,000	
	Truck (old)			35,000
	Cash			20,000
	Note Payable			13,000

- *Truck* is an **asset** account that is **increasing.**
- *Accumulated Dep.* is a contra *asset* account that is **decreasing.**
- *Truck* is an *asset* account that is **decreasing.**
- *Cash* is an **asset** account that is **decreasing.**
- *Note Payable* is a *liability* account that is **increasing.**

EXCHANGING A FIXED ASSET (LOSS WITH A LOAN) EXAMPLE

A truck that was purchased on 1/1/2010 at a cost of $35,000 has a $28,000 credit balance in Accumulated Depreciation as of 12/31/2013. The truck is traded in on 12/31/2013, four years after it was purchased, for a new truck that costs $40,000. The company receives a $5,000 trade-in allowance for the old truck. The company pays $20,000 in cash and takes out a loan for the remainder.

Solution Facts

- No additional adjusting entry is necessary since the truck was traded in fter a full year of depreciation
- Book value is $7,000
- Trade-in allowance is $5,000
- Loss of $2,000 since book value is more than the amount of cash received
- Cost of the new truck is $40,000. The trade-in allowance of $5,000 plus the cash payment of $20,000 covers $25,000 of the cost. The company must take out a loan for $15,000 to cover the $40,000 cost.

Date	Account		Debit	Credit
12/31	Loss on Exchange of Asset		2,000	
	Truck (new)		40,000	
	Accumulated Depreciation		28,000	
	Truck (old)			35,000
	Cash			20,000
	Note Payable			15,000

- *Loss* is an **expense** account that is **increasing.**
- *Truck* is an *asset* account that is **increasing.**
- *Accumulated Dep.* is a contra *asset* account that is **decreasing.**
- *Truck* is an *asset* account that is **decreasing.**
- *Cash* is an **asset** account that is **decreasing.**
- *Note Payable* is a **liability** account that is **increasing.**

EXCHANGING A FIXED ASSET (GAIN WITH A LOAN) EXAMPLE

A truck that was purchased on 1/1/2010 at a cost of $35,000 has a $28,000 credit balance in Accumulated Depreciation as of 12/31/2013. The truck is traded in on 12/31/2013, four years after it was purchased, for a new truck that costs $40,000. The company receives a $10,000 trade-in allowance for the old truck. The company pays $20,000 in cash and takes out a loan for the remainder.

Solution Facts

- No additional adjusting entry is necessary since the truck was traded in after a full year of depreciation
- Book value is $7,000
- Trade-in allowance is $10,000
- Gain of $3,000 since the amount of cash received is more than the book value
- Cost of the new truck is $40,000. The trade-in allowance of $10,000 plus the cash payment of $20,000 covers $30,000 of the cost. The company must take out a loan for $10,000 to cover the $40,000 cost.

Date	Account		Debit	Credit
12/31	Truck (new)		40,000	
	Accumulated Depreciation		28,000	
	Truck (old)			35,000
	Cash			20,000
	Note Payable			10,000
	Gain on Exchange of Asset			3,000

- *Truck* is an **asset** account that is **increasing.**
- *Accumulated Dep.* is a **contra asset** account that is **decreasing.**
- *Truck* is an **asset** account that is **decreasing.**
- *Cash* is an **asset** account that is **decreasing.**
- *Note Payable* is a **liability** account that is **increasing.**
- *Gain* is a **revenue** account that is **increasing.**

EXCHANGING A FIXED ASSET (PARTIAL YEAR) EXAMPLE

A truck that was purchased on 1/1/2010 at a cost of $35,000 has a $28,000 credit balance in Accumulated Depreciation as of 12/31/2013. The truck is traded in on 7/1/2014, four years and six months after it was purchased, for a new truck that costs $40,000. The company receives a $5,000 trade-in allowance for the old truck. The company pays $20,000 in cash and takes out a loan for the remainder.

The following adjusting entry updates the Accumulated Depreciation account to its current balance as of 7/1/2014, the date of the sale. Normally the adjusting entry is made only on 12/31 for the full year, but this is an exception since the asset is being traded in. It is necessary to know the exact book value as of 7/1/2014, and the accumulated depreciation credit amount is part of the book value calculation.

Date	Account		Debit	Credit
7/1	Depreciation Expense		3,500	
	Accumulated Depreciation			3,500

- *Depreciation Expense* is an **expense** account that is **increasing.**
- *Accumulated Dep.* is a contra **asset** account that is **increasing.**

The Accumulated Depreciation credit balance as of 7/1/2014 is $28,000 + $3,500, or $31,500.

Solution Facts

- Journalize the adjusting entry for the additional six months' depreciation since the last 12/31 adjusting entry. The amount is $7,000 x 6/12 = $3,500.
- Book value is $3,500 ($35,000 – $31,500)
- Trade-in allowance is $5,000

The Accumulated Depreciation credit balance as of 7/1/2014 is $28,000 + $3,500, or $31,500.

Solution Facts

- Journalize the adjusting entry for the additional six months' depreciation since the last 12/31 adjusting entry. The amount is $7,000 x 6/12 = $3,500.
- Book value is $3,500 ($35,000 – $31,500)
- Trade-in allowance is $5,000

Date	Account		Debit	Credit
12/31	Truck (new)		40,000	
	Accumulated Depreciation		31,500	

	Truck (old)			35,000
	Cash			20,000
	Note Payable			15,000
	Gain on Exchange of Asset			1,500

- *Truck* is an **asset** account that is **increasing.**
- *Accumulated Dep.* is a contra **asset** account that is **decreasing.**
- *Truck* is an **asset** account that is **decreasing.**
- *Cash* is an **asset** account that is **decreasing.**
- *Note Payable* is a **liability** account that is **increasing.**
- *Gain* is a **revenue** account that is **increasing.**

Partial-year depreciation to update the truck's book value at the time of trade-in could also result in a loss or break-even situation.

4.8 GAINS AND LOSSES ON THE INCOME STATEMENT

Gains and losses are reported on the income statement. However, since they are not transactions that normally occur in the day-to-day operations of a business, they are listed below a new line entitled "Net income from operations." Net income from operations summarizes revenue and expenses from operational transactions. Gains are added to that amount and losses are deducted to arrive at the final net Income result.

Notice how gains and losses are presented on the income statement:

Jonick Company
Income Statement
For the Year Ended December 31, 2012

Sales		$150,000	
Cost of merchandise sold		50,000	
Gross Profit			$100,000
Operating Expenses			
Salaries expense		$13,000	
Rent expense		8,000	
Insurance expense		6,000	
Supplies expense		5,000	
Depreciation expense		3,000	
Miscellaneous expense		1,000	
Total operating expenses			36,000
Net income from operations			$64,000
Gain on sale of investments		3,000	
Loss on sale of equipment		-2,000	1,000
Net income			$65,000

4.8.1 Amortization of an Intangible Asset

Other longer-term assets that a business may possess and use for its operations are not physical items. These are therefore called intangible assets and may include patents, copyrights, internet domain names, franchises, trademarks, and goodwill. Patents and copyrights, for example, represent a business's exclusive right to use or do something that other businesses cannot, at least not without permission.

Intangible assets that have finite, or defined useful lives are expensed off over time, similar to fixed assets. This expense for fixed assets is called depreciation; however, for intangible assets it is called amortization. There is no separate contra asset account used when amortizing an intangible asset. Instead, the value of the asset is credited and declines over time.

The maximum legal life of a patent is 20 years, but a company can assign a useful period of less than that based on its planned usage. Copyrights and franchises also have specific useful lives. Therefore, these assets may be amortized.

The following annual adjusting entry is an example of the amortization of a patent that cost $12,000 to purchase and that has a useful life of 12 years.

Date	Account		Debit	Credit
12/31	Amortization Expense		1,000	
	Patents			1,000

- *Amortization Expense* is an **expense** account that is **increasing.**
- *Patents* is an **asset** account that is **decreasing.**

Internet domain names and trade names are considered to have infinite useful lives since they are continuously renewable. Only if a company assigns a specific usage period to either of these would the intangible asset be amortized.

Goodwill is the most common intangible asset with an indefinite useful life. Goodwill results only when a business buys another company and pays more than the fair value of all of the assets and liabilities it acquires. No useful life can reasonably be determined; therefore, goodwill is not amortized.

The balances of both fixed and intangible assets are presented in the assets section of the balance sheet at the end of each accounting period. When a company has a significant number of assets, they are typically presented in categories for clearer presentation. A financial statement that organizes its asset (and liability) accounts into categories is called a **classified balance sheet.**

The partial classified balance sheet that follows shows the assets section only. Note that there are four sections. **Current assets** itemizes relatively liquid assets that will be converted to cash or used within one year. Long-term assets presents financial assets that are intended to be held for more than one year. These will be discussed in a later section of this document. **Property, plant and equipment** lists physical assets with a useful life greater than one year, as well as the associated Accumulated Depreciation account for each fixed asset that is depreciated. The property, plant and equipment category reports the original cost of each fixed asset, the total amount of that cost that has been expensed off over time to date, and the resulting book value. **Intangible assets** are then presented.

The total of asset for each category appears in the far right column of the classified balance sheet, and the sum of these totals appears as **total assets.**

Jonick Company Balance Sheet June 30, 2018			
Assets			
Current assets:			
Cash		$40,000	
Accounts receivable	$28,000		
Less: Allowance for doubtful accounts	3,000	25,000	
Merchandise Inventory		60,000	
Supplies		18,000	
Prepaid Rent		12,000	
Total current assets			$155,000
Long-term assets:			
Investment in equity securities			18,000
Property, plant and equipment:			
Equipment	$16,000		
Less: accumulated depreciation	2,000	$14,000	
Building	200,000		
Less: accumulated depreciation	70,000	130,000	
Land		110,000	
Total property, plant and equipment			254,000
Intangible assets:			
Patents			13,000
Total assets			$440,000

ACCOUNT TYPE	ACCOUNTS	TO INCREASE	TO DECREASE	NORMAL BALANCE	FINANCIAL STATEMENT	CLOSE OUT?
Asset	Building Land Truck Equipment Patent Copyright Trademark Goodwill	debit	credit	debit	Balance Sheet	NO
Contra Asset	Accumulated Depreciation	credit	debit	credit	Balance Sheet	NO
Liability	Note Payable	credit	debit	credit	Balance Sheet	No
Revenue or Gain	Gain on Disposal of Fixed Asset	credit	debit	credit	Income Statement	YES
Expense or Loss	Depreciation Expense Loss on Disposal of Fixed Asset	debit	debit	credit	Income Statement	YES

Topics – Fixed assets	Fact	Journal Entry	Calculate Amount	Format
Concept of fixed assets and depreciation	x			
Calculate the cost basis of a fixed asset			x	
Calculate full-year depreciation using straight-line method			x	
Calculate partial-year depreciation using straight-line method			x	
Calculate full-year depreciation using units of production method			x	
Calculate partial-year depreciation using units of production method			x	
Calculate full-year depreciation using declining balance method			x	
Calculate partial-year depreciation using declining balance method			x	
Calculate book value				
Journalize disposal of a fully-depreciated fixed asset		x	x	
Journalize disposal of a partially-depreciated fixed asset at a loss		x	x	
Journalize sale of a fixed asset for its book value		x	x	
Journalize sale of a fixed asset at a loss		x	x	
Journalize sale of a fixed asset at a gain		x	x	
Journalize exchange of a fixed asset for its book value		x	x	

Topics – Fixed assets	Fact	Journal Entry	Calculate Amount	Format
Journalize exchange of fixed asset at a loss		X	X	
Journalize exchange of a fixed asset at a gain		X	X	
Journalize amortization of an intangible asset		X	X	
Financial statements			X	X
Journalize closing entries		X		
Post closing entries to ledgers			X	
Journal entry for dividends		X		
Total stockholders' equity			X	
Accounting equation	X		X	
Changes in stockholders' equity			X	
Retained earnings statement			X	X
Balance sheet			X	X
Financial statements connected	X		X	

The accounts that are highlighted in bright yellow are the new accounts you just learned. Those in highlighted in light yellow are the ones you learned previously.

#3

Jonick Corporation
Balance Sheet
June 30, 2014

ASSETS			
Current assets:			
Cash		$40,000	
Accounts receivable	$28,000		
Less: Allowance for doubtful accounts	3,000	25,000	
Merchandise inventory		60,000	
Supplies		18,000	
Prepaid rent		12,000	
Prepaid insurance		6,000	
Prepaid taxes		4,000	
Note receivable		2,000	
Total current assets			$167,000
Fixed assets:			
Equipment	$16,000		
Less: Accumulated depreciation	2,000	14,000	
Van	30,000		
Less: Accumulated depreciation	5,000	25,000	
Building	200,000		
Less: Accumulated depreciation	70,000	130,000	
Land		110,000	
Total fixed assets			279,000
Intangible assets:			
Patents			14,000
Total assets			$460,000

LIABILITIES			
Current liabilities:			
Accounts payable	$14,000		
Unearned fees	13,000		
Wages payable	12,000		
Salaries payable	11,000		
Taxes payable	10,000		
Interest payable	9,000		
Notes payable	8,000		
Sales tax payable	7,000		
Social security tax payable	6,000		
Medicare tax payable	5,000		
Federal withholding tax payable	4,000		
State withholding tax payable	3,000		
Federal unemployment tax payable	2,000		
State unemployment tax payable	1,000		
Total current liabilities		$105,000	
Long-term liabilities:			
Mortgage note payable	$56,000		
Bonds payable	40,000		
Less: Discount on bonds payable	(6,000)		
Total long-term liabilities		90,000	
Total liabilities			$195,000
STOCKHOLDERS' EQUITY			
Common stock		$80,000	
Paid-in-capital in excess of par - common stock		34,000	
Preferred stock		50,000	
Paid-in-capital in excess of par - preferred stock		18,000	
Paid-in-capital from sale of treasury stock		13,000	
Retained earnings		90,000	
Treasury stock		(20,000)	
Total stockholders' equity			265,000
Total liabilities and stockholders' equity			$460,000

#2

Jonick Corporation
Retained Earnings Statement
For the Month Ended June 30, 2014

Retained earnings, June 1, 2014			$60,000
Net income		$40,000	
Less: Cash dividends	$6,000		
Stock dividends	4,000	10,000	
Increase in retained earnings			30,000
Retained earnings, June 30, 2014			$90,000

#1

Jonick Corporation
Income Statement
For the Month Ended June 30, 2014

Operating REVENUES:			
Fees Earned		$200,000	
Sales	$150,000		
Less: Sales returns	10,000		
Less: Sales discounts	5,000		
Net sales	135,000		
Cost of merchandise sold	55,000		
Gross profit		80,000	
Gross operating revenues			$280,000
Operating EXPENSES:			
Salaries expense		$25,000	
Wages expense		22,000	
Rent expense		20,000	
Insurance expense		19,000	
Supplies expense		18,000	
Advertising expense		17,000	
Maintenance expense		16,000	
Depreciation expense		15,000	
Taxes expense		14,000	
Utilities expense		13,000	
Payroll tax expense		12,000	
Bad debt expense		11,000	
Bank card expense		10,000	
Vehicle expense		9,000	
Delivery expense		8,000	
Amortization expense		7,000	
Miscellaneous expense		6,000	
Total operating expenses			242,000
Net income from operations			$38,000
Other revenue and expenses:			
Interest revenue		$5,000	
Interest expense		(4,000)	
Gain on sale of equipment		3,000	
Loss on redemption of bonds		(2,000)	2,000
Net income			$40,000

4.9 INVESTMENTS

4.9.1 Investments Overview

A company may have idle cash that it does not need immediately for its current operations. Just like individuals, a company may seek to invest this money so that its value grows over time. Rather than placing the cash in checking or savings accounts in banks, where interest rates are relatively low, companies may choose to invest in other corporations or government entities for potentially higher rates of return.

One option is for the company to invest in **equity securities,** which involves purchasing stock in other corporations. Equity is actual ownership, and stock can be considered a receipt that confirms that ownership. The investor buys a number of shares of stock at a purchase price per share. The investor becomes a partial owner of the corporation and is called a stockholder.

The stock investor may then benefit in two ways. First, the investee (company invested in) may pay dividends, which are payouts of profits, to stockholders. Secondly, the market value per share may increase over time, and the investor may experience a gain on the value of the shares owned. Although there is not necessarily a guarantee of dividends or appreciation of the value of the shares of stock owned, these are the two main incentives that attract companies and individuals to invest in stock. There is no repayment due date on the ownership of shares of stock.

Investments in stock may be classified as either short or long-term assets, depending on the length of time that the buyer intends to hold the equities. Short-term stock investments held for less than one year may be called **marketable securities** and appear as a current asset on the investor's balance sheet. **Long-term investments in stocks** are held for more than one year—often many years—by the investing corporation. These are listed in the Investments section of the firm's balance sheet.

A second investment choice for the company is **debt** securities, such as corporate or governmental **bonds.** Bonds are loans made collectively by smaller lenders, such as other corporations and individual people, to a corporation. The people or companies who invest in corporate bonds are called **bondholders.** They do not become owners of a corporation like stockholders do; they are just lenders. Bondholders lend their money to corporations in order to be paid interest on the loan amount throughout the number of years in the term of the bond. Interest on corporate bonds is often paid semi-annually—every six months. On the maturity date, bondholders are repaid the original amount that they loaned the corporation. Investments in bonds may be classified as either short or long-term assets, depending on the length of time that the buyer intends to hold the investment. Short-term bond investments held for less than one year may be called **marketable securities** or **trading securities** and appear as a current asset on the investor's balance sheet. Long-term investments in bonds are held for more than one year—usually many years—by the investing corporation. These are listed in the Investment section of the firm's balance sheet for most of their life and only become current assets within one year of their maturity date. Long-term investments in bonds are classified as either **held-to-maturity** or **available-for-sale** securities, which will be explained in the following section.

Certain types of stock and bond investments may be sold at breakeven, at a gain, or at a loss, similar to the sale of fixed assets. Again, it is important to note that any gain or loss is incurred on an investment transaction is outside of what occurs in normal business operations. When a gain or loss on the sale of an investment is recognized in the same transaction as the receipt of cash, it is considered a realized gain or loss, because it occurs only at the time of the sale and is based on the amount of cash received.

Other types of stock and bond investments are adjusted to fair value, or the current trading price on the open market, throughout the time they are owned by the investor. Adjustments just prior to preparing financial statements may result in reporting a gain or loss, but in this case any gain or loss is considered **unrealized** since a sale has not transpired and no cash has been received yet. These concepts will be elaborated on in the discussions of investments that follow.

The following Accounts Summary Table summarizes the accounts relevant to investing in stocks and bonds.

ACCOUNT TYPE	ACCOUNTS	TO INCREASE	TO DECREASE	NORMAL BALANCE	FINANCIAL STATEMENT	CLOSE OUT?
Asset	Investment in ABC Stock Investment in ABC Bonds	debit	credit	debit	Balance Sheet	NO
Stockholders' Equityt	Unrealized Holding Gain - Available-for-Sale Securities	credit	debit	credit	Balance Sheet	NO
Contra Stockholders' Equity	Unrealized Holding Loss - Available-for-Sale Securities	debit	credit	debit	Balance Sheet	No

ACCOUNT TYPE	ACCOUNTS	TO INCREASE	TO DECREASE	NORMAL BALANCE	FINANCIAL STATEMENT	CLOSE OUT?
Revenue or Gain	Dividends Revenue Investment Income Interest Revenue Gain on Sale of Investment Unrealized Holding Gain/ Loss - Net Income (if credit balance)	credit	debit	credit	Income Statement	YES
Expense or Loss	Loss on Sale of Investment Unrealized Holding Gain/ Loss - Net Income (if debit balance)	debit	credit	debit	Income Statement	YES

4.9.2 Investments in Stock

A company may invest in the stock of other corporations if it has no immediate need for its cash. A separate account that mentions the unique name of the corporation for each stock investment is used. For example, a company might invest in the stock of three other corporations and use Investment in ABC Stock, Investment in *Home Depot Stock, and Investment in Delta Airlines Stock* as their three distinct asset account names. (On the balance sheet, these individual investment accounts may be combined in the Marketable Securities listing for short-term investments and/or the *Equities Securities* listing for long-term investments for an efficient presentation.)

FAIR VALUE THROUGH NET INCOME method

Your Corporation purchases 5,000 shares of **ABC Stock for $10 per share. ABC Corporation has 50,000 shares outstanding,** so Your purchases 10% of those shares.

Account		Debit	Credit
Investment in ABC Stock		50,000	
Cash			50,000

- *Investment in ABC Stock* is an **asset** account that is **increasing.**

- *Cash* is an **asset** account that is **decreasing.**

Investment in ABC Stock debit balance: $50,000 Carrying amount per share: $10.00 ($50,000 / 5,000) Number of shares owned: 5,000

Percentage of shares owned to outstanding: 10% (5,000 / 50,000)

Amount: $10 x 5,000

EQUITY method

Your Corporation purchases 5,000 shares of **ABC Stock for $10 per share. ABC Corporation has 20,000 shares outstanding,** so Your purchases 25% of those shares.

Account		Debit	Credit
Investment in ABC Stock		50,000	
Cash			50,000

- *Investment in ABC* Stock is an **asset** account that is **increasing.**
- *Cash* is an **asset** account that is **decreasing.**

Investment in ABC Stock debit balance: $50,000 Carrying amount per share: $10.00 ($50,000 / 5,000) Number of shares owned: 5,000

Percentage of shares owned to outstanding: 25% (5,000 / 20,000)

Calculation: $10 x 5,000

Ledger account balance:

Investment in ABC Stock					
Date	Item	Debit	Credit	Debit	Credit
		50,000		50,000	

Ledger account balance:

Investment in ABC Stock					
Date	Item	Debit	Credit	Debit	Credit
		50,000		50,000	

1. RECEIVE DIVIDEND PAYMENTS

One difference between the fair value through net income and equity methods is seen when the issuing corporation pays cash dividends.

Fair value through net income method

Under the fair value through net income method, the investor simply reports dividend receipts as revenue. The Dividends Revenue account is credited.

Equity method

Under the equity method, dividend receipts are reported as a reduction of the investment account. The investing company's significant ownership percentage results in a transaction that is analogous to the corporation paying itself.

FAIR VALUE THROUGH NET INCOME method

Your Corporation receives $5,000 in dividends from ABC Corporation.

Account		Debit	Credit
Cash		5,000	
Dividends Revenue			5,000

- *Cash* is an **asset** account that is **increasing.**
- *Dividends Revenue* is a **revenue** account that is **increasing.**

Investment in ABC Stock debit balance: $50,000 Carrying amount per share: $10.00 ($50,000 / 5,000) Number of shares owned: 5,000

Percentage of shares owned to outstanding: 10% (5,000 / 50,000)

EQUITY method

Your Corporation receives $5,000 in dividends from ABC Corporation.

Account		Debit	Credit
Cash		5,000	
Investment in ABC Stock			5,000

- *Cash* is an **asset** account that is **increasing.**
- *Investment* in ABC Stock is an **asset** account that is **decreasing.**

Investment in ABC Stock debit balance: $45,000 Carrying amount per share: $9.00 ($45,000 / 5,000) Number of shares owned: 5,000

Percentage of shares owned to outstanding: 25% (5,000 / 20,000)

Ledger account balance:

Investment in ABC Stock					
Date	Item	Debit	Credit	Debit	Credit
		50,000		50,000	

Ledger account balance:

Investment in ABC Stock					
Date	Item	Debit	Credit	Debit	Credit
		50,000		50,000	
			5,000	45,000	

2. RECOGNIZE NET INCOME OF THE ISSUING CORPORATION

Another difference between the fair value through net income and equity methods is seen when the issuing corporation reports net income.

Fair value through net income method

There is no journal entry under the fair value through net income method, where the percentage of investor ownership is not considered significant enough to participate in the issuing company's earnings.

Equity method

Under the equity method, the investing corporation owns such a significant percentage of the issuing corporation's shares that it actually takes ownership of its percentage of the issuing corporation's net income and reports it as its own. In this case, Your Corporation owns 25% of ABC Corporation's outstanding shares, so it recognizes 25% of ABC Corporation's net income ($100,000 x 25% = $25,000). This results in an increase in the value of the investment account as well.

FAIR VALUE THROUGH NET INCOME method

ABC Corporation reports net income of $100,000.

Account		Debit	Credit
Investment in ABC Stock		50,000	
Cash			50,000

NO JOURNAL ENTRY REQUIRED to account for ABC net income

EQUITY method

ABC Corporation reports net income of $100,000.

Account		Debit	Credit
Investment in ABC Stock		25,000	
Investment in ABC Stock			25,000

- *Investment* in ABC Stock is an **asset** account that is **increasing.**
- *Investment Income* is a **revenue** account that is **increasing.**

Investment in ABC Stock new debit balance: $70,000 Carrying amount per share: $14.00 ($70,000 / 5,000) Number of shares owned: 5,000

Percentage of shares owned to outstanding: 25% (5,000 / 20,000)

Calculation: $100,000 x 25%

Ledger account balance:

Investment in ABC Stock					
Date	Item	Debit	Credit	Debit	Credit
		50,000		50,000	

Ledger account balance:

Investment in ABC Stock					
Date	Item	Debit	Credit	Debit	Credit
		50,000		50,000	
			5,000	45,000	
		25,000		70,000	

3. ADJUST TO FAIR VALUE

Fair value through net income method

A third difference between the two methods is that the carrying value of the investment under the fair value through net income method must be adjusted to fair value at the end of each accounting period. Fair value is the current trading price of the stock on the market, which is readily available for public corporations in financial newspapers and online sites.

For investments that involve less than 20% of the issuing corporation's outstanding stock, a gain or loss is recorded if fair value is different than carrying value. However, it is an unrealized gain or loss since the investment has not yet been sold and there are no cash proceeds yet. The investment account is debited if the fair value increases, and an **unrealized** gain is recognized by crediting the Unrealized Holding Gain/Loss – Net Income account. These accounts in the journal entry are reversed and an unrealized loss results if the fair value of the investment declines.

The Unrealized Holding Gain/Loss – Net Income account appears on the income statement under a category heading called other comprehensive income section, after the net income line. An unrealized gain is added to net

income and/or an unrealized loss is deducted from it to arrive at the final income statement amount of **comprehensive income.** Unrealized gains and losses are treated similarly to **realized** gains and losses—which occur when the stock is actually sold for cash—in terms of arriving at the final income statement amount. The Unrealized Holding Gain/Loss – Net Income account is adjusted at least annually to reflect the current trading price of the stock investment.

Equity method

For investments that involve 20% or more of the issuing corporation's outstanding stock, there is no adjustment to fair value.

FAIR VALUE THROUGH NET INCOME method

The fair value of the 5,000 shares of ABC Corporation stock is $12.00 per share at the end of the accounting period.

Account		Debit	Credit
Investment in ABC Stock		10,000	
Unrealized holding Gain/ Loss - Net Income			10,000

- *Investment* in ABC Stock is an **asset** account that is **increasing.**
- *Unrealized Holding Gain/Loss – Net Income* is a gain that is **increasing.**

Investment in ABC Stock debit balance: $60,000 Carrying amount per share: $12.00 ($60,000 / 5,000) Number of shares owned: 5,000

Percentage of shares owned to outstanding: 10% (5,000 / 50,000)

Amount: 5,000 x ($12.00 fair value – $10.00 cost)

Ledger account balance:

Investment in ABC Stock					
Date	**Item**	**Debit**	**Credit**	**Debit**	**Credit**
		50,000		50,000	
		10,000		60,000	

Ledger account balance:

Investment in ABC Stock					
Date	**Item**	**Debit**	**Credit**	**Debit**	**Credit**
		50,000		50,000	
			5,000	45,000	
		25,000		70,000	

Ledger account balance:

Unrealized Holding Gain/Loss - Net Income					
Date	**Item**	**Debit**	**Credit**	**Debit**	**Credit**
			10,000		10,000

4. SELL THE STOCK INVESTMENT

Fair value through net income method

A final difference between the two methods is on the sale of the investment. The carrying value of the investment under the fair value through net income method must be adjusted to fair value at the time the shares are sold. The investment account is debited if the fair value increases, and an unrealized gain is recognized by crediting the Unrealized Holding Gain/Loss – Net Income account. These accounts in the journal entry are reversed if the fair value of the investment declines.

Equity method

For investments that use the equity method, there is no adjustment to fair value at the time of sale.

FAIR VALUE THROUGH NET INCOME method

The fair value of the 5,000 shares of ABC Corporation stock is $11.60 per share at the time the shares are sold.

Account		Debit	Credit
Unrealized Holding Gain/Loss – Net Income		10,000	
Investment in ABC Stock			10,000

- *Unrealized Holding Gain/Loss – Net Income* is a loss that is **increasing.**
- *Investment* in ABC Stock is an **asset** account that is **decreasing.**

EQUITY method

NO JOURNAL ENTRY REQUIRED to adjust to fair value

Account		Debit	Credit

Amount: 5,000 x ($12.00 carrying value – $11.60 fair value)

Your Corporation sells all 5,000 shares of ABC Corporation stock for the fair value of $11.60 per share.

Account		Debit	Credit
Cash		58,000	
Investment in ABC Stock			58,000

- *Cash* is an **asset** account that is **increasing.**
- *Investment* in ABC Stock is an **asset** account that is **decreasing.**

Your Corporation sells all 5,000 shares of ABC Corporation stock for $15.00 per share.

Account		Debit	Credit
Cash		75,000	
Investment in ABC Stock			70,000
Gain on Sale of Investment			5,000

- *Cash* is an **asset** account that is **increasing.**
- *Investment in ABC* Stock is an **asset** account that is **decreasing.**
- *Gain on Sale of Investment* is a **revenue** account that is **increasing.**

Investment in ABC Stock debit balance: $58,000 Carrying amount per share: $11.60 ($58,000 / 5,000) Number of shares owned: 5,000

Percentage of shares owned to outstanding: 10% (5,000 / 50,000)

Amount: 5,000 x $11.60

Ledger account balance:

Investment in ABC Stock					
Date	Item	Debit	Credit	Debit	Credit
		50,000		50,000	
			58,000	0	

Ledger account balance:

Investment in ABC Stock					
Date	**Item**	**Debit**	**Credit**	**Debit**	**Credit**
		50,000		50,000	
			5,000	45,000	

3. RECOGNIZE NET INCOME OF THE ISSUING CORPORATION

Another difference between the fair value through net income and equity methods is seen when the issuing corporation reports net income.

Fair value through net income method

There is no journal entry under the fair value through net income method, where the percentage of investor ownership is not considered significant enough to participate in the issuing company's earnings.

Equity method

Under the equity method, the investing corporation owns such a significant percentage of the issuing corporation's shares that it actually takes ownership of its percentage of the issuing corporation's net income and reports it as its own. In this case, Your Corporation owns 25% of ABC Corporation's outstanding shares, so it recognizes 25% of ABC Corporation's net income ($100,000 x 25% = $25,000). This results in an increase in the value of the investment account as well.

FAIR VALUE THROUGH NET INCOME method

ABC Corporation reports net income of $100,000.

Account		Debit	Credit

NO JOURNAL ENTRY REQUIRED to account for ABC net income

EQUITY method

ABC Corporation reports net income of $100,000.

Account		Debit	Credit
Investment in ABC Stock		25,000	
Investment in ABC Stock			25,000

- *Investment in ABC Stock* is an **asset** account that is **increasing.**
- *Investment Income* is a **revenue** account that is **increasing.**

Investment in ABC Stock new debit balance: $70,000 Carrying amount per share: $14.00 ($70,000 / 5,000) Number of shares owned: 5,000

Percentage of shares owned to outstanding: 25% (5,000 / 20,000)

Calculation: $100,000 x 25%

Ledger account balance:

Investment in ABC Stock					
Date	**Item**	**Debit**	**Credit**	**Debit**	**Credit**
		50,000		50,000	

Ledger account balance:

Investment in ABC Stock					
Date	**Item**	**Debit**	**Credit**	**Debit**	**Credit**
		50,000		50,000	
			5,000	45,000	
		25,000		70,000	

4. ADJUST TO FAIR VALUE

Fair value through net income method

A third difference between the two methods is that the carrying value of the investment under the fair value through net income method must be adjusted to fair value at the end of each accounting period. Fair value is the current trading price of the stock on the market, which is readily available for public corporations in financial newspapers and online sites.

For investments that involve less than 20% of the issuing corporation's outstanding stock, a gain or loss is recorded if fair value is different than carrying value. However, it is an **unrealized** gain or loss since the investment has not yet been sold and there are no cash proceeds yet. The investment account is debited if the fair value increases, and an unrealized gain is recognized by crediting the *Unrealized Holding Gain/Loss – Net Income* account. These accounts in the journal entry are reversed and an unrealized loss results if the fair value of the investment declines.

The Unrealized Holding Gain/Loss - Net Income account appears on the income statement under a category heading called other comprehensive income section, after the net income line. An unrealized gain is added to net income and/or an unrealized loss is deducted from it to arrive at the final income statement amount of comprehensive income. Unrealized gains and losses are treated similarly to realized gains and losses—which occur when the stock is actually sold for cash—in terms of arriving at the final income statement amount. The Unrealized Holding Gain/Loss - Net Income account is adjusted at least annually to reflect the current trading price of the stock investment.

Equity method

For investments that involve 20% or more of the issuing corporation's outstanding stock, there is no adjustment to fair value.

FAIR VALUE THROUGH NET INCOME method

The fair value of the 5,000 shares of ABC Corporation stock is $12.00 per share at the end of the accounting period.

Account		Debit	Credit
Investment in ABC Stock		10,000	
Unrealized holding Gain/ Loss - Net Income			10,.000

- *Investment in ABC Stock* is an **asset** account that is **increasing.**
- *Unrealized Holding Gain/Loss - Net Income* is a gain that is **increasing.**

Investment in ABC Stock debit balance: $60,000 Carrying amount per share: $12.00 ($60,000 / 5,000) Number of shares owned: 5,000

Percentage of shares owned to outstanding: 10% (5,000 / 50,000)

Amount: 5,000 x ($12.00 fair value - $10.00 cost)

EQUITY method

Account		Debit	Credit

NO JOURNAL ENTRY REQUIRED to adjust to fair value.

Ledger account balance:

Investment in ABC Stock					
Date	Item	Debit	Credit	Debit	Credit
		50,000		50,000	
		10,000		60,000	

Ledger account balance:

Investment in ABC Stock					
Date	Item	Debit	Credit	Debit	Credit
		50,000		50,000	
			5,000	45,000	
		25,000		70,000	

Ledger account balance:

Unrealized Holding Gain/Loss - Net Income					
Date	Item	Debit	Credit	Debit	Credit
			10,000		10,000

5. SELL THE STOCK INVESTMENT

Fair value through net income method

A final difference between the two methods is on the sale of the investment. The carrying value of the investment under the fair value through net income method must be adjusted to fair value at the time the shares are sold. The investment account is debited if the fair value increases, and an unrealized gain is recognized by crediting the Unrealized Holding Gain/Loss – Net Income account. These accounts in the journal entry are reversed if the fair value of the investment declines.

Equity method

For investments that use the equity method, there is no adjustment to fair value at the time of sale.

FAIR VALUE THROUGH NET INCOME method

The fair value of the 5,000 shares of ABC Corporation stock is $11.60 per share at the time the shares are sold.

Account		Debit	Credit
Unrealized Holding Gain/Loss – Net Income	10,000		
Investment in ABC Stock			10,000

- *Unrealized Holding Gain/Loss – Net Income* is a loss that is **increasing.**
- *Investment* in ABC Stock is an asset account that is **decreasing.**

EQUITY method

NO JOURNAL ENTRY REQUIRED to adjust to fair value

Account		Debit	Credit

Amount: 5,000 x ($12.00 carrying value – $11.60 fair value)

Your Corporation sells all 5,000 shares of ABC Corporation stock for the fair value of $11.60 per share.

Account		Debit	Credit
Cash		58,000	
Investment in ABC Stock			58,000

- *Cash* is an **asset** account that is **increasing.**
- *Investment in ABC Stock* is an **asset** account that is **decreasing.**

Your Corporation sells all 5,000 shares of ABC Corporation stock for $15.00 per share.

Account		Debit	Credit
Cash		75,000	
Investment in ABC Stock			70,000
Gain on Sale of Investment			5,000

- *Cash* is an **asset** account that is **increasing.**
- *Investment in ABC Stock* is an **asset** account that is **decreasing.**
- *Gain on Sale of Investment* is a **revenue** account that is **increasing.**

Investment in ABC Stock debit balance: $58,000 Carrying amount per share: $11.60 ($58,000 / 5,000) Number of shares owned: 5,000

Percentage of shares owned to outstanding: 10% (5,000 / 50,000)

Amount: 5,000 x $11.60

Ledger account balance:

Investment in ABC Stock					
Date	Item	Debit	Credit	Debit	Credit
		50,000		50,000	
		10,000		60,000	
			2,000	58,000	
			58,000	0	

Ledger account balance:

Investment in ABC Stock					
Date	Item	Debit	Credit	Debit	Credit
		50,000		50,000	
			5,000	45,000	
		25,000		70,000	
			70,000	0	

Ledger account balance:

Unrealized Holding Gain/Loss - Net Income					
Date	Item	Debit	Credit	Debit	Credit
			10,000		10,000
		2,000			8,000

4.9.3 Investments in Stock on the Financial Statements

The investment in stock accounts appear in the assets section of the balance sheet. Those that are intended to be sold or traded within one year are current assets. Those that are intended to be held for more than one year are categorized as long-term investments.

LESS THAN 20% OWNERSHIP (FAIR VALUE THROUGH NET INCOME METHOD)

The Unrealized Holding Gain/Loss – Net Income account appears on the income statement as part of other comprehensive income. It represents the amount of gain or loss on investments that have not yet been sold, but whose fair value has changed since their initial cost. A fair value greater than cost represents an unrealized gain; a fair value less than cost represents an unrealized loss. The Unrealized Holding

Gain/Loss – Net Income account is adjusted over time, particularly before financial statements are prepared, to update the unrealized gain or loss amount based on the most current fair value.

The *Gain on Sale of Investment and Loss on Sale of Investment* accounts that represent actual gains and losses from the sale of investments are not used for stock investments that are less than 20% of outstanding shares. This is because the Unrealized Holding Gain/Loss – Net Income account is updated just prior to the sale to bring the investment account to fair value, which is the amount of cash received from the sale. Therefore, no realized gain or loss is recognized at that time.

20% TO 50% OWNERSHIP (EQUITY METHOD)

For investments that involve 20% or more of the issuing corporation's outstanding stock, there is no adjustment to fair value and the *Unrealized Holding Gain/Loss – Net Income* account is not used.

The *Gain on Sale of Investment and/or Loss on Sale of Investment* accounts appear on the income statement as other income. These represent realized gains or losses that result from the sale of stock investments under the equity method.

The following table includes financial statements with select accounts for a company that holds equity investments.

Comprehensive Income Statement		Balance Sheet	
Revenues	$XXX,XXX	ASSETS	
Expenses	XXX,XXX	Current assets:	
Income from operations	$XXX,XXX	Marketable securities	$XXX,XXX
Other income and expenses:		Long-term investments: Equity securities	XXX,XXX
Dividends revenue	XXX,XXX		
Investment Income[2]	XXX,XXX		
Gain on sale of investment[2]	XXX,XXX		
Loss on sale of investment[2]	(XXX,XXX)		
Net income	$XXX,XXX		
Other comprehensive income:			
Unrealized holding gain/loss on investments 1	XXX,XXX		

[1] *related to fair value through net income method securities*

[2] *related to equity method securities*

4.10 INVESTMENTS IN BONDS

A company may invest in the bonds of another corporation if it has no immediate need for its cash, just like it can invest in another corporation's stock. An investor in bonds is lending money to another corporation. A separate account that mentions the unique name of the corporation for each bond investment is used.

For example, a company might invest in the bonds of three other corporations and use Investment in ABC Bonds, Investment in Home Depot Bonds, and Investment in Delta Airlines Bonds as their three distinct asset account names.

There are five possible journal entries related to investing in bonds, as follows:

1. Purchase the bonds investment
2. Record the semi-annual interest receipts
3. Amortize the discount or premium
4. Adjust to fair value
5. Sell the bonds investment

Investments in bonds are accounted for in three different ways, depending on how long the investor intends to hold the investment. Bonds are classified as one of three types of securities.

The debt is classified as (a) held-to-maturity when the investor has the intent and ability to hold the bond full term.

The debt is classified as (b) trading when the intent is to sell it in the short term for profit and own it less than one year.

The debt is classified as (c) available-for-sale when it is neither held-to- maturity nor trading.

The investment in bonds accounts appear in the assets section of the balance sheet. Those that are classified as trading securities to be sold or traded within one year are current assets. Held-to-maturity and available-for-sale securities that are intended to be owned for more than one year are categorized as long-term investments.

Bonds have a face value, which is the amount that will be repaid on the maturity date. In the example that follows, the face amount is $5,000,000. In addition, the bond investment will show a contract rate, which is the percent of interest that will be paid annually to investors. In the example, the interest rate is 8%. Bonds also are in effect for a stated period of time and have a maturity date. In the example, the term of the bonds is four years, so the maturity date is December 31, 2021. On that date, investors are repaid the face amount of the bond investment.

4.10.1 Held-to-Maturity Securities

Bond investments are classified as held-to-maturity when the investor has the intent and ability to hold the bond full term. Two versions of the journal entries related to investing in held-to-maturity bond securities are illustrated side by side in the journal entries that follow. The transactions on the left illustrate transactions for bond investments purchased at a discount. On the right are journal entries for bonds purchased at a premium. Explanations are included.

Held-to-maturity bond securities appear under the Long-Term Investments caption in the assets section of the balance sheet. They are reported at their amortized cost, as explained below. They are not adjusted to fair value.

1A. PURCHASE THE BOND INVESTMENT OF HELD-TO-MATURITY SECURITIES

Bonds may be purchased for their face amount. They may also be purchased at either a discount or a premium; that is, for less or more than the face amount, respectively. If the contract interest rate that the issuing corporation is offering is less than the going market rate, investors purchase the bonds at a discount (for less than face amount). If the contract interest rate that the issuing corporation is offering is more than the going market rate, investors purchase the bonds at a premium (for more than face amount).

The following bonds are purchased on January 1, 2018.

At a Discount (market rate is lower)

1/1/2018 Your Corporation purchases $5,000,000 of four-year, 6% ABC Co. bonds for $4,700,000. (The bond investment is purchased at a discount of $300,000).

Account		Debit	Credit
Investment in ABC Stock		4,700,000	
Cash			4,700,000

- *Investment in ABC Bonds* is an **asset** account that is **increasing.**
- *Cash* is an **asset** account that is **decreasing.**

At a Premium (market rate is higher)

1/1/2018 Your Corporation purchases $5,000,000 of four-year, 6% ABC Co. bonds for $5,300,000. (The bond investment is purchased at a premium of $300,000).

Account		Debit	Credit
Investment in ABC Bonds		5,300,000	
Cash			5,300,000

- *Investment in ABC Bonds* is an **asset** account that is **increasing.**
- *Cash* is an **asset** account that is **decreasing.**

Ledger account balance:

Investment in ABC Stock					
Date	Item	Debit	Credit	Debit	Credit
		4,700,000		4,700,000	

Ledger account balance:

Investment in ABC Stock					
Date	Item	Debit	Credit	Debit	Credit
		5,300,000		5,300,000	

2A. RECORD INTEREST FOR SEMI-ANNUAL INTEREST RECEIPTS FOR HELD-TO-MATURITY SECURITIES

The corporation that issued the bond securities pays interest to the investor semi-annually, or every six months. The issuing company pays semi-annual interest on June 30 and December 31 each year. The amount is determined by multiplying the face amount of the bonds by half of the annual contract rate.

At a Discount (market rate is lower)

EVERY SIX MONTHS Your Corporation records semi- annual interest received and discount amortized.

Account		Debit	Credit
Cash		15,000	
Investment Revenue			15,000

- *Cash* is an **asset** account that is **increasing.**
- *Interest Revenue* is a **revenue** account that is **increasing.**

At a Premium (market rate is higher)

EVERY SIX MONTHS Your Corporation records semi- annual interest received and premium amortized.

Account		Debit	Credit
Cash		15,000	
Interest Revenue			15,000

- *Cash* is an **asset** account that is **increasing.**
- *Interest Revenue* is a **revenue** account that is **increasing.**

Cash and Interest Revenue amounts = ($5,000,000 x 6%) / 2 Cash and Interest Revenue amounts = ($5,000,000 x 6%) / 2

The investment account balances are not affected by the receipt of the interest. This transaction is recorded every six months as the cash is received for the interest revenue for as long as the investment is held.

3A. AMORTIZATION OF DISCOUNT OR PREMIUM FOR HELD-TO-MATURITY SECURITIES JUST PRIOR TO FINANCIAL STATEMENTS

If bonds are purchased at a discount or premium, there is a difference between the amount paid for the investment and the face amount. That difference is accounted for over time as Interest Revenue rather than recorded as Interest Revenue all at once at the time of purchase. This process is called amortization; it is similar to depreciation but for non-physical assets. Assume that the investor prepares financial statements at the end of each calendar year. The straight-line method will be used to amortize the discount or premium amount at the end of each year, which involves dividing the discount or premium amount by the number of years in the term of the bond.

At a Discount (market rate is lower)
EVERY YEAR END Your Corporation records semi-annual interest received and discount amortized.

Account		Debit	Credit
Investment in ABC Bonds		75,000	
Investment Revenue			75,000

- *Cash* is an **asset** account that is **increasing.**
- *Interest Revenue* is a **revenue** account that is **increasing.**

At a Premium (market rate is higher)
EVERY YEAR END Your Corporation records semi-annual interest received and premium amortized.

Account		Debit	Credit
Interest Revenue		75,000	
Interest in ABC Bonds			75,000

- *Interest Revenue* is a **revenue** account that is **decreasing.**
- *Investment in ABC Bonds* is an **asset** account that is **decreasing.**

Investment amortization amount = ($5,000,000 - $4,700,000) / 4 years = $75,000

Investment amortization amount = ($5,000,000 - $5,300,000) / 4 years = $75,000

The journal entry above is repeated every year end for a total of four years in the term of the bond.

The ledgers that follow show the change over time in the carrying amount of the bond investment as the discount or premium is amortized every year.

With each entry in the investment account's ledger, the running debit balances moves closer and closer to the face amount of the bonds. The debit balance of an investment purchased at a discount continuously increases. The debit balance of an investment purchased at a premium continuously decreases.

Ledger account balance:

Investment in ABC Stock					
Date	**Item**	**Debit**	**Credit**	**Debit**	**Credit**
1/1/18		4,700,000		4,700,000	
12/31/18		75,000		4,775,000	
12/31/19		75,000		4,850,000	
12/31/20		75,000		4,925,000	
12/31/21		75,000		5,000,000	

Ledger account balance

Investment in ABC Stock					
Date	**Item**	**Debit**	**Credit**	**Debit**	**Credit**
1/1/18		5,300,000		5,300,000	
12/31/18			75,000	5,225,000	
12/31/19			75,000	5,150,000	
12/31/20			75,000	5,075,000	
12/31/21			75,000	5,000,000	

4A. ADJUST TO FAIR VALUE—NOT APPLICABLE FOR HELD-TO-MATURITY SECURITIES

Held-to-maturity investments are not adjusted to fair value over time since the intent is not to sell them at a gain or loss prior to the maturity date of the bonds. Therefore, there is no journal entry to adjust held-to-maturity investments to fair value.

5A. ALTERNATIVE #1 - SELL THE BONDS INVESTMENT OF HELD-TO-MATURITY SECURITIES ON MATURITY DATE

Investors receive the full face amount on the maturity date. Held-to-maturity securities are typically repaid on the maturity date, so this is the more common transaction for the repayment.

At a Discount (market rate is lower)
12/31/21 ABC Co. redeems the bonds and pays back the face amount of $5,000,000 to Your Corporation after the full term of the bond.

Account		Debit	Credit
Cash		5,000,000	
Investment in ABC Bonds			5,000,000

- *Cash* is an **asset** account that is **increasing.**
- *Investment in ABC Bonds* is an **asset** account that is **decreasing.**

At a Premium (market rate is higher)
12/31/21 ABC Co. redeems the bonds and pays back the face amount of $5,000,000 to Your Corporation after the full term of the bond.

Account		Debit	Credit
Cash		5,000,000	
Interest in ABC Bonds			5,000,000

- *Cash* is an **asset** account that is **increasing.**
- **Investment in ABC Bonds** is an asset account that is **decreasing.**

Ledger account balance:

Investment in ABC Stock					
Date	Item	Debit	Credit	Debit	Credit
1/1/18		4,700,000		4,700,000	
12/31/18		75,000		4,775,000	
12/31/19		75,000		4,850,000	
12/31/20		75,000		4,925,000	
12/31/21		75,000		5,000,000	
12/31/21			5,000,000		0

Ledger account balance:

Investment in ABC Stock					
Date	Item	Debit	Credit	Debit	Credit
1/1/18		5,300,000		5,300,000	
12/31/18			75,000	5,225,000	
12/31/19			75,000	5,150,000	
12/31/20			75,000	5,075,000	
12/31/21			75,000	5,000,000	
12/31/21			5,000,000	0	

5A. ALTERNATIVE #2—SELL THE BONDS INVESTMENT OF HELD- TO-MATURITY SECURITIES PRIOR TO MATURITY DATE

Investors may receive more or less than the face amount of the bond if they sell the investment prior to the maturity date. A gain or loss on the sale may occur. The examples that follow show a bond purchased at a discount that is sold for a gain and a bond purchased at a premium that is sold at a loss. The gain and loss may be reversed for a premium and discount, respectively, as well.

Held-to-maturity securities are typically repaid on the maturity date, so this is the less common transaction for the repayment.

At a Discount (market rate is lower)

12/31/20 Your Corporation sells the bond after three full years for $4,945,000 when the carrying amount of the investment is $4,925,000.

Account		Debit	Credit
Cash		4,945,000	
Gain on Sale of Investment			20,000
Investment in ABC Bonds			4,925,000

- *Cash* is an **asset** account that is **increasing.**
- *Gain on Sale of Investment* is a **revenue** account that is **increasing.**
- *Investment in ABC Bonds* is an **asset** account that is **decreasing.**

At a Premium (market rate is higher)

12/31/20 Your Corporation sells the bond after three full years for $5,055,000 when the carrying amount of the investment is $5,075,000.

Account		Debit	Credit
Cash		5,000,000	
Interest in ABC Bonds			5,000,000

- *Cash* is an **asset** account that is **increasing.**
- *Loss on Sale of Investment* is a **revenue** account that is **increasing.**
- *Investment in ABC Bonds* is an **asset** account that is **decreasing.**

Ledger account balance:

Investment in ABC Stock					
Date	Item	Debit	Credit	Debit	Credit
1/1/18		4,700,000		4,700,000	
12/31/18		75,000		4,775,000	
12/31/19		75,000		4,850,000	
12/31/20		75,000		4,925,000	
12/31/20			4,925,000	0	

Ledger account balance:

Investment in ABC Stock					
Date	Item	Debit	Credit	Debit	Credit
1/1/18		5,300,000		5,300,000	
12/31/18			75,000	5,225,000	
12/31/19			75,000	5,150,000	
12/31/20			75,000	5,075,000	
12/31/20			5,075,000	0	

Ledger account balance:

Date	Item	Debit	Credit	Debit	Credit
12/31/20			20,000		20,000

Ledger account balance:

Date	Item	Debit	Credit	Debit	Credit
12/31/20		20,000		20,000	

4.10.2 Purchasing Bond Investments with Accrued Interest and Partial-Year Amortization

In the previous held-to-maturity examples, the investments were purchased on January 1 and sold on December 31. Each year the investor owned the bond securities for the full 12 months of the calendar year.

This, obviously, is not always the case. Bond investments may be purchased and sold any time during the year. Assuming that the investing corporation prepares annual financial statements on December 31 each calendar year, the corporation may need to pro-rate the amounts received for semi-annual interest and amounts amortized to adjust for a partial year of ownership.

The examples below show a comparison of full-year transactions on the left and partial-year transactions on the right.

Full Year

1/1/2018 Your Corporation purchases $5,000,000 of four-year, 6% ABC Co. bonds for $4,700,000. (The bond investment is purchased at a discount of $300,000).

Account		Debit	Credit
Investment in ABC Bonds		4,700,000	
Cash			4,700,000

- *Investment in ABC Bonds* is an **asset** account that is **increasing.**
- *Cash* is an **asset** account that is **decreasing.**

Partial Year

3/1/2018 Your Corporation purchases $5,000,000 of four-year, 6% ABC Co. bonds for $4,700,000. (The bond investment is purchased at a discount of $300,000).

Account		Debit	Credit
Interest in ABC Bonds		4,700,000	
Interest Revenue		5,000	
Cash			4,705,000

- *Investment in ABC Bonds* is an **asset** account that is **increasing.**
- *Interest Revenue* is a **revenue** account that is **decreasing.**
- *Cash* is an **asset** account that is **decreasing.**

Interest is paid each year on June 30 and December 31. Since Your Corporation will be the owner of the bond on June 30, Your will receive the full six-month payment of $15,000 ($5,000,000 x 3%). However, Your is only entitled to one- third of it, or $5,000, since the investor only owned the bond four months (March, April, May, and June) during the six-month period. The party Your purchased the bond from is entitled to the other two months' worth, or $5,000.

Therefore, at the time of the closing on the bond on March 1, Your Corporation advances the seller his $5,000 portion of the $15,000 interest payment that will be paid on June 30. As you see from the transaction that follows, Your receives the full $15,000 from the company that issued the bond on June 30, and Your keeps it all—$10,000 is for the four months when Your owned the bond, and the other $5,000 is to reimburse Your for the amount it paid the seller on March 1.

2. RECEIVE SEMI-ANNUAL INTEREST PAYMENT ON 6/30/18 AND 12/31/18

Full Year

EVERY SIX MONTHS Your Corporation records semi- annual interest received.

Account		Debit	Credit
Cash		15,000	
Interest Revenue			15,000

- *Cash* is an **asset** account that is **increasing.**
- *Interest Revenue* is a **revenue** account that is **increasing.**

Cash and Interest Revenue amounts = ($5,000,000 x 6%) / 2

Partial Year

EVERY SIX MONTHS Your Corporation records semi- annual interest received.

Account		Debit	Credit
Cash		15,000	
Interest Revenue			15,000

- *Cash* is an **asset** account that is **increasing.**
- *Interest Revenue* is a **revenue** account that is **increasing.**

Cash and Interest Revenue amounts = ($5,000,000 x 6%) / 2

Full Year

EVERY YEAR END Your Corporation amortizes the discount on the investment.

Account		Debit	Credit
Investment in ABC Bonds		75,000	
Interest Revenue			75,000

- *Investment in ABC Bonds* is an **asset** account that is **increasing.**
- *Interest Revenue* is a *revenue* account that is **increasing.**

($5,000,000 - $4,700,000) / 4 years = $75,000

Partial Year

EVERY YEAR END Your Corporation amortizes the premium on the investment.

Account		Debit	Credit
Investment in ABC Bonds		62,500	
Interest Revenue			62,500

- *Investment in ABC Bonds is* an **asset** account that is **increasing.**
- *Interest Revenue is a* revenue account that is **increasing.**

($5,000,000 - $4,700,000) / 4 years = $75,000 x 10/12 = 62,500

Cash and Interest Revenue amounts = ($5,000,000 x 6%)/2

The investor can only amortize the discount over the period it owns the bonds. In this partial-year case, the investor can amortize 10 months out of 12 months in the year (March through December).

4.10.3 Selling Bond Investments with Accrued Interest and Partial-Year Amortization

An investor must also pro-rate interest and amortization amounts if it sells the investment during a calendar year. The examples below show a comparison of full-year transactions on the left and partial-year transactions on the right.

Full Year

On January 1, 2016, Your Corporation had purchased $5,000,000 of four-year, 6% ABC Co. bonds for $4,700,000. (The bond investment was purchased at a discount of $300,000). Your amortized the discount on 12/31 at the end of 2016 and 2017. The carrying amount on the investment on December 31, 2017 is $4,850,000 ($4,700,000 + $75,000 for 2016 + $75,000 for 2017).

It is now December 31, 2018 and Your Corporation amortizes the discount to date in 2018 and sells the investment for $4,875,000.

12/31/18 Your Corporation amortizes the discount on the investment for 2018, just before the sale.

Account		Debit	Credit
Investment in ABC Bonds		75,000	
Interest Revenue			75,000

- *Investment in ABC Bonds* is an asset account that is **increasing.**
- *Interest Revenue* is a **revenue** account that is **increasing.**

($5,000,000 - $4,700,000) / 4 years = $75,000

Partial Year

On January 1, 2016, Your Corporation had purchased $5,000,000 of four-year, 6% ABC Co. bonds for $4,700,000. (The bond investment was purchased at a discount of $300,000). Your amortized the discount on 12/31 at the end of 2016 and 2017. The carrying amount on the investment on December 31, 2017 is $4,850,000 ($4,700,000 + $75,000 for 2016 + $75,000 for 2017).

It is now April 30, 2018 and Your Corporation amortizes the discount to date in 2018 and sells the investment for $4,875,000.

4/30/18 Your Corporation amortizes the additional discount on the investment for 2018, just before the sale.

Account		Debit	Credit
Investment in ABC Bonds		62,500	
Interest Revenue			62,500

- *Investment in ABC Bonds* is an **asset** account that is **increasing.**
- *Interest Revenue* is a **revenue** account that is **increasing.**

($5,000,000 - $4,700,000) / 4 years = $75,000 x 4/12 = 25,000

Ledger account balance:

Investment in ABC Stock					
Date	Item	Debit	Credit	Debit	Credit
1/1/16		4,700,000		4,700,000	
12/31/16		75,000		4,775,000	
12/31/17		75,000		4,850,000	
12/31/18		75,000		4,925,000	

Ledger account balance:

Investment in ABC Stock					
Date	Item	Debit	Credit	Debit	Credit
1/1/16		4,700,000		4,700,000	
12/31/16		75,000		4,775,000	
12/31/17		75,000		4,850,000	
4/30/18		25,000		4,825,000	

In the case of the partial year where the investment was sold on April 30, 2018, the seller receives two-thirds of the $15,000 bond interest amount that the issuing company will pay on June 30. This is because the seller owned the investment four months during the six-month interest period. The buyer pays this $10,000 to the seller at the closing and the buyer is reimbursed on June 30 when he receives and keeps the full $15,000 interest payment.

Full Year

12/31/18 Your Corporation sells the bond after three full years for $4,875,000 when the carrying amount of the investment is $4,925,000.

Account		Debit	Credit
Cash		4,885,000	
Loss on Sale of Investment		50,000	
Investment in ABC Bonds			4,925,000
Interest Revenue			10,000

- *Cash* is an **asset** account that is **increasing.**
- *Loss on Sale of Investment* is a **loss** that is **increasing.**
- *Investment in ABC Bonds* is an **asset** account that is **decreasing.**
- *Interest Revenue* is a *revenue* account that is **increasing.**

Partial Year

4/30/18 Your Corporation sells the bond after two years and four months for $4,875,000 when the carrying amount of the investment is $4,825,000.

Account		Debit	Credit
Cash		4,885,000	
Gain on Sale of Investment			50,000
Investment in ABC Bonds			4,825,000
Interest Revenue			10,000

- *Cash* is an **asset** account that is **increasing.**
- *Gain on Sale of Investment* is a **gain** that is **increasing.**
- *Investment in ABC Bonds* is an **asset** account that is **decreasing.**
- *Interest Revenue* is a **revenue** account that is **increasing.**

Ledger account balance

Investment in ABC Stock					
Date	**Item**	**Debit**	**Credit**	**Debit**	**Credit**
1/1/16		4,700,000		4,700,000	
12/31/16		75,000		4,775,000	
12/31/17		75,000		4,850,000	
12/31/18		75,000		4,925,000	
12/31/18			4,925,000	0	

Ledger account balance

Investment in ABC Stock					
Date	**Item**	**Debit**	**Credit**	**Debit**	**Credit**
1/1/16		4,700,000		4,700,000	
12/31/16		75,000		4,775,000	
12/31/17		75,000		4,850,000	
4/30/18		25,000		4,825,000	
4/30/18			4,825,000	0	

Ledger account balance:

Investment in ABC Stock					
Date	**Item**	**Debit**	**Credit**	**Debit**	**Credit**
12/31/18		50,000		50,000	

Ledger account balance:

Investment in ABC Stock					
Date	**Item**	**Debit**	**Credit**	**Debit**	**Credit**
4/30/18			50,000		50,000

4.10.4 Trading Securities

A bond investment is classified as trading when the investor intends to sell it quickly within one year. Trading bond securities appear in the current assets section on the balance sheet at their fair value. Unrealized gains or losses due to a difference between cost and fair value are reported on the investor's income statement as a component of **comprehensive income** in the *Unrealized Holding Gain/Loss - Net Income* account.

AVAILABLE-FOR-SALE SECURITIES

A bond investment is classified as **available-for-sale** when it is neither held- to-maturity nor trading. Available-for-sale bond securities typically appear under the **Long-Term Investments** caption in the assets section of the balance sheet at their fair value. Unrealized gains or losses due to a difference between cost and fair value are reported on the investor's balance sheet in the stockholders' equity section under the caption **Other Accumulated Comprehensive Income** in the *Unrealized Holding Gain/Loss - Available-for-Sale Securities account.*

Two versions of the transactions related to investing in bonds are illustrated side by side in the journal entries that follow. The transactions on the left illustrate transactions for bond investments classified as trading securities. On the right are transactions for bonds classified as available-for-sale securities. Explanations are included.

1. PURCHASE THE BOND INVESTMENT OF TRADING OR AVAILABLE-FOR-SALE SECURITIES

Notice in this example that the bonds are purchased on July 1, halfway through the calendar year.

Trading Securities

7/1/2018 Your Corporation purchases $5,000,000 of four-year, 6% ABC Co. bonds for their face amount. The investment is classified as a trading security since the investor expects to sell it in approximately 9 months.

Account		Debit	Credit
Investment in ABC Bonds		5,000,000	
Cash			5,000,000

- *Investment in ABC Bonds* is an **asset** account that is **increasing.**
- *Cash* is an **asset** account that is **decreasing.**

Available-for-Sale Securities

7/1/2018 Your Corporation purchases $5,000,000 of four-year, 6% ABC Co. bonds for their face amount. The investment is classified as an available-for-sale security since the expected sale date is uncertain.

Account		Debit	Credit
Investment in ABC Bonds		5,000,000	
Cash			5,000,000

- *Investment in ABC Bonds* is an **asset** account that is **increasing.**
- *Cash* is an **asset** account that is **decreasing.**

Ledger account balance

Investment in ABC Stock					
Date	Item	Debit	Credit	Debit	Credit
7/1/18		5,000,000		5,000,000	

Ledger account balance

Investment in ABC Stock					
Date	Item	Debit	Credit	Debit	Credit
7/1/18		5,000,000		5,000,000	

2. RECORD INTEREST FOR SEMI-ANNUAL INTEREST RECEIPTS

The corporation that issued the bond securities pays interest to the investor semi-annually, or every six months. The issuing company pays semi-annual interest on June 30 and December 31 each year. The semi-annual amount is determined by multiplying the face amount of the bonds by half of the annual contract rate.

Trading Securities

12/31/2018 Your Corporation records semi-annual interest received.

Account		Debit	Credit
Cash		15,000	
Interest Revenue			15,000

- *Cash* is an **asset** account that is **increasing.**
- *Interest Revenue* is a *revenue* account that is **increasing.**

Cash and Interest **Revenue** amounts = ($5,000,000 x 6%) / 2

Available-for-Sale Securities

12/31/2018 Your Corporation records semi-annual interest received.

Account		Debit	Credit
Cash		15,000	
Interest Revenue			15,000

- *Cash* is an **asset** account that is **increasing.**
- *Interest* Revenue is a **revenue** account that is **increasing.**

Cash and Interest Revenue amounts = ($5,000,000 x 6%) / 2

The investment account balance is not affected by the receipt of the interest. This transaction is recorded every six months as the cash is received for the interest revenue for as long as the investment is held.

3. AMORTIZATION OF DISCOUNT OR PREMIUM FOR TRADING OR AVAILABLE-FOR-SALE SECURITIES

There is no discount or premium for either security since the bonds were purchased at their face amounts.

4. ADJUST TRADING OR AVAILABLE-FOR-SALE SECURITIES TO FAIR VALUE JUST PRIOR TO FINANCIAL STATEMENTS

Trading securities and available-for-sale securities are adjusted to fair value at least once annually. In these examples, that adjustment will occur on December 31, 2018, just before the financial statements are prepared for the year.

Trading Securities

12/31/18 The fair value of the trading securities is $5,010,000.

Account		Debit	Credit
Investment in ABC Bonds	10,000		
Unrealized Holding Gain/Loss — Net Income			10,000

- *Investment in ABC Bonds* is an **asset** account that is **increasing.**
- *Unrealized Holding Gain/Loss – Net Income* is a gain account that is **increasing.**

Amount = $5,010,000 fair value - $5,000,000 cost

Available-for-Sale Securities

12/31/18 The fair value of the available-for-sale securities is $5,010,000.

Account		Debit	Credit
Investment in ABC Bonds		10,000	
Unrealized Holding Gain/Loss — Available-for-Sale			10,000

- *Investment in ABC Bonds* is an **asset** account that is **increasing.**
- *Unrealized Holding Gain/Loss – Available-for-Sale* is a gain that is **increasing.**

Amount = $5,010,000 fair value - $5,000,000 cost

Ledger account balance

Investment in ABC Stock (trading)					
Date	Item	Debit	Credit	Debit	Credit
7/1/18		5,000,000		5,000,000	
12/31/18		10,000		5,010,000	

Ledger account balance:

Investment in ABC Stock (available-for-sale)					
Date	Item	Debit	Credit	Debit	Credit
7/1/18		5,000,000		5,000,000	
12/31/18		10,000		5,010,000	

Ledger account balance:

Unrealized Holding Gain/Loss — Net Income					
Date	**Item**	**Debit**	**Credit**	**Debit**	**Credit**
12/31/18		10,000		10,000	

Ledger account balance:

Unrealized Holding Gain/Loss — Available-For-Sale					
Date	**Item**	**Debit**	**Credit**	**Debit**	**Credit**
12/31/18		10,000		10,000	

The following table includes financial statements with select accounts for a company that holds debt investments.

Comprehensive Income Statement		Balance Sheet	
Revenues	$XXX,XXX	ASSETS	
Expenses	XXX,XXX	Current assets:	
Income from operations	$XXX,XXX	Trading securities	$XXX,XXX
Other income and expenses:		Long-term investments:	
Investment Income	XXX,XXX	Available-for-sale securities	XXX,XXX
Gain on sale of investment[3]	XXX,XXX	Held-to-maturity securities	XXX,XXX
Loss on sale of investment[3]	(XXX,XXX)	LIABILITIES	
Net income	$XXX,XXX	STOCKDOLERS' EQUITY	
		Common Stock	XXX,XXX
Other comprehensive income:		Retained Earnings	XXX,XXX
Unrealized holding gain/loss on investments[1]	XXX,XXX	Other accumulated comprehen- sive income:	
Comprehensive income	$XXX,XXX	Unrealized holding gain/ loss on available-for-sale securities[2]	XXX,XXX

[1]related to trading securities

[2]related to available-for-sale securities

[3]related to held-to-maturity securities

After financial statements are prepared, income statement accounts are closed to Retained Earnings.

Income statement accounts, such as *Unrealized Holding Gain/Loss - Net Income, are closed to Retained Earnings after the financial statements are prepared. Unrealized Holding Gain/Loss - Available-for-Sale Securities* is a balance sheet account and therefore is not closed.

Trading Securities

12/31/18 Close the income statement account.

Account		Debit	Credit
Unrealized Holding Gain/Loss — Net Income		10,000	
Retained Earnings			10,000

- *Unrealized Holding Gain/Loss - Net Income* is a gain set to zero by **decreasing.**
- *Retained* Earnings is a stockholders' equity account that is **increasing.**

Available-for-Sale Securities

Account		Debit	Credit

No Journal Entry.

Ledger account balance:

Investment in ABC Stock (trading)					
Date	Item	Debit	Credit	Debit	Credit
7/1/18		5,000,000		5,000,000	
12/31/18		10,000		5,010,000	

Ledger account balance:

Investment in ABC Stock (available-for-sale)					
Date	Item	Debit	Credit	Debit	Credit
7/1/18		5,000,000		5,000,000	
12/31/18		10,000		5,010,000	

Ledger account balance:

Unrealized Holding Gain/Loss — Net Income					
Date	Item	Debit	Credit	Debit	Credit
12/31/18		10,000		10,000	
12/31/18			10,000	0	

Ledger account balance:

Unrealized Holding Gain/Loss — Available-For-Sale					
Date	Item	Debit	Credit	Debit	Credit
12/31/18		10,000		10,000	

5. SELL THE BONDS INVESTMENT OF TRADING SECURITIES OR AVAILABLE-FOR SALE SECURITIES

The trading securities are sold on March 31, 2019. The available for sale securities are sold on October 31, 2019.

The first step in the sale of each of the debt securities is to bring the carrying amount of the investment to its fair value on the date of the sale. This may also impact the amount of unrealized holding gain or loss balance.

Trading Securities

3/31/19 Your Corporation sells the bond trading securities when the fair value is $5,008,000.

Account		Debit	Credit
Unrealized Holding Gain/Loss— Net Income		2,000	
Retained Earnings			2,000

- *Unrealized Holding Gain/Loss – Net Income* is a loss account that is **increasing.**
- *Investment in ABC Bonds* is an **asset** account that is **decreasing.**

Amount = $5,008,000 fair value - $5,010,000 carrying amount

Available-for-Sale Securities

10/31/19 Your Corporation sells the bond available-for-sale securities when the fair value is $5,008,000.

Account		Debit	Credit
Unrealized Holding Gain/Loss – Available-for-Sale		2,000	
Investment in ABC Bonds			2,000

- *Unrealized Holding Gain/Loss – Net Income* is a loss account that is **increasing.**
- *Investment in ABC Bonds* is an asset account that is **decreasing.**

Amount = $5,008,000 fair value - $5,010,000 carrying amount

Ledger account balance:

Investment in ABC Stock (trading)					
Date	Item	Debit	Credit	Debit	Credit
7/1/18		5,000,000		5,000,000	
12/31/18		10,000		5,010,000	
3/31/19			2,000	5,008,000	

Ledger account balance:

Investment in ABC Stock (available-for-sale)					
Date	Item	Debit	Credit	Debit	Credit
7/1/18		5,000,000		5,000,000	
12/31/18		10,000		5,010,000	
10/31/19			2,000	5,008,000	

Ledger account balance:

Unrealized Holding Gain/Loss — Net Income					
Date	Item	Debit	Credit	Debit	Credit
7/1/18		5,000,000		5,000,000	
12/31/18		10,000		5,010,000	
10/31/19			2,000	5,008,000	

Ledger account balance:

Unrealized Holding Gain/Loss — Available-For-Sale					
Date	Item	Debit	Credit	Debit	Credit
12/31/18		10,000		10,000	
10/31/19		2,000		8,000	

The second step in the sale of available-for-sale securities is to transfer the unrealized gain/loss amount from the balance sheet account to the Gain (or Loss) on Sale of Investment account on the income statement so it can be included in the net income amount for the year.

There is no such transfer for trading securities since the *Unrealized Holding Gain/ Loss – Net Income* account is already an income statement account.

Trading Securities

3/31/19 Your Corporation sells the bond trading securities when the fair value is $5,008,000.

Account		Debit	Credit

No Journal entry.

Available-for-Sale Securities

10/31/19 Your Corporation sells the bond available-for-sale securities when the fair value is $5,008,000. Transfer the unrealized gain.

Account		Debit	Credit
Unrealized Holding Gain/Loss– Available-for-Sale		8,000	
Gain on Sale of Investment			2,000

- *Unrealized Holding Gain/Loss – Net Income* is set to zero by **decreasing.**
- *Gain on Sale of Investment* is a gain that is **increasing.**

Amount = $5,008,000 fair value - $5,010,000 carrying amount

Ledger account balance:

Investment in ABC Stock (trading)					
Date	Item	Debit	Credit	Debit	Credit
7/1/18		5,000,000		5,000,000	
12/31/18		10,000		5,010,000	
3/31/19			2,000	5,008,000	

Ledger account balance:

Investment in ABC Stock (available-for-sale)					
Date	Item	Debit	Credit	Debit	Credit
7/1/18		5,000,000		5,000,000	
12/31/18		10,000		5,010,000	
10/31/19			2,000	5,008,000	

Ledger account balance:

Unrealized Holding Gain/Loss — Net Income					
Date	Item	Debit	Credit	Debit	Credit
3/31/19		2,000		2,000	
12/31/18		10,000		10,000	
12/31/18			10,000	0	
3/31/19		2,000		2,000	

Ledger account balance:

Unrealized Holding Gain/Loss — Available-For-Sale					
Date	Item	Debit	Credit	Debit	Credit
12/31/18		10,000		10,000	
12/1/19		2,000		8,000	
10/31/19			8,000	0	

Ledger account balance:

Gain on Sale of Investment					
Date	Item	Debit	Credit	Debit	Credit
10/31/19		8,000		8,000	

The third step is to receive the cash from the sale of the investment at fair value.

Trading Securities

3/31/19 Your Corporation sells the bond trading securities when the fair value is $5,008,000.

Account		Debit	Credit
Cash		5,008,000	
Investment in ABC Bonds			5,008,000

- *Cash* is an **asset** account that is **increasing.**
- *Investment in ABC Bonds* is an **asset** account that is **decreasing.**

Available-for-Sale Securities

10/31/19 Your Corporation sells the bond available-for-sale securities when the fair value is $5,008,000.

Account		Debit	Credit
Cash		5,008,000	
Investment in ABC Bonds			5,008,000

- **Cash** is an *asset* account that is **increasing.**
- **Investment in ABC Bonds** is an **asset** account that is **decreasing.**

Ledger account balance:

Investment in ABC Stock (trading)					
Date	Item	Debit	Credit	Debit	Credit
7/1/18		5,000,000		5,000,000	
12/31/18		10,000		5,010,000	
3/31/19			2,000	5,008,000	
3/31/19		5,008,000		0	

Ledger account balance:

Investment in ABC Stock (available-for-sale)					
Date	Item	Debit	Credit	Debit	Credit
7/1/18		5,000,000		5,000,000	
12/31/18		10,000		5,010,000	
10/31/19			2,000	5,008,000	
10/31/19			5,008,000	0	

Ledger account balance (on income statement):

Unrealized Holding Gain/Loss — Net Income					
Date	Item	Debit	Credit	Debit	Credit
3/31/19		2,000		2,000	
12/31/18		10,000		10,000	
12/31/18			10,000	0	
3/31/19		2,000		2,000	

Ledger account balance (on balance sheet):

Unrealized Holding Gain/Loss — Available-For-Sale					
Date	Item	Debit	Credit	Debit	Credit
12/31/18		10,000		10,000	
12/1/19		2,000		8,000	
10/31/19			8,000	0	

Ledger account balance (on income statement):

Unrealized Holding Gain/Loss — Available-For-Sale					
Date	Item	Debit	Credit	Debit	Credit
10/31/19		8,000		8,000	

The *Unrealized Holding Gain/Loss - Net Income* account appears on the income statement as part of other comprehensive income. It represents that amount of gain or loss on investments that have not yet been sold, but whose fair value is different than their initial cost. A fair value greater than cost represents an unrealized gain; a fair value less than cost represents an unrealized loss. The *Unrealized Holding Gain/Loss - Net Income* account is adjusted before financial statements are prepared to update the unrealized gain or loss amount based on the most current fair value.

The *Gain on Sale of Investment and Loss on Sale of Investment* accounts that represent actual gains and losses from the sale of investments is not used for trading securities. This is because the *Unrealized Holding Gain/Loss - Net Income* account is updated just prior to the sale, which at the same time brings the investment account to fair value. Since the cash received equals the fair value amount, there is no gain or loss recognized at that time. SALES TAX

05 Liabilities in More Detail

5.1 SALES TAX

Merchandising businesses that sell product to end-users (customers that intend to use it themselves rather than sell it to another party) often are required to collect state sales tax. Sales tax collected accumulates in a liability account called Sales Tax Payable. Periodically (every two weeks, month, or quarter, depending on size and location of the business) the balance in the Sales Tax Payable account is sent to the state sales tax agency.

19a. Sale on account without sales tax

Date	Account		Debit	Credit
19a	Accounts Receivable		1,000	
	Sales			1,000

20a. Sale on account with 8% sales tax

Date	Account		Debit	Credit
20a	Accounts Receivable		1,080	
	Sales			1,000
	Sales Tax Payable			80

19b. Sale for cash without sales tax

Date	Account		Debit	Credit
19b	Cash		1,000	
	Sales			1,000

20b. Sale for cash with 8% sales tax

Date	Account		Debit	Credit
20b	Cash		1,080	
	Sales			1,000
	Sales Tax Payable			80

Notice that the **sales** tax does not become part of the Sales account.

The following journal entry would be made when the monthly sales tax is due if the **Sales Tax Payable** balance was $5,500

21. Paid sales tax of $5,500.

Date	Account		Debit	Credit
21	Sales Tax Payable		5,500	
	Cash			5,500

- *Sales Tax Payable* is a **liability** account that is **decreasing.**
- *Cash* is an **asset** account that is **decreasing.**

Sales tax is NOT a business expense since it is a payment of customers' money to the sales tax agency rather than the business's money.

5.2 PAYROLL

Employee salaries and wages are usually one of the highest expenses that an employer has. These notes will provide a simplified discussion of payroll and payroll taxes. There can be many variations, exceptions, and complexities. However, knowing the basic elements is a very good start to understanding payroll.

A **salary** is typically an amount an employee earns annually, such as $52,000 per year.

A **wage** is typically an amount an employee earns hourly, such as $10 per hour. The hourly rate is then multiplied by the number of hours in the pay period to determine total earnings for that period.

A **pay period** is the span of time that is included in each paycheck that an employee receives. Typical pay periods are weekly, bi-weekly, semi-monthly, and monthly.

Gross pay is the amount that an employee earns in a pay period before any payroll taxes or other deductions are subtracted. EXAMPLES: (1) The gross pay of an employee who is paid weekly and who earns $52,000 per year is $1,000 per week. (2) The gross pay of an employee who is paid weekly and who earns $10 per hour for a 40-hour work week is $400 per week.

Employees are required by law to have certain taxes withheld (taken out) of their gross pay as they earn it. Therefore, rather than receiving the entire amount of their gross pay in each paycheck, they receive less. Employers are required by law to withhold these taxes from an employee's gross pay and then pay them to federal and state government agencies on the employee's behalf.

Employees in the state of Georgia typically must pay the following taxes, which are withheld from their gross pay:

How much?		What for?
Federal income tax	Use IRS tax tables	Needs of the population in the United States
Social Security tax	6.2% of gross pay	Monthly income when employee reaches retirement age
Medicare tax	1.45% of gross pay	Health insurance benefits when employee reaches retirement age
Georgia State income tax	Use GA Dept. of Revenue tax tables	Needs of the population in the State of Georgia

The federal and state governments provide tax tables so an employee's withholding tax amount can simply be looked up. Four pieces of information about the employee are needed to use the tables.

1. Gross pay amount
2. Pay period
3. Marital status (single or married)
4. Number of allowances (employee fills out a Form W4 on the hire date and provides this information

Department of the Treasury
Internal Revenue Service

Publication 15
Cat. No. 10000W

(Circular E), Employer's Tax Guide

For use in **2013**

You can download a copy of Publication 15, Circular E, Employer's Tax Guide (2013) that contains the federal income tax withholding tables, beginning on page 46.

State of Georgia
Department of Revenue

CURRENT INCOME TAX PAYMENT ACT OF 1960

EMPLOYER'S TAX GUIDE

Revised January 2011

You can download a copy of the State of Georgia Employer Tax Guide that contains the state income tax withholding tables, beginning on page 22

To use the tax tables, you need to locate the page with the employee's correct pay period and marital status on the top. Next, look down the first two columns on the page and locate the row in which the employee's gross pay amount would fall. Finally, look across the row and locate the amount that falls under the number of allowances that the employee has claimed.

Net pay is the amount of cash the employee receives in his/her paycheck. It is gross pay minus taxes withheld.

Gross pay - Federal income tax - Social Security tax - Medicare tax - State tax = Net pay

EXAMPLE

Excess Company has two employees, Marta Stoward and Ronald Tramp. Here are facts about their compensation:

	Compensation	Pay Period	Number of Allowances	Marital Status
Marta	Salary: $48,000 per year	Monthly	0	Single
Ronald	Wage: $15 per hour 40-hour work week	Weekly	2	Married
(his wife works too)				

Here are the calculations to determine how much each is paid per paycheck:

Marta Stoward (monthly)			Ronald Tramp (weekly)	
Gross pay	$4,000.00		Gross pay	$600.00
Federal tax	620.00	(page 59)	Federal tax	30.00
S.S. tax	248.00		S.S. tax	37.20
Medicare tax	58.00		Medicare tax	8.70
State tax	215.19	(page 25)	State tax	26.14
Net pay	2,858.81		Net pay	497.96

Let's assume for a moment Marta is the only employee.

Marta Stoward (monthly)		
Gross pay	$4,000.00	
Federal tax	620.00	(page 59)
S.S. tax	248.00	(6.2% x 4,000)
Medicare tax	58.00	(1.45% x 4,000)
State tax	215.19	(page 25)
Net pay	2,858.81	

Using Marta as an example, here is one of the journal entries that Excess Company would make when Marta is paid. The payment of the federal and state taxes is not due until the 15th of the following month.

Date	Account		Debit	Credit
10/31	Salary Expense		4,000.00	
	Federal Income Tax Payable			620.00
	Social Security Tax Payable			248.00
	Medicare Tax Payable			58.00
	State Income Tax Payable			215.19
	Cash			2,858.81

- *Salary Expense* is an **expense** account that is **increasing.**
- *Fed. Income Tax Payable* is a **liability** account that is **increasing.**
- *Soc. Sec. Tax Payable* is a **liability** account that is **increasing.**
- *Medicare Tax Payable* is a **liability** account that is **increasing.**
- *State Income Tax Payable* is a **liability** account that is **increasing.**
- *Cash* is an asset **account** that is **decreasing.**

Below is an excerpt from the federal income tax tables:

SINGLE Persons—MONTHLY Payroll Period
(For Wages Paid through December 2013)

And the wages are—		And the number of withholding allowances claimed is—										
At least	But less than	0	1	2	3	4	5	6	7	8	9	10
		The amount of income tax to be withheld is—										
3,960	4,000	610	529	447	386	337	289	240	191	142	94	55
4,000	4,040	620	539	457	392	343	295	246	197	148	100	59
4,040	4,080	630	549	467	398	349	301	252	203	154	106	63
4,080	4,120	640	559	477	404	355	307	258	209	160	112	67
4,120	4,160	650	569	487	410	361	313	264	215	166	118	71
4,160	4,200	660	579	497	416	367	319	270	221	172	124	75

Below is an excerpt from the state of Georgia income tax tables:

Table A: Single - Monthly

Wages		Allowances										
Greater Than	But Less Than	0	1	2	3	4	5	6	7	8	9	10
3,977.00	4,042.00	215.19	201.69	188.19	174.69	161.19	147.69	134.19	120.69	107.19	93.69	80.19
4,042.00	4,106.00	219.03	205.53	192.03	178.53	165.03	151.53	138.03	124.53	111.03	97.53	84.03
4,106.00	4,170.00	222.87	209.37	195.87	182.37	168.87	155.37	141.87	128.37	114.87	101.37	87.87
4,170.00	4,234.00	226.71	213.21	199.71	186.21	172.71	159.21	145.71	132.21	118.71	105.21	91.71
4,234.00	4,298.00	230.55	217.05	203.55	190.05	176.55	163.05	149.55	136.05	122.55	109.05	95.55

By law, the employer must match and contribute what an employee pays in Social Security and Medicare taxes. Since Marta paid $248.00 and $58.00 of her salary, the company must also pay $248.00 and $58.00 toward her retirement benefits. Also, an employer is required to pay federal and state unemployment insurance taxes for the employee, and these amounts are based on a percentage of gross pay. We will use .8% for federal unemployment insurance and 5.4% for state unemployment insurance.

Therefore, here is the second journal entry that Excess Company would make when Marta is paid to account for the expenses that the company itself must absorb.

Date	Account		Debit	Credit
10/31	Payroll Tax Expense		554.00	
	Social Security Tax Payable			248.00
	Medicare Tax Payable			58.00
	Federal Unemployment Insurance Tax Payable			32.00
	State Unemployment Insurance Tax Payable			216.00

- *Payroll Tax Expense* is an **expense** account that is **increasing.**
- *Soc. Sec. Tax Payable* is a **liability** account that is **increasing.**
- *Medicare Tax Payable* is a **liability** account that is **increasing.**
- *FUTA Payable* is a **liability** account that is **increasing.**
- *SUTA* Payable is a **liability** account that is **increasing.**

Notice that every month that Marta is paid $4,000, she actually costs the company $4,554.00 due to the payroll taxes it must pay!

Finally, you must actually pay all of these payables. Let's say you do so 15 days later. The federal income tax, Social Security Tax, Medicare tax, and federal unemployment tax would be sent to the Internal Revenue Service. The state income tax and the state unemployment tax would be sent to the Georgia Department of Revenue. Here is the journal entry to reflect all these payments.

Date	Account		Debit	Credit
11/15	Federal Income Tax Payable		620.00	
	Social Security Tax Payable		496.00	
	Medicare Tax Payable		116.00	
	Federal Unemployment Insurance Tax Payable		32.00	
	State Income Tax Payable		215.19	
	State Unemployment Insurance Tax Payable		216.00	
	Cash			1,695.19

- *Fed. Income Tax Payable* is a **liability** account that is **decreasing.**
- *Soc. Sec. Tax Payable* is a **liability** account that is **decreasing.**
- *Medicare Tax Payable* is a **liability** account that is **decreasing.**
- *FUTA Payable* is a **liability** account that is **decreasing.**
- *State Income Tax Payable* is a **liability** account that is **decreasing.**
- *SUTA Payable* is a **liability** account that is **decreasing.**
- *Cash* is an *asset* account that is **decreasing.**

Notice that the Social Security tax and Medicare tax amounts include both what Marta paid in and what the company contributed. The total cash that the company paid out for Marta is the $2,858.81 paid to her and the $1,695.19 paid to the government revenue agencies, for a total of $4,554.00.

5.3 NOTES PAYABLE

A business may borrow money from a bank, vendor, or individual to finance operations on a temporary or long-term basis or to purchase assets. Note **Payable** is used to keep track of amounts that are owed as short-term or long- term business loans.

A note payable is a loan contract that specifies the principal (amount of the loan), the interest rate stated as an annual percentage, and the terms stated in number of days, months, or years. A note payable may be either short term (less than one year) or long term (more than one year).

5.3.1 Short-Term Note Payable

Loans may be short term, due to be repaid by the business within one year. These are current liabilities. There are two types of short-term notes payable: interest bearing and discounted. The difference lies basically in when the borrower pays the interest to the lender. For an interest-bearing note, the interest is paid at the end of the term of the loan. For a discounted note, the interest is paid up front when the note is issued.

SHORT-TERM NOTE PAYABLE – INTEREST BEARING

In the following example, a company issues a 60-day, 12% **interest-bearing** note for $1,000 to a bank on January 1. The company is borrowing $1,000.

Date	Account		Debit	Credit
1/1	Cash		1,000	
	Note Payable			1,000

- *Cash* is an **asset** account that is **increasing.**
- *Note Payable* is a **liability** account that is **increasing.**

Cash is debited to recognize the receipt of the loan proceeds. Note Payable is credited for the principal amount that must be repaid at the end of the term of the loan.

An interest-bearing note payable may also be issued on account rather than for cash. In this case, a company already owed for a product or service it previously was invoiced for on account. Rather than paying the account off on the due date, the company requests an extension and converts the accounts payable to a note payable.

Date	Account		Debit	Credit
1/1	Accounts Payable		1,000	
	Note Payable			1,000

- *Accounts Payable* is a **liability** account that is **decreasing.**
- *Note Payable* is a **liability** account that is **increasing.**

At the end of the term of the loan, on the maturity date, the note is void. At that time the **Note Payable** account must be debited for the principle amount. In addition, the amount of interest charged must be recorded in the journal entry as **Interest Expense.** The interest amount is calculated using the following equation:

Principal x Rate x Time = Interest Earned

To simplify the math, we will assume every month has 30 days and each year has 360 days.

For a 12% interest rate on a 60-day note, the interest on a 1,000 note would be $20, calculated as follows:

1,000 x 12% x 60/360 = $20

Note that since the 12% is an annual rate (for 12 months), it must be prorated for the number of months or days (60/360 days or 2/12 months) in the term of the loan.

On the maturity date, both the Note Payable and Interest Expense accounts are debited. Note Payable is debited because it is no longer valid and its balance must be set back to zero. Interest Expense is debited because it is now a cost of business. Cash is credited since it is decreasing as the loan is repaid.

Date	Account		Debit	Credit
2/28	Note Payable		1,000	
	Interest Expense		20	
	Cash			1,020

- *Note Payable* is a **liability** account that is **decreasing.**

- *Interest Expense* is an **expense** account that is **increasing.**
- *Cash* is an **asset** account that is **decreasing.**

SHORT-TERM NOTE PAYABLE – DISCOUNTED

In the following example, a company issues a 60-day, 12% **discounted note** for $1,000 to a bank on January 1. The company is borrowing $1,000.

Date	Account		Debit	Credit
1/1	Cash		980	
	Interest Expense		20	
	Note Payable			1,000

- *Cash* is an **asset** account that is **increasing.**
- *Interest Expense* is an **expense** account that is **increasing.**
- *Note Payable* is a **liability** account that is **increasing.**

Cash is debited to recognize the receipt of the loan proceeds. Note Payable is credited for the principal amount that must be repaid at the end of the term of the loan.

In addition, the amount of interest charged is recorded as part of the initial journal entry as Interest Expense. The amount of interest reduces the amount of cash that the borrower receives up front.

The interest amount is calculated using the following equation: Principal x Rate x Time = Interest Earned.

To simplify the math, we will assume every month has 30 days and each year has 360 days.

For a 12% interest rate on a 60-day note, the interest on a 1,000 note would be $20, calculated as follows:

1,000 x 12% x 60/360 = $20

Note that since the 12% is an annual rate (for 12 months), it must be prorated for the number of months or days (60/360 days or 2/12 months) in the term of the loan.

On the maturity date, only the **Note Payable** account is debited for the principal amount. **Note Payable** is debited because it is no longer valid and its balance must be set back to zero. **Cash** is credited since it is decreasing as the loan is repaid.

Date	Account		Debit	Credit
2/28	Note Payable		1,000	
	Cash			1,000

- *Note Payable* is a **liability** account that is **decreasing.**
- *Cash* is an **asset** account that is **decreasing.**

5.3.2 Long-Term Note Payable

Long-term notes payable are often paid back in periodic payments of equal amounts, called installments. Each installment includes repayment of part of the principal and an amount due for interest. The principal is repaid annually over the life of the loan rather than all on the maturity date. To determine the amount of the annual payment, divide the face amount of the note (the amount borrowed) by one of the factors in the present value of an annuity of $1 to be paid in the future shown in the table below. Select the amount in the table at the intersection of the interest rate and number of years of the loan. For example, a $10,000, 4%, 10-year loan would have an annual payment of $1,232 (rounded to the nearest dollar.) The calculation is 10,000 / 8.11090.

EXAMPLE

Assume a company borrows $50,000 for five years at an annual interest rate of 5%. The journal entry would be as follows:

Date	Account		Debit	Credit
1/1	Cash		50,000	
	Note Payable			50,000
	Cash			1,020

- *Cash* is an **asset** account that is **increasing.**
- *Note Payable* is a **liability** account that is **increasing.**

Installment payments of $11,549 will be made once a year on December 31. This amount is determined by dividing the $50,000 principal by the present value of an annuity of $1 factor of 4.32948 and rounding to the nearest dollar.

The breakout of the year 1 installment payment of $11,549 is as follows:

Interest on amount owed: $50,000 x 5% = $2,500

Reduction of principal: $11,549 - $2,500 = $9,049

The company owes $40,951 after this payment, which is $50,000 - $9,049.

Date	Account		Debit	Credit
12/31	Note Payable		9,049	
	Interest Expense		2,500	
	Cash			11,549

- *Note Payable* is a **liability** account that is **decreasing.**
- **Interest Expense** is an **expense** account that is **increasing.**
- Cash is an **asset** account that is **decreasing.**

Periods	3.00%	3.50%	4.00%	4.50%	5.00%	5.50%	6.00%	6.50%	7.00%	7.50%	8.00%	8.50%	9.00%	9.50%	10.00%
1	0.96087	0.96618	0.96154	0.95694	0.95238	0.94787	0.94340	0.93897	0.93458	0.93023	0.92593	0.92166	0.91743	0.91324	0.90909
2	1.91347	1.89969	1.88610	1.87267	1.85941	1.84632	1.83339	1.82063	1.80802	1.79557	1.78327	1.77111	1.75911	1.74725	1.73554
3	2.82861	2.80164	2.77509	2.74896	2.72325	2.69793	2.67301	2.64848	2.62432	2.60053	2.57710	2.55402	2.53130	2.50891	2.48685
4	3.71710	3.67308	3.62990	3.58753	3.54595	3.50515	3.46511	3.42580	3.38721	3.34933	3.31213	3.27560	3.23972	3.20448	3.16987
5	4.57971	4.51505	4.45182	4.38998	4.32948	4.27028	4.21236	4.15568	4.10020	4.04589	3.99271	3.94064	3.88965	3.83971	3.79079
6	5.41719	5.32855	5.24214	5.15787	5.07569	4.99553	4.91732	4.84101	4.76654	4.69385	4.62288	4.55359	4.48592	4.41983	4.35526
7	6.23028	6.11454	6.00206	5.89270	5.78637	5.68297	5.58238	5.48452	5.38929	5.29660	5.20637	5.11851	5.03295	4.94961	4.86842
8	7.01969	6.87396	6.73275	6.59589	6.46321	6.33457	6.20979	6.08875	5.97130	5.85730	5.74664	5.63918	5.53482	5.43344	5.33493
9	7.78611	7.60769	7.43533	7.26879	7.10782	6.95220	6.80169	6.65610	6.51523	6.37889	6.24689	6.11906	5.99525	5.87528	5.75902
10	8.53020	8.31661	8.11090	7.91272	7.72174	7.53763	7.36009	7.18883	7.02358	6.86408	6.71008	6.56135	6.41766	6.27880	6.14457
11	9.25262	9.00155	8.76048	8.52892	8.30641	8.09254	7.88688	7.68904	7.49867	7.31542	7.13896	6.96898	6.80519	6.64730	6.49506
12	9.95400	9.66333	9.38507	9.11858	8.86325	8.61852	8.38384	8.15873	7.94269	7.73528	7.53608	7.34469	7.16073	6.98384	6.81369

The breakout of the year 2 installment payment of $11,549 is as follows:

Interest on amount owed: $40,951 x 5% = $2,048

Reduction of principal: $11,549 - $2,048 = $9,501

The company owes $31,450 after this payment, which is $40,951 - $9,501.

Date	Account		Debit	Credit
12/31	Note Payable		9,501	
	Interest Expense		2,048	
	Cash			11,549

- *Note Payable* is a **liability** account that is **decreasing.**
- *Interest Expense* is an **expense** account that is **increasing.**
- *Cash* is an **asset** account that is **decreasing.**

The breakout of the year 3 installment payment of $11,549 is as follows:

Interest on amount owed: $31,450 x 5% = $1,573

Reduction of principal: $11,549 - $1,573 = $9,976

The company owes $21,474 after this payment, which is $31,450 - $9,976.

Date	Account		Debit	Credit
12/31	Note Payable		9,976	
	Interest Expense		1,573	
	Cash			11,549

- *Note Payable* is a **liability** account that is **decreasing.**
- *Interest Expense* is an **expense** account that is **increasing.**
- *Cash* is an **asset** account that is **decreasing.**

The breakout of the year 4 installment payment of $11,549 is as follows:

Interest on amount owed: $21,474 x 5% = $1,074

Reduction of principal: $11,549 - $1,074 = $10,475

The company owes $10,999 after this payment, which is $21,474 - $10,475.

Date	Account		Debit	Credit
12/31	Note Payable		10,475	
	Interest Expense		1,074	
	Cash			11,549

- *Note Payable* is a **liability** account that is **decreasing.**
- *Interest Expense* is an **expense** account that is **increasing.**
- *Cash* is an **asset** account that is **decreasing.**

The breakout of the year 5 installment payment of $11,549 is as follows:

Interest on amount owed: $10,999 x 5% = $550

Reduction of principal: $11,549 - $550 = $10,999

The company owes $0 after this payment, which is $10,999 - $10,999.

Date	Account		Debit	Credit
12/31	Note Payable		10,999	
	Interest Expense		550	
	Cash			11,549

- *Note Payable* is a **liability** account that is **decreasing.**
- *Interest Expense* is an **expense** account that is **increasing.**
- *Cash* is an **asset** account that is **decreasing.**

Installments that are due within the coming year are classified as a current liability on the balance sheet. Installments due after the coming year are classified as a long-term liability on the balance sheet.

Using the example above, **Notes Payable** would be listed on the balance sheet that is prepared at the end of year 3 as follows:

LIABILITIES			
Current liabilities:			
Accounts Payable	$18,769		
Salaries Payable	14,904		
Taxes Payable	12,582		
Note payable (current)	10,475	←	
Sales tax payable	7,163		
Total current liabilities		$97,893	
Long-term liabilities:			
Note Payable		10,999	←
Total liabilities			$108,892

The principal of $10,475 due at the end of year 4—within one year—is current.

The principal of $10,999 due at the end of year 5 is classified as long term.

5.4 BONDS

A corporation often needs to raise money from outside sources for operations, purchases, or expansion. One way to do this is to issue stock. Investors contribute cash to the business and are issued stock in return to recognize their shares of ownership.

Another alternative for raising cash is to borrow the money and to pay it back at a future date. Banks and other traditional lending sources are one option where the corporation may go to take out a loan for the full amount needed.

Another possibility is for the corporation to issue bonds, which are also a form of debt. **Bonds** are loans made by smaller lenders, such as other corporations and individual people. Corporate bonds are usually issued in $1,000 increments. A corporation may borrow from many different smaller investors and collectively raise the amount of cash it needs. Corporate bonds are traded on the bond market similar to the way corporate stock is traded on the stock market. They are long-term liabilities for most of their life and only become current liabilities as of one year before their maturity date.

The people or companies who purchase bonds from a corporation are called bondholders, and they are essentially lending their money as an investment. The reason bondholders lend their money is because they are paid interest by the corporation on the amount they lend throughout the term of the bond. Bondholders do not become owners of a corporation like stockholders do.

A **bond** is a loan contract, called a **debenture**, which spells out the terms and conditions of the loan agreement. At the very least, the debenture states the face amount of the bond, the interest rate, and the term. The face amount is the amount that the bondholder is lending to the corporation. The contract rate of interest is similar to a rental fee that the corporation commits to pay for use of the lenders' money. It is quoted as an annual percentage, such as 6% per year. Finally, the **term** is the number of years that the bond covers. **The maturity** date is the date that the corporation must pay back the full face amount to the bondholders. None of the face amount of the bond is repaid before the maturity date.

There is one other important number to look for: the **market rate of interest.** Think of it as the interest rate that the competition (other corporations) is offering to the same prospective investors. It may be the same, higher, or lower than an issuing corporation's contract interest rate.

EXAMPLE

A corporation's contract rate is 8%.

The market rate is 8%.	The contract rate is equal to the market rate.
The market rate is 6%.	The contract rate is more than the market rate.
The market rate is 10%.	The contract rate is less than the market rate.

These are new accounts related to issuing bonds:

Account	Type	Financial Statement	To Increase
Bonds Payable	Liability	Balance Sheet	credit
Discount on Bonds Payable	Contra liability	Balance Sheet	debit
Premium on Bonds Payable	Contra liability	Balance Sheet	credit
Interest Expense	Expense	Income Statement	debit

Account	Type	Financial Statement	To Increase
Gain on Redemption of Bonds	Revenue	Income Statement	credit
Loss on Redemption of Bonds	Expense	Income Statement	debit

ACCOUNT TYPE	ACCOUNTS	TO INCREASE	TO DECREASE	NORMAL BALANCE	FINANCIAL STATEMENT	CLOSE OUT?
Liability	Bonds Payable Premium on Bonds Payable	credit	debit	credit	Balance Sheet	NO
Contra Liability	Discount on Bonds Payable	credit	debit	credit	Balance Sheet	NO
Revenue	Gain on Redemption of Bonds	credit	debit	credit	Balance Sheet	YES
Expense	Interest Expense Loss on Redemption of Bonds	credit	debit	credit	Balance Sheet	YES

There are four journal entries related to issuing bonds, as follows:

1. Issuing the bond - accepting cash from bondholders and incurring the debt to pay them back
2. Paying semi-annual interest - recording the expense of paying bondholders the contract interest rate every six months
3. Amortizing the discount or premium - recording the expense or revenue associated with issuing a bond below or above face amount
4. Redeeming the bond - paying back the bondholders on or before the maturity date of the bond

Besides keeping a running balance of each of the new accounts, the key number to determine is the **carrying amount** of a bond at any point in time. This is the bond's book value, or what it is worth at the moment.

5.4.1 Bond Transactions When Contract Rate Equals Market Rate

A corporation may borrow money by issuing bonds. In return the corporation will pay the bondholders interest every six months and, at the end of the term, repay the bondholders the face amount. The number of payments bondholders will receive in the future from the corporation is always twice the number of years in the term plus 1.

EXAMPLE

$100,000 of five-year, 12% bonds when the market rate is 12%.

Number of payments

Over the five-year term of the bond, the bondholders will receive 11 payments: 10 semi-annual interest payments and the one final repayment of the face amount of the bonds.

Semi-annual interest payment amount

To calculate the semi-annual interest, first multiply the face amount of $100,000 by the **contract** rate of 12% to get the annual amount of interest. Then divide the result by 2 since interest is paid semiannually. The result is (100,000 x 12%)/2 = $6,000 every six months.

Here is a comparison of the 10 interest payments if a company's contract rate **equals** the market rate.

Corporation (pays 12% interest)	Market (pays 12% interest)
$6,000 every six months x 10 semi-annual payments **$60,000** over the five-year period	$6,000 every six months x 10 semi-annual payments **$60,000** over the five-year period

Since the total interest payments are equal, the corporation's bond is competitive with other bonds on the market and the bond can be issued at face amount.

Issuing bonds - A journal entry is recorded when a corporation issues bonds.

1/1/11: Issued $100,000 of five-year, 12% bonds when the market rate was 12%.

Account		Debit	Credit
Cash		100,000	
Bands Payable			100,000

Issuing bonds is selling them to bondholders in return for cash. The issue price is the amount of cash collected from bondholders when the bond is sold. Cash is debited for the amount received from bondholders; the liability (debt) from bonds increases for the face amount.

- *Cash* is an **asset** account that is **increasing.**
- *Bonds Payable* is a **liability** account that is **increasing.**

Paying semi-annual interest

A corporation typically pays interest to bondholders semi-annually, which is twice per year. In this example the corporation will pay interest on June 30 and December 31.

6/30/11: Paid the semi-annual interest to the bondholders.

Account		Debit	Credit
Interest Expense		6,000	
Cash			6,000

(100,000 x 12%) / 2

This same journal entry for $6,000 is made every six months, on 6/30 and 12/31, for a total of 10 times over the term of the five-year bond.

- *Interest Expense* is an **expense** account that is **increasing.**
- *Cash* is an **asset** account that is **decreasing.**

Redeeming bonds - A journal entry is recorded when a corporation redeems bonds.

1/1/16: Redeemed $100,000 of five-year bonds on the maturity date.

Account		Debit	Credit
Bonds Payable		100,000	
Cash			100,000

Redeeming means paying the bond debt back on the maturity date. The bonds liability decreases by the face amount. Cash decreases and is credited for what is paid to redeem the bonds. In this case, it is the $100,000 face amount. This is the 11th payment by the corporation to the bondholders.

- *Bonds Payable* is a **liability** account that is **decreasing.**
- *Cash* is an **asset** account that is **decreasing.**

A bond's contract rate of interest may be equal to, less than, or more than the going market rate.

Compare the contract rate with the market rate since this will impact the selling price of the bond when it is issued.

Example: Three interest rate scenarios **A three-year, $100,000 bond's contract rate is 8%.**	
The market rate is 8%.	Contract rate equals market rate Bond sells at face amount
The market rate is 10%.	Contract rate is less than market rate Bond sells at a discount, which is less than face amount
The market rate is 6%.	Contract rate is greater than market rate Bond sells at a premium, which is more than face amount

5.4.2 Bond Transactions When Contract Rate is Less Than Market Rate

There are times when the contract rate that your corporation will pay is less than the market rate that other corporations will pay. As a result, your corporation's semi-annual interest payments will be lower than what investors could receive elsewhere. To be competitive and still attract investors, the bond must be issued at a discount. This means the corporation receives less cash than the face amount of the bond when it issues the bond. This difference is the discount. The corporation still pays the full face amount back to the bondholders on the maturity date.

EXAMPLE

$100,000 of five-year, 11% bonds when the market rate was 12%.

Here is a comparison of the 10 interest payments if a company's contract rate is **less than** the market rate.

Corporation (pays 11% interest)	Market (pays 12% interest)
$5,500 every six months x 10 semi-annual payments **$55,000** over the five-year period	$6,000 every six months x 10 semi-annual payments **$60,000** over the five-year period

In this case, the corporation is offering an 11% interest rate, or a payment of $5,500 every six months, when other companies are offering a 12% interest rate, or a payment of $6,000 every six months. As a result, the corporation will pay out $55,000 in interest over the five-year term. Comparable bonds on the market will pay out $60,000 over this same time frame. This is a difference of $5,000 over ten years.

To compensate for the fact that the corporation will pay out $5,000 less in interest, it will charge investors $5,000 less to purchase the bonds and collect

$95,000 instead of $100,000. This is essentially paying them the $5,000 difference in interest up front since it will still pay bondholders the full $100,000 face amount at the end of the five-year term.

INCENTIVES TO BUY A CAR: ZERO-PERCENT INTEREST VS. A REBATE

You may have heard of ways car manufacturers encourage people to buy vehicles. One is zero-percent financing, which is essentially an interest-free loan. This saves borrowers money because they do not have to pay interest on their loans, which can amount to quite a savings. Another incentive car manufacturers may offer is a rebate, which is an up-front reduction off the purchase price, similar to a coupon for a food purchase.

If a manufacturer offers both zero-percent interest and a rebate, the car buyer can choose one or the other—but not both. Guess what—both deals are probably about equal in terms of savings. So why would both be offered? Because some people will be attracted to buy because of lower payments over time and others will be interested due to the lower up- front purchase price. The deals are designed to appeal to different types of people with different buying preferences.

It is similar with bonds. Some investors prefer to pay full price and have higher interest payments every six months. Others are attracted by paying less up front and being paid back the full face amount at maturity and are willing to live with the lower semi-annual interest payments. Both deals are equal in value but are structured to appeal to different markets.

There are four journal entries that relate to bonds that are issued at a discount.

1. Issuing bonds

A journal entry is recorded when a corporation issues bonds.

1/1/11: Issued $100,000 of five-year, 11% bonds when the market rate was 12% for $95,000.

Account		Debit	Credit
Cash		95,000	
Discount on Bonds Payable		5,000	
Bonds Payable			100,000

(100,000 – 5,000)

The company receives cash from bondholders and its liability (debt) from bonds increases for the face amount. The difference between the face amount and the lesser amount of cash received is a discount.

- Cash is an **asset** account that is **increasing.**
- *Discount on Bonds Payable* is a **contra liability** account that is **increasing.**
- *Bonds Payable* is a **liability** account that is **increasing.**

The corporation will be paying out $5,000 less in interest over the next five years, so to compensate it reduces the purchase price of the bonds by $5,000. Now the value of the corporation's bond is comparable in value to other bonds on the market.

IMPORTANT: There is one final step to properly issuing bonds at a discount. The Cash and Discount on Bonds Payable amounts must be adjusted to their present value. In this example, the amount of cash received is $96,321, and the discount amount is $3,679.

This is the correct journal entry for issuing the bonds at a discount in this example.

1/1/11: Issued $100,000 of five-year, 11% bonds when the market rate was 12% for $96,321.

Account		Debit	Credit
Cash		96,321	
Discount on Bonds Payable		3,679	
Bonds Payable			100,000

(100,000 – 3,679)

- **Cash** is an **asset** account that is **increasing.**
- *Discount on Bonds Payable* is a **contra liability** account that is **increasing.**
- *Bonds Payable* is a **liability** account that is **increasing.**

Although it may not seem so, the $96,321 is the $95,000 from above and the $3,679 is the $5,000 from above. These differences are a result of a financial concept called the time value of money, which states that $1 today is worth more than $1 in the future.

2. Paying semi-annual interest

The corporation pays interest of 11% annually, which is the rate it promises to pay in the contract, in spite of the fact that the market rate is 12%.

6/30/11: Paid the semi-annual interest to the bondholders.

Account		Debit	Credit
Interest Expense		5,500	
Cash			5,500

(100,000 x 11%) / 2

This same journal entry for $5,500 is made every six months, on 6/30 and 12/31, for a total of 10 times over the term of the five-year bond.

- *Interest Expense* is an **expense** account that is **increasing.**
- *Cash* is an **asset** account that is **decreasing.**

3. Amortizing the discount

The corporation issued the bond January 1 at a $3,679 discount: it received $96,321 in cash on the issue date but will pay back $100,000 on the maturity date. That $3,679 difference is a cost of doing business for this company. Instead of claiming this entire discount amount as interest expense when the bond is issued, the company records it in the *Discount on Bonds Payable* account.

At the end of each year, the corporation will make an adjusting entry that amortizes the discount, or expenses part of it off. The discount amount is divided by the number of years in the term of the bond, and that amount is removed from the *Discount on Bonds Payable* account and recorded as Interest Expense. Amortization is similar to depreciation in terms of expensing a transaction off over time; it applies to an intangible rather than a physical product.

In this case, the $3,679 discount is divided by 5, the number of years of the term of the bond, resulting in $736 per year (rounded to the nearest dollar.) This becomes a debit to interest expense each year. The original debit balance in the *Discount on Bonds Payable account* is reduced by a credit of $736 each year.

12/31/11: Amortized the discount for the year.

Account		Debit	Credit
Interest Expense		736	
Discount on Bonds Payable			736

3,679 / 5 (rounded)

This same journal entry for $736 made at the end of each year on 12/31, for a total of five times over the term of the five-year bond. After recording this adjusting entry at the end of each of five years, the balance in Discount on Bonds Payable will be zero.

- *Interest Expense* is an **expense** account that is **increasing.**
- *Discount on Bonds Payable* is a **contra liability** account that is **decreasing.**

4. Redeeming bonds

A journal entry is recorded when a corporation redeems bonds.

12/31/15: Redeemed the $100,000 five-year bonds on the maturity date.

Account		Debit	Credit
Bonds Payable		100,000	
Cash			100,000

Redeeming means paying the bond debt back on the maturity date. The bonds liability decreases by the face amount. Cash decreases and is credited for what is paid to redeem the bonds. In this case, it is the $100,000 face amount. This is the 11th payment by the corporation to the bondholders.

- *Bonds* Payable is a **liability** account that is **decreasing.**
- *Cash* is an **asset** account that is **decreasing.**

After five years the *Discount on Bonds Payable* account has a zero balance, so nothing needs to be done with this account at this time.

5.4.3 Carrying Amount of Bonds Issued at a Discount

The carrying amount can be thought of as "what the bond is worth" at a given point in time. Initially, the carrying amount is the amount of cash received when the bond is issued.

Calculate the carrying amount as follows:

Bonds Payable credit balance - *Discount on Bonds* Payable debit balance = Carrying amount Each year the discount is amortized, the carrying amount changes. The Discount on Bonds Payable debit balance decreases, so the carrying amount increases and gets closer and closer to the face amount over time. At the maturity date, the carrying amount equals the face amount.

In this example, the Bonds Payable credit balance is always $100,000. Notice on the ledger at the right below that each time the end-of-year adjusting entry is posted, the debit balance of the *Discount on Bonds Payable* decreases. As a result, the carrying amount increases and gets closer and closer to face amount over time.

***Last credit amount differs due to rounding**

Carrying amount = 100,000 – Discount on BP balance			
			Carrying amount
1/1/11	100,000 – 3,679	=	96,321
12/31/11	100,000 – 2,943	=	97,057
12/31/12	100,000 – 2,207	=	97,793
12/31/13	100,000 – 1,471	=	98,529
12/31/14	100,000 – 735	=	99,265
12/31/15	100,000 – 0	=	100,000

Discount on Bonds Payable					
Date	**Item**	**Debit**	**Credit**	**Debit**	**Credit**
1/1/11		3,679		3,679	
12/31/11			736	2,943	
12/31/12			736	2,207	
12/31/13			736	1,471	
12/31/14			736	735	
12/31/15			735	0	

Besides keeping a running balance of each of the new accounts, the key number to determine is the **carrying amount** of a bond at any point in time. This is the bond's book value, or what it is worth at the moment.

5.4.4 Bond Transactions When Contract Rate is More Than Market Rate

There are times when the contract rate that your corporation will pay is more than the market rate that other corporations will pay. As a result, your corporation's semi-annual interest payments will be higher than what investors could receive elsewhere. Since its future interest payments will be higher in comparison to other bonds on the market, the corporation can command a higher amount up front when the bond is issued, and the bond is sold at a **premium**. This means the corporation receives more cash than the face amount of the bond when it issues the bond. This difference is the premium. The corporation still pays the face amount back to the bondholders on the maturity date.

EXAMPLE

$100,000 of five-year, 12% bonds when the market rate was 11%.

Here is a comparison of the 10 interest payments if a company's contract rate **is more than** the market rate.

Corporation (pays 12% interest)	Market (pays 11% interest)
$6,000 every six months x 10 semi-annual payments **$60,000** over the five-year period	$5,500 every six months x 10 semi-annual payments **$55,000** over the five-year period

In this case, the corporation is offering a 12% interest rate, or a payment of $6,000 every six months, when other companies are offering an 11% interest rate, or a payment of $5,500 every six months. As a result, the corporation will pay out $60,000 in interest over the five-year term. Comparable bonds on the market will pay out $55,000 over this same time frame. This is a difference of $5,000 over five years.

To compensate for the fact that the corporation will pay out $5,000 more in interest, it will charge investors $5,000 more to purchase the bonds and will collect $105,000 instead of $100,000. This is essentially collecting the $5,000 difference in interest up front from investors and essentially using it to pay them the higher interest rate over time. The corporation will still pay bondholders the $100,000 face amount at the end of the five-year term.

There are four journal entries that relate to bonds that are issued at a premium.

1. Issuing bonds

A journal entry is recorded when a corporation issues bonds.

1/1/11: Issued $100,000 of five-year, 12% bonds when the market rate was 11% for $105,000.

Account		Debit	Credit
Cash		105,000	
Premium on Bonds Payable			5,000
Bonds Payable			100,000

(100,000 + 5,000)

The company receives cash from bondholders and its liability (debt) from bonds increases for the face amount. The difference between the amount of cash received and the lesser face amount is a premium. Cash is an asset account that is increasing.

- *Cash* is an **asset** account that is **increasing.**
- *Premium on Bonds Payable* is a **contra liability** account that is **increasing.**
- **Bonds** Payable is a **liability** account that is **increasing.**

The corporation will be paying out $5,000 more in interest over the next five years, so to compensate it increases the purchase price of the bonds by $5,000. Now the value of the corporation's bond is comparable in value to other bonds on the market.

IMPORTANT: There is one final step to properly issuing bonds at a premium. The Cash and Premium on Bonds Payable amounts must be adjusted to their present value. In this example, the amount of cash received is $103,769, and the premium amount is $3,679.

This is the correct journal entry for issuing the bonds at a premium in this example.

1/1/11: Issued $100,000 of five-year, 12% bonds when the market rate was 11% for $103,769.

Account		Debit	Credit
Cash		103,769	
Premium on Bonds Payable			3,769
Bonds Payable			100,000

(100,000 + 3,769)

- *Cash* is an **asset** account that is **increasing.**
- *Premium on Bonds Payable* is a contra liability account that is increasing.
- Bonds Payable is a liability account that is increasing.

Although it may not seem so, the $103,769 is the $105,000 from above and the $3,679 is the $5,000 from above. These differences are a result of a financial concept called the time value of money, which states that $1 today is worth more than $1 in the future.

2. Paying semi-annual interest

The corporation pays interest of 12% annually, which is the rate it promised to pay in the contract, in spite of the fact that the market rate is 11%.

6/30/11: Paid the semi-annual interest to the bondholders.

Account		Debit	Credit
Interest Expense		6,000	
Cash			6,000

(100,000 x 12%) / 2

This same journal entry for $6,000 is made every six months, on 6/30 and 12/31, for a total of 10 times over the term of the five-year bond.

- *Interest* Expense is an **expense** account that is **increasing.**
- *Cash* is an **asset** account that is **decreasing.**

3. Amortizing the premium

The corporation issued the bond January 1 at a $3,769 premium: it received $103,769 in cash on the issue date but will pay back $100,000 on the maturity date. That $3,769 difference is income for this company. Instead of claiming this entire premium amount as a reduction of interest expense when the bond is issued, the company records it in the *Premium on Bonds Payable* account.

At the end of each year, the corporation will make an adjusting entry that amortizes the premium, or expense part of it off. The premium amount is divided by the number of years in the term of the bond, and that amount is removed from the *Premium on Bonds Payable* account and recorded an *Interest Expense* (as a credit, similar to recognizing it as revenue.) Amortization is similar to depreciation in terms of expensing a transaction off over time; it applies to an intangible rather than a physical product.

In this case, the $3,769 premium is divided by 5, the number of years of the term of the bond, resulting in $754 per year (rounded to the nearest dollar.) This becomes a credit to interest expense each year. The original credit balance in the Premium on Bonds Payable account is reduced by a credit of $754 each year.

12/31/11: Amortized the premium for the year.

Account		Debit	Credit
Premium on Bonds Payable		754	
Interest Expense			754

3,769 / 5 (rounded)

This same journal entry for $754 made at the end of each year on 12/31, for a total of five times over the term of the five-year bond. After recording this adjusting entry at the end of each of five years, the balance in Premium on Bonds Payable will be zero.

- *Premium on Bonds Payable* is a **contra liability** account that is **decreasing**
- *Interest Expense* is an **expense** account that is **decreasing.**

4. Redeeming bonds

A journal entry is recorded when a corporation redeems bonds.

12/31/15: Redeemed the $100,000 five-year bonds on the maturity date.

Account		Debit	Credit
Bonds Payable		100,000	
Cash			100,000

Redeeming means paying the bond debt back on the maturity date. The bonds liability decreases by the face amount. Cash decreases and is credited for what is paid to redeem the bonds. In this case, it is the $100,000 face amount. This is the 11th payment by the corporation to the bondholders.

- *Bonds* Payable is a **liability** account that is **decreasing.**
- *Cash* is an **asset** account that is **decreasing.**

After five years the *Premium on Bonds Payable* account has a zero balance, so nothing needs to be done with this account at this time

5.4.5 Carrying Amount of Bonds Issued at a Premium

The **carrying amount** can be thought of as "what the bond is worth" at a given point in time. Initially, the carrying amount is the amount of cash received when the bond is issued.

Calculate the carrying amount as follows:

Bonds Payable credit balance + *Premium on Bonds Payable* credit balance = Carrying amount

Each year the premium is amortized, the carrying amount changes. The *Premium on Bonds Payable* credit balance decreases, so the carrying amount decreases and gets closer and closer to the face amount over time. At the maturity date, the carrying amount equals the face amount.

In this example, the *Bonds Payable* credit balance is always $100,000. Notice on the ledger at the right below that each time the end-of-year adjusting entry is posted, the credit balance of the *Premium on Bonds Payable* decreases. As a result, the carrying amount decreases and gets closer and closer to face amount over time.

***Last debit amount differs due to rounding**

Carrying amount = 100,000 + Premium on BP balance			
			Carrying amount
1/1/11	100,000 + 3,769	=	103,769
12/31/11	100,000 + 3,015	=	103,015
12/31/12	100,000 + 2,261	=	102,261
12/31/13	100,000 + 1,507	=	101,507
12/31/14	100,000 + 735	=	100,753
12/31/15	100,000 + 0	=	100,000

Discount on Bonds Payable					
Date	Item	Debit	Credit	Debit	Credit
1/1/11			3,769		3,769
12/31/11		754			3,015
12/31/12		754			2,261
12/31/13		754			1,507
12/31/14		754			753
12/31/15		753			0

Besides keeping a running balance of each of the new accounts, the key number to determine is the **carrying amount** of a bond at any point in time. This is the bond's book value, or what it is worth at the moment.

5.4.6 Calling Bonds

Calling bonds means that a company pays them back early, before the maturity date. Not all bonds are callable; this must be a stipulation in the bond contract. The conditions of the contract will also determine how much the bond will be called for: exactly face amount, less than face amount, or more than face amount.

1. The company may pay bondholders the face amount of $100,000.
2. The company may call the bonds for less than face amount and, for example, pay bondholders $99,000 for a $100,000 bond. This could also be worded as "called the bond at 99," which means 99% of the face amount.
3. The company may call the bonds for more than face amount and, for example, pay bondholders $102,000 for a $100,000 bond. This could also be worded as "called the bond at 102," which means 102% of the face amount.

Take the following steps in preparing the journal entry for calling a bond.

1. Determine the carrying amount of the bond - what it is currently worth
2. Determine how much the company will pay to redeem the bond early
3. Determine the amount of any gain or loss by comparing the carrying amount to the redemption amount
4. Debit *Bonds Payable* for the face amount to zero out its credit balance
5. Credit Discount on Bonds Payable for its debit balance to zero out the account OR Debit Premium on Bonds Payable for its credit balance to zero out the account
6. Credit Cash for the amount paid to bondholders
7. Debit *Loss on Redemption of Bonds* OR credit Gain on *Redemption of Bonds* if either applies

Bonds may be redeemed at breakeven, at a gain, or at a loss. As with the sale of fixed assets or investments, it is important to note that any gain or loss when bonds are repaid early is incurred on a transaction that is outside of what occurs in normal business operations.

If a corporation redeems a bond prior to its maturity date, the carrying amount at the time should be compared to the amount of cash the issuing company must pay to call the bond. If the corporation pays **more** cash than what the bond is worth (the carrying amount), it experiences a **loss.** If it pays less cash than the bond's carrying amount, there is a **gain.**

It is important to note that a gain or loss is incurred on a transaction that is outside of what occurs in normal business operations and therefore is not categorized as an operating revenue or expense. A loss is similar to an expense, except it involves a transaction that is not directly related to the business' operations. A gain is similar to revenue. It too involves a non-operational transaction. Redeeming bonds is not a corporation's primary line of business, so these transactions are non-operational.

ANALOGY

Let's say you purchase an airline ticket from Atlanta to San Francisco for $400. While in flight, you learn that the person sitting next to you paid $250 for the same flight. You would probably feel badly and a little cheated for having paid too much. That is similar to paying more than carrying amount to redeem a bond, and that is a loss. On the flip side, you would feel pretty pleased if you were the one who paid $250 rather than the other passenger's $400 fare. That is similar to a gain on redemption of bonds, when you pay less than carrying amount to redeem a bond. The following four examples show bonds at both a discount and a premium that are called at both a gain and a loss.

EXAMPLE 1

Bond issued at a discount, called at a loss

Facts	Calculations
Bonds Payable balance: 100,000 credit	Carrying amount is **97,000** (100,000 - 3,000)
Discount on Bonds Payable balance: 3,000 debit	Redemption amount is **102,000** (100,000 x 102%)
Bonds are called at 102	Loss on Redemption of Bonds is **5,000** (97,000 - 102,000)

Calling bonds - A journal entry is recorded when a corporation redeems bonds early.

Account		Debit	Credit
Bonds Payable		100,000	
Loss on Redemption of Bonds		5,000	
Discount on Bonds Payable			3,000
Cash			102,000

Given (100,000 - 3,000) - 102,000

Given 100,000 x 102%

EXAMPLE 2

Bond issued at a discount, called at a gain

Facts	Calculations
Bonds Payable balance: 100,000 credit Discount on Bonds Payable balance: 3,000 debit Bonds are called at 96	Carrying amount is 97,000 (100,000 - 3,000) Redemption amount is 96,000 (100,000 x 96%) Gain on Redemption of Bonds is 1,000 (97,000 - 96,000)

Calling bonds - A journal entry is recorded when a corporation redeems bonds early.

Account		Debit	Credit
Bonds Payable		100,000	
Gain on Redemption of Bonds			1,000
Discount on Bonds Payable			3,000
Cash			96,000

Given (100,000 - 3,000) - 96,000

Given 100,000 x 96%

EXAMPLE 3

Bond issued at a premium, called at a loss

Facts	Calculations
Bonds Payable balance: 100,000 credit Premium on Bonds Payable balance: 3,000 credit Bonds are called at 104	Carrying amount is 103,000 (100,000 + 3,000) Redemption amount is 104,000 (100,000 x 104%) Loss on Redemption of Bonds is 1,000 (103,000 - 104,000)

Calling bonds - A journal entry is recorded when a corporation redeems bonds early.

Account		Debit	Credit
Bonds Payable		100,000	
Premium on Bonds Payable		3,000	
Loss on Redemption of Bonds		1,000	
Cash			104,000

Given (100,000 - 3,000) - 102,000

Given 100,000 x 102%

EXAMPLE 4

Bond issued at a premium, called at a gain

Facts	Calculations
Bonds Payable balance: 100,000 credit Premium on Bonds Payable balance: 3,000 credit Bonds are called at 98	Carrying amount is 103,000 (100,000 + 3,000) Redemption amount is 98,000 (100,000 x 98%) Gain on Redemption of Bonds is 5,000 (103,000 - 98,000)

Calling bonds - A journal entry is recorded when a corporation redeems bonds early.

Account		Debit	Credit
Bonds Payable		100,000	
Gain on Redemption of Bonds			1,000
Discount on Bonds Payable			3,000
Cash			96,000

Given Given (100,000 + 3,000) - 98,000

Given Given 100,000 x 98%

100,000 x 98%

5.4.7 Partial Years

In all the previous examples, bonds were issued on January 1 and redeemed on December 31 several years later. In all cases, the bonds were held for full calendar years.

Bonds may also be issued during a calendar year rather than on January 1. They may also be redeemed during a calendar year rather than on December 31. Since the adjusting entries to amortize the discount or premium occur on December 31 of each calendar year, it will be necessary to pro-rate the amortization amount to properly reflect the time during the year that the bond was held.

EXAMPLE 1

Issuing bonds mid-year

A five-year bond is issued on April 1, 2012 at a $60,000 premium. The premium is $12,000 per year, or $1,000 per month.

The adjusting entry to amortize the premium on December 31, 2012 is as follows:

Account		Debit	Credit
Premium on Bonds Payable		9,000	
Interest Expense			9,000

The bond was held for 9 months in 2012, so the amount amortized is $9,000 (1,000 x 9).

Account		Debit	Credit
Interest Expense		3,000	
Discount on Bonds Payable			3,000

The bond was held for 3 months in 2012, so the amount amortized is $3,000 (1,000 x 3).

Normally the adjusting entry is recorded on December 31 each year. However, if a bond is redeemed mid-year, an adjusting entry is recorded to bring the carrying up to date as of the date of redemption.

5.4.8 Partial Redemptions

It is possible for a corporation to redeem only some of the bonds that it holds.

EXAMPLE 2

Bonds Payable credit balance = $600,000. Discount on Bonds Payable debit balance = $30,000 One-third of the bonds are redeemed for $195,000

Account		Debit	Credit	
Bonds Payable		200,000		600,000 / 3
Loss on Redemption of Bonds		5,000		195,000 - (200,000 - 10,000)
Discount on Bonds Payable			10,000	30,000 / 3
Cash			195,000	Given

The balances of both current and long-term liabilities are presented in the liabilities section of the balance sheet at the end of each accounting period. When a company has a significant number of liabilities, they are typically presented in categories for clearer presentation. As mentioned previously, a financial statement that organizes its liability (and asset) accounts into categories is called a **classified balance sheet.**

The partial classified balance sheet that follows shows the liabilities section only. Note that there are two sections. **Current liabilities** itemizes relatively liabilities that will be converted paid within one year. **Long-term liabilities** lists liabilities with repayment dates that extend beyond one year. For bond issuances, any unamortized discount or premium amount associated with the debt is listed in conjunction with the bonds payable face amount, and the carrying amount of the bonds is also presented.

The total of each liability category appears in the far-right column of the classified balance sheet, and the sum of these totals appears as **total liabilities.**

Jonick Corporation
Balance Sheet
June 30, 2018

LIABILITIES			
Current liabilities:			
Accounts payable		$15,000	
Unearned fees		13,000	
Wages payable		12,000	
Taxes payable		10,000	
Interest payable		9,000	
Note payable		8,000	
Sales tax payable		7,000	
Total current liabilities			$74,000
Long-term liabilities:			
Mortgage note payable		$56,000	
Bonds payable	$40,000		
Less: Discount on bonds payable	(5,000)	35,000	
Total long-term liabilities			91,000
Total liabilities			$165,000

The following Accounts Summary Table summarizes the accounts relevant to issuing bonds.

ACCOUNT TYPE	ACCOUNTS	TO INCREASE	TO DECREASE	NORMAL BALANCE	FINANCIAL STATEMENT	CLOSE OUT?
Liability	Sales Tax Payable Federal Income Tax Payable State Income Tax Pay- able Social Security Tax Payable Medicare Tax Payable Federal Unemployment Tax Payable State Unemployment Tax Payable Note Payable Bonds Payable Premium on Bonds Payable	credit	debit	credit	Balance Sheet	NO

ACCOUNT TYPE	ACCOUNTS	TO INCREASE	TO DECREASE	NORMAL BALANCE	FINANCIAL STATEMENT	CLOSE OUT?
Contra Liability	Discount on Bonds Payable	debit	credit	credit	Balance Sheet	NO
Revenue or Gain	Gain on Redemption of Bonds	credit	debit	debit	Income Statement	YES
Expense or Loss	Interest Expense Payroll Tax Expense Loss on Redemption of Bonds	credit	debit	debit	Income Statement	YES

The accounts that are highlighted in bright yellow are the new accounts you just learned. Those highlighted in light yellow are the ones you learned previously.

#1

Jonick Corporation
Income Statement
For the Month Ended June 30, 2014

Operating REVENUES:			
Fees Earned		$200,000	
Sales	$150,000		
Less: Sales returns	10,000		
Less: Sales discounts	5,000		
Net sales	135,000		
Cost of merchandise sold	55,000		
Gross profit		80,000	
Gross operating revenues			$280,000
Operating EXPENSES:			
Salaries expense		$25,000	
Wages expense		22,000	
Rent expense		20,000	
Insurance expense		19,000	
Supplies expense		18,000	
Advertising expense		17,000	
Maintenance expense		16,000	
Depreciation expense		15,000	
Taxes expense		14,000	
Utilities expense		13,000	
Payroll tax expense		12,000	
Bad debt expense		11,000	
Bank card expense		10,000	
Vehicle expense		9,000	
Delivery expense		8,000	
Amortization expense		7,000	
Miscellaneous expense		6,000	
Total operating expenses			242,000
Net income from operations			$38,000
Other revenue and expenses:			
Interest revenue		$5,000	
Interest expense		(4,000)	
Gain on sale of equipment		3,000	
Loss on redemption of bonds		(2,000)	2,000
Net income			$40,000

#3

Jonick Corporation
Balance Sheet
June 30, 2014

ASSETS			
Current assets:			
Cash		$40,000	
Accounts receivable	$28,000		
Less: Allowance for doubtful accounts	3,000	25,000	
Merchandise inventory		60,000	
Supplies		18,000	
Prepaid rent		12,000	
Prepaid insurance		6,000	
Prepaid taxes		4,000	
Note receivable		2,000	
Total current assets			$167,000
Fixed assets:			
Equipment	$16,000		
Less: Accumulated depreciation	2,000	14,000	
Van	30,000		
Less: Accumulated depreciation	5,000	25,000	
Building	200,000		
Less: Accumulated depreciation	70,000	130,000	
Land		110,000	
Total fixed assets			279,000
Intangible assets:			
Patents			14,000
Total assets			$460,000

LIABILITIES			
Current liabilities:			
Accounts payable	$14,000		
Unearned fees	13,000		
Wages payable	12,000		
Salaries payable	11,000		
Taxes payable	10,000		
Interest payable	9,000		
Notes payable	8,000		
Sales tax payable	7,000		
Social security tax payable	6,000		
Medicare tax payable	5,000		
Federal withholding tax payable	4,000		
State withholding tax payable	3,000		
Federal unemployment tax payable	2,000		
State unemployment tax payable	1,000		
Total current liabilities		$105,000	
Long-term liabilities:			
Mortgage note payable	$56,000		
Bonds payable	40,000		
Less: Discount on bonds payable	(6,000)		
Total long-term liabilities		90,000	
Total liabilities			$195,000
STOCKHOLDERS' EQUITY			
Common stock		$60,000	
Paid-in-capital in excess of par - common stock		34,000	
Preferred stock		50,000	
Paid-in-capital in excess of par - preferred stock		18,000	
Paid-in-capital from sale of treasury stock		13,000	
Retained earnings		90,000	
Treasury stock		(20,000)	
Total stockholders' equity			265,000
Total liabilities and stockholders' equity			$460,000

#2

Jonick Corporation
Retained Earnings Statement
For the Month Ended June 30, 2014

Retained earnings, June 1, 2014			$60,000
Net income		$40,000	
Less: Cash dividends	$6,000		
Stock dividends	4,000	10,000	
Increase in retained earnings			30,000
Retained earnings, June 30, 2014			$90,000

06 Stockholders' Equity in More Detail

6.1 ACCOUNTING EQUATION

The **accounting equation** is the basis for all transactions in accounting. It must be in balance at all times. It involves the three types of accounts that appear on the balance sheet.

The accounting equation is **Assets = Liabilities + Stockholders' Equity**. The corporation has assets, and it must pay for these assets. It can do so in two ways. The corporation can use its own money or it can borrow and use other people's money, incurring liabilities, or debts.

Indirectly, revenue and expense accounts are part of this accounting equation since they impact the value of stockholders' equity through closing entries, which move revenue and expense account balances into Retained Earnings.

```
ACCOUNTING EQUATION: Assets = Liabilities + Stockholders' Equity
                                                /          \
                                       Common Stock    Retained Earnings
                                                            /        \
                                                       Revenue     Expenses
```

Retained earnings is a company's accumulated profit since it began operations minus any dividends distributed over that time.

Stockholders' equity (account category) is the amount of a business's total assets that is owned by the stockholders. Two accounts that you know so far fall in this category: stockholders' equity is the total of the balances in the *Common Stock* and *Retained Earnings* accounts.

Common Stock (account) is the ownership value in the business that comes from outside the company - investors put their own money into the business.

Retained Earnings (account) is the ownership value in the business that comes from inside the company - the business makes a profit that is shared by its stockholders.

Dividends (account) are distributions of profits from *Retained Earnings* to stockholders.

Any change in the *Common Stock*, Retained Earnings, or Dividends accounts affects total stockholders' equity.

Stockholders' Equity can increase in two ways:

1. Stock is issued and Common Stock increases *and*/or
2. Business makes a profit and Retained Earnings increases

Stockholders' Equity can decrease in two ways:

1. Dividends are distributed and Retained Earnings decreases and/or
2. Business takes a loss and Retained Earnings decreases

6.2 CORPORATIONS AND STOCKHOLDERS' EQUITY

A **corporation** is a form of business organization that is a separate legal entity; it is distinct from the people who own it. The corporation can own property, enter into contracts, borrow money, conduct business, earn profit, pay taxes, and make investments similar to the way individuals can.

The **owners** of a corporation are called **stockholders.** These are people who have invested cash or contributed other assets to the business. In return, they receive **shares of stock**, which are transferable units of ownership in a corporation. Stock can also be thought of as a receipt to acknowledge ownership in the company. The value of the stock that a stockholder receives equals the value of the asset(s) that were contributed.

A corporation may be owned by one stockholder or by millions. Very small companies can incorporate by filing articles of incorporation with a state in the

U.S. and being granted corporate status. Corporations are **ongoing.** Stockholders can buy and sell their shares of stock without interrupting the operation of the company. Another characteristic of a corporation is **limited liability.** Stockholders can lose no more than the amount they invested in the corporation. If the corporation fails, the individuals who own it do not personally have to cover the corporation's liabilities.

Up to this point, the stockholders' equity section of the balance sheet has included two accounts: *Common* Stock and *Retained* Earnings. Common Stock is value that the owners have in the business because they have contributed their own personal assets. Retained earnings is value the owners have in the corporation because the business has been operating – doing what it was set up to do - and as a result it has generated a profit that the owners share. It is preferable, of course, for stockholder wealth to increase due to net income over time. That earnings potential is, in fact, what attracts stockholders to invest their own money into a business in the first place.

The following Accounts Summary Table summarizes the accounts relevant to issuing stock.

ACCOUNT TYPE	ACCOUNTS	TO INCREASE	TO DECREASE	NORMAL BALANCE	FINANCIAL STATEMENT	CLOSE OUT?
Asset	Organization Costs	debit	debit	debit	Balance Sheet	NO
Liability	Cash Dividends Payable	credit	debit	credit	Balance Sheet	NO
Stockholders' Equity	Common Stock (CS) Paid-in Capital in Excess of Par - CS Preferred Stock (PS) Paid-in Capital in Excess of Par - PS Paid-in Capital from Sale of Treasury Stock Stock Dividends Distributable	credit	debit	credi	Balance Sheet	YES
Contra Stockholders' Equity	Treasury Stock	debit	debit	debit	Balance Sheet	YES
Contra Stockholders' Equity	Cash Dividends Stock Dividends	debit	credit	debit	Retained Earning Statement	

NOTE: *Common Stock, Preferred Stock,* and Stock *Dividends Distributable* amounts can only be in multiples of par value. Use Paid-In Capital in Excess of Par for any differences between issue price and par value.

We will be using the accounts above in numerous journal entries. The point of these journal entries is to ultimately arrive at one number: total stockholders' equity. Owners of a business are very interested in knowing what they are worth, and that final result is the answer to that question.

The new material we will cover next involves the stockholders' equity section of the balance sheet. The generic *Common Stock* account will no longer be the only account used for owner investments: six new accounts will be added that describe a corporation's equity in more specific detail. In addition, a second type of dividends will be covered: Stock Dividends.

The income statement is not affected by these new accounts. The retained earnings and balance sheet are. The statements on the left show account names in blue that you learned previously. The statements on the right show account names in blue that will replace those on the left as we take a more detailed look at stockholders' equity.

Celebrity Inn
Retained Earnings Statement
For the Month Ended June 30, 2012

Retained earnings, June 1, 2012		$ 40,000
Net income for the month	$ 11,000	
Less Cash dividends	5,000	
Increase in retained earnings		6,000
Retained earnings, June 30, 2012		$ 46,000

Celebrity Inn
Retained Earnings Statement
For the Month Ended June 30, 2012

Retained earnings, June 1, 2012			$ 40,000
Net income for the month		$ 11,000	
Less	Cash dividends	2,000	
	Stock dividends	3,000	
Increase in retained earnings			6,000
Retained earnings, June 30, 2012			$ 46,000

Celebrity Inn
Balance Sheet
June 30, 2012

	ASSETS	
Cash	$ 38,000	
Accounts receivable	11,000	
Truck	32,000	
Total Assets		$ 81,000
	LIABILITIES	
Accounts payable	$ 3,000	
Note payable	2,000	
	STOCKHOLDERS' EQUITY	
Common Stock	$ 30,000	
Retained earnings	46,000	
Total liabilities and stockholders' equity		$ 81,000

Celebrity Inn
Balance Sheet
June 30, 2012

	ASSETS	
Cash	$ 38,000	
Accounts receivable	11,000	
Truck	32,000	
Total Assets		$ 81,000
	LIABILITIES	
Accounts payable	$ 3,000	
Note payable	2,000	
	STOCKHOLDERS' EQUITY	
Paid-in capital:		
Common stock, $5 par		
(20,000 shares authorized, 4,000 shares issued)		$ 20,000
Paid-in capital in excess of par - common stock		3,000
Preferred stock $1, $10 par		
(10,000 shares authorized, 500 shares issued)		5,000
Paid-in capital in excess of par - preferred stock		1,000
Paid-in capital from sale of treasury stock		4,000
Retained earnings		46,000
Deduct treasury stock		3,000
Total liabilities and stockholders' equity		$ 81,000

The first five stockholders' equity accounts shown on the balance sheet above track owner investments. The total value of these seven account balances is called **paid-in capital.** Total paid-in capital plus *Retained Earnings,* which is still used to keep a running balance of a company's accumulated profit on hand, equals total stockholders' equity.

Shares authorized is the number of shares a corporation is allowed to issue (sell). For a large corporation this is based on a decision by its Board of Directors, a group elected to represent and serve the interest of the stockholders. Authorization is just permission to sell shares of stock; no action has actually taken place yet. Therefore, there is no journal entry for a stock authorization.

Shares issued is the number of shares a corporation has sold to stockholders for the first time. The number of shares issued cannot exceed the number of shares authorized.

The terms above may be better understood with an analogy to a credit card. If you are approved for a credit card, the terms will include a credit limit, such as $5,000, which is the maximum that you are allowed to charge on the card. This is similar to "shares authorized," the maximum number of shares a company is allowed to issue. The credit limit on a card does not mean that you have to charge $5,000 on your first purchase, but instead that you may continue to charge purchases up until you have reached a $5,000 maximum. The same holds true for shares issued. Smaller numbers of shares may be sold over time up to the maximum of the number of shares authorized.

If you wish to charge more than your credit limit on a credit card, you may contact the company that issued the card and request an increase in your credit limit. They may or may not grant this request. The same is true for a corporation. If it wishes to issue more shares than the number authorized, it may approach the Board of Directors with this request.

6.3 ISSUING STOCK FOR CASH

A corporation may issue stock to raise money. "Issue" means to sell the shares of stock for the first time. If the company issues only one type of stock, it is common stock. The investors become owners of the company and are called stockholders. A journal entry must be recorded when a corporation issues stock.

1. Issued 15,000 shares of $10 par common stock for $10 per share.

Account		Debit	Credit
Cash		150,000	
Common Stock			150,000

Cash 150,000

Common Stock 150,000

Par value is an amount assigned to each share of stock when it is authorized. Notice in this case the par value equals the issue price per share.

- *Cash* is an **asset** account that is **increasing.**
- *Common* Stock is a **stockholders' equity** account that is **increasing.**

2. Issued 15,000 shares of $10 par common stock for $12 per share.

Account		Debit	Credit
Cash		180,000	
Common Stock			150,000
Paid-in Capital in Excess of Par - Common Stock			30,000

(15,000 x $12) - Cash received

(15,000 x $10) - Stock issued at par value

(15,000 x $ 2) - Premium on the common stock issued

Here the issue price is greater than the par value. The Common Stock account can only be credited in multiples of the par value per share. The other $2 per share is credited to the Paid-in Capital in Excess of Par - Common Stock account.

- *Cash* is an **asset** account that is **increasing.**
- *Common Stock* is a **stockholders'** equity account that is **increasing.**
- *Paid-in Capital in Excess of Par - Common* Stock is a **stockholders' equity** account that is **increasing.**

Besides common stock, a corporation may also issue preferred stock. This type of stock has a more predictable dividend payment, which will be covered later.

3. Issued 1,000 shares of $100 par preferred stock for $105 per share.

Account		Debit	Credit
Cash		105,000	
Common Stock			100,000
Paid-in Capital in Excess of Par - Common Stock			5,000

(1,000 x $105) - Cash received

(1,000 x $100) - Stock issued at par value

(1,000 x $5) - Premium on the preferred stock issued

The journal entry for issuing preferred stock is very similar to the one for common stock. This time *Preferred Stock* and *Paid-in Capital in Excess of Par - Preferred Stock* are credited instead of the accounts for common stock.

- *Cash* is an **asset** account that is **increasing.**
- *Preferred Stock is a stockholders'* equity **account** that is **increasing.**
- *Paid-in Capital in Excess* of *Par - Preferred* **Stock is a stockholders' equity**

account that is **increasing.**

Information about preferred stock might also be presented in one of the following two ways:

Example 1: A corporation issues 1,000 shares of $1 preferred, $100 par stock for $105 per share.

Example 2: A corporation issues 1,000 shares of 1% preferred, $100 par stock for $105 per share.

The extra dollar or percentage information given relates to the cash dividend amount per share on the preferred stock. It may be stated directly as a dollar amount, such as $1. It may also be stated as a percentage, such as 1% of the par value of $100, which also results in $1 per share. This $1 or 1% is not a factor in the journal entry for issuing the preferred stock.

6.4 ISSUING STOCK FOR NON-CASH ASSETS

Stock may be issued for assets other than cash, such as services rendered, land, equipment, vehicles, accounts receivable, and inventory. This is more common in small corporations than in larger ones. The journal entries are similar to those for issuing stock for cash. In this case, the value of either the stock or the asset must be known. The assumption is that both the asset and the stock have the same value.

1. Issued 10,000 shares of $20 par common stock for land. The fair market value of the stock is $20 per share.

Account		Debit	Credit
Land		200,000	
Common Stock			200,000

(10,000 x $20) - Value of the land

(10,000 x $20) - Stock issued at par value

When issuing stock for non-cash assets, it is assumed the value of the asset (land) and the value of the stock are equal. Notice that the par value equals the issue price per share. The value of the stock can be calculated and the value of the land is set equal to that same amount.

- *Land* is an **asset** account that is **increasing.**
- *Common* Stock is a **stockholders' equity** account that is **increasing.**

2. Issued 10,000 shares of $20 par common stock for land. The fair market value of the stock is $25 per share.

Account		Debit	Credit
Land		250,000	
Common Stock			200,000
Paid-in Capital in Excess of Par - Common Stock			50,000

(10,000 x $20) - Value of the land

(10,000 x $20) - Stock issued at par value

When issuing stock for non-cash assets, it is assumed the value of the asset (land) and the value of the stock are equal. Notice that the par value equals the issue price per share. The value of the stock can be calculated and the value of the land is set equal to that same amount.

- *Land* is an **asset** account that is **increasing.**
- *Common Stock* is a *stockholders' equity* account that is **increasing.**

3. Issued 10,000 shares of $20 par common stock for land. The fair market value of the land is $250,000.

Account		Debit	Credit
Land		250,000	
Common Stock			200,000
Paid-in Capital in Excess of Par - Common Stock			50,000

$250,000 - Value of the land

(10,000 x $20) - Stock issued at par value

$250,000 - 200,000 - Premium on the common stock issued

The value of the land is given; the value of the stock equals that of the land. Remember, the Common Stock account can only be credited for the par value per share. The Paid-in Capital in Excess of Par - Common Stock account is used for the difference between the value of the land and the stock's total par value.

- *Land* is an **asset** account that is **increasing.**
- *Common Stock* is a **stockholders' equity** account that is **increasing.**
- *Paid-in Capital in Excess of Par - Common Stock* is a **stockholders' equity** account that is **increasing.**

4. Issued 1,000 shares of $10 par common stock for services provided by an attorney. The fair market value of the stock is $10 per share.

Account	Debit	Credit
Organization Costs	10,000	
Common Stock		10,000

(1,000 x $10) - Value of the services provided

(1,000 x $10) - Stock issued at par value

Organization Costs are expenses incurred to start a business, such as legal fees. This is an asset account. Sometimes the service providers are given stock rather than cash for their services. When issuing stock for non-cash assets, it is assumed the value of the asset (organization costs) and the value of the stock that is issued are equal. Notice that the par value equals the issue price per share.

- *Organization Costs* is an **asset** account that is **increasing.**
- *Common Stock* is a stockholders' **equity** account that is **increasing.**

5. Issued 1,000 shares of $10 par common stock for services provided by an engineer. The fair market value of the stock is $12 per share.

Account	Debit	Credit
Organization Costs	12,000	
Common Stock		10,000
Paid-in Capital in Excess of Par - Common Stock		2,000

(1,000 x $12) - Value of the land

(1,000 x $10) - Stock issued at par value

(1,000 x $ 2) - Premium on the common stock issued

The market value per share of the stock, $12, is given. Therefore, the value of the organization costs can be calculated by multiplying the $12 times the number of shares issued. Remember, the *Common Stock* account can only be credited for the par value of $10 per share, so the *Paid-in Capital in Excess of Par - Common Stock* account is used for the $2 per share difference.

- *Organization* Costs is an **asset** account that is **increasing.**
- *Common Stock* is a stockholders' **equity** account that is **increasing.**
- *Paid-in Capital in Excess of Par - Common Stock* is a **stockholders' equity** account that is **increasing.**

TREASURY STOCK

Treasury stock is stock that is repurchased by the same corporation that issued it. The corporation is buying back its own stock from the stockholders. Since treasury stock shares are no longer owned by stockholders, but by the corporation itself, total stockholders' equity decreases.

Shares outstanding equals the number of shares issued (sold for the first time) minus the number of shares of treasury stock a corporation has reacquired. When treasury stock is purchased, the number of shares issued remains unchanged, but the number of shares outstanding decreases.

When treasury stock is purchased, the *Treasury Stock* account is debited for the number of shares purchased times the purchase price per share. Treasury Stock is a contra stockholders' equity account and increases by debiting. It is not an asset account.

Treasury stock may be resold to stockholders at the same, a higher, or a lower price than it was purchased for. When sold, the *Treasury Stock* account can only be credited in multiples of its original purchase price per share. Use the *Paid-in Capital from Sale of Treasury Stock* account for differences between purchase and selling prices. *Paid-in Capital from Sale of Treasury Stock* is credited for any amount above the original purchase price (similar to a gain) and is debited for any amount below the original purchase price (similar to a loss).

The sale of treasury stock increases the number of shares outstanding and increases total stockholders' equity. The par value of the stock is not a factor in the purchase or sale of treasury stock.

EXAMPLE

Assume there were 10,000 shares of common stock issued before any treasury stock transaction. That would mean there were also 10,000 shares outstanding.

1. **Purchased 1,000 shares of treasury stock at $45 per share.**

Account		Debit	Credit
Treasury Stock		45,000	
Cash			45,000

(1,000 x $45) - Purchase price time number of shares

(1,000 x $45) - Purchase price time number of shares

Buying treasury stock reduces the number of shares outstanding (the number of shares stockholders own). Prior to purchasing the 1,000 shares of treasury stock there were 10,000 shares of common stock outstanding. After purchasing the treasury stock, there are 9,000 shares outstanding.

- *Treasury Stock* is a **contra stockholders' equity** account that is **increasing.**
- *Cash* is an **asset** account that is **decreasing.**

NOTE: Another way this same transaction could be stated is as follows:

Purchased 1,000 shares of treasury stock for $45,000.

To determine the purchase price per share, divide $45,000 by 1,000 shares to get $45 per share. Treasury stock may be resold to stockholders for more than its purchase price per share.

2. Sold 200 shares of treasury stock at $60 per share OR sold 200 shares of treasury stock for $12,000.

Account		Debit	Credit
Cash		12,000	
Paid-in Capital from Sale of Treasury Stock			3,000
Treasury Stock			9,000

(200 x $60) - Total amount received

(200 x $15) - More than purchase price on the sale

(200 x $45) - Multiple of $45 purchase price

Notice that the treasury stock is sold for $60, MORE than it was purchased for per share ($45). The $15 per share difference is recorded as a credit to the *Paid-in Capital from Sale of Treasury Stock* account.

Selling treasury stock increases the number of shares outstanding (the number of shares stockholders own). Prior to selling these 200 shares of treasury stock there were 9,000 shares of common stock outstanding (see #1). After selling these shares of treasury stock, there are 9,200 shares outstanding.

- *Cash* is an **asset** account that is **increasing.**
- **Paid-in Capital from Sale of Treasury Stock** is a **stockholders' equity** account that is **increasing.**
- *Treasury Stock* is a **contra stockholders' equity** account that is **decreasing.**

Treasury stock may be resold to stockholders for less than its purchase price per share.

3. Sold 200 shares of treasury stock at $40 per share OR sold 200 shares of treasury stock for $8,000.

Account		Debit	Credit
Cash		8,000	
Paid-in Capital from Sale of Treasury Stock		1,000	
Treasury Stock			9,000

(200 x $40) - Total amount received

(200 x $ 5) - Less than purchase price on the sale

(200 x $45) - Multiple of $45 purchase price

Notice that the treasury stock is sold for $40, LESS than it was purchased for per share ($45). The $5 per share difference is recorded as a debit to the *Paid-in Capital from Sale of Treasury Stock* account.

Selling treasury stock increases the number of shares outstanding (the number of shares stockholders own). Prior to selling these additional 200 shares of treasury stock there were 9,200 shares of common stock outstanding (see #2). After selling these additional shares of treasury stock, there are 9,400 shares outstanding.

- *Cash* is an **asset** account that is **increasing.**
- **Paid-in Capital from Sale of Treasury Stock** is a **stockholders' equity** account that is **decreasing.**
- *Treasury Stock* is a **contra stockholders' equity** account that is **decreasing.**

6.5 CASH DIVIDENDS

Cash dividends are corporate earnings that are paid out to stockholders. They are pay payouts of retained earnings, which is accumulated profit. Therefore, cash dividends reduce both the **Retained Earnings** and Cash account balances.

Cash Dividends is a contra stockholders' equity account that temporarily substitutes for a debit to the *Retained Earnings* account. At the end of the accounting period, *Cash Dividends* is closed to *Retained Earnings.*

There are three prerequisites to paying a cash dividend: a decision by the Board of Directions, sufficient cash, and sufficient retained earnings.

Cash dividends are only paid on shares outstanding. No dividends are paid on treasury stock, or the corporation would essentially be paying itself.

Three dates are associated with a cash dividend. The **date of declaration** is the date the corporation commits to paying the stockholders. On that date, a liability is incurred and the *Cash Dividends Payable* is used to record the amount owed to the stockholders until the cash is actually paid. The *date of record* is the date on which ownership is determined. Since shares of stock may be traded, the corporation names a specific date, and whoever owns the shares on that date will receive the dividend. There is no journal entry on the date of record. Finally, the *date of payment* is the date the cash is actually paid out to stockholders.

1. Date of Declaration

Declared a cash dividend of $32,000. **OR**

Declared a cash dividend of $2 per share on 10,000 shares of preferred stock outstanding (total $20,000) and $.50 per share on 24,000 shares of common stock outstanding (total $12,000). NOTE: The $20,000 for preferred and $12,000 for common dividends can be combined into one journal entry.

Account		Debit	Credit
Cash Dividends		32,000	
Cash Dividends Payable			32,000

(10,000 x $2) + (24,000 x $.50)

- *Cash Dividends* is a **contra stockholders' equity** account that is **increasing.**
- *Cash Dividends Payable* is a **liability** account that is **increasing.**

2. Date of Record - no journal entry

3. Date of Payment

Paid the amount that had been declared. The Cash Dividends Payable account balance is set to zero.

Account		Debit	Credit
Cash Dividends Payable		32,000	
Cash			32,000

(10,000 x $2) + (24,000 x $.50)

- *Cash Dividends* Payable is a **liability** account that is **decreasing.**
- *Cash* is an **asset** account that is **decreasing.**

NOTE: Many times the challenge with dividend declarations is to first determine the number of shares outstanding.

For example, if a company issued 30,000 shares of common stock, reacquired 10,000 as treasury stock, and then sold 1,000 shares of the Treasury Stock, there would be 21,000 shares outstanding (30,000 - 10,000 + 1,000). If a cash dividend of $2 per share were declared, the total cash dividends would be $42,000 (21,000 x $2).

6.6 STOCK DIVIDENDS

Stock dividends are corporate earnings that are distributed to stockholders. They are distributions of retained earnings, which is accumulated profit. With a stock dividend, stockholders receive additional shares of stock instead of cash. Stock dividends transfer value from *Retained Earnings* to the *Common Stock and Paid-in Capital in Excess of Par – Common Stock* accounts, which increases total paid-in capital.

Stock Dividends is a contra stockholders' equity account that temporarily substitutes for a debit to the *Retained Earnings* account. At the end of the accounting period, *Stock Dividends* is closed to *Retained Earnings*. Stock dividends are only declared on shares outstanding, not on treasury stock shares.

Three dates are associated with a stock dividend. The **date of declaration** is the date the corporation commits to distributing additional shares to stockholders. On that date, the stockholders' equity account *Stock Dividends Distributable* is used to record the value of the shares due to the stockholders until the shares are distributed. The **date of record** is the date on which ownership is determined. Since shares of stock may be traded, the corporation names a specific date, and whoever owns the shares on that date will receive the dividend. There is no journal entry on the date of record. Finally, the **date of distribution** is the date the shares are actually distributed to stockholders.

1. Date of Declaration

Declared a 2% stock dividend on 21,000 shares of $10 par common stock outstanding. The fair market value is $15 per share.

Account		Debit	Credit
Stock Dividends		6,300	
Stock Dividends Distributable			4,200
Paid-in Capital in Excess of Par - Common Stock			2,100

21,000 x 2% x $15 (fair market value)

21,000 x 2% x $10 (par value)

21,000 x 2% x $5 (premium)

- *Stock Dividends* is a **contra stockholders' equity** account that is **increasing.**
- *Stock Dividends Distributable* is a **stockholders' equity** account that is **increasing.**

Stock Dividends is calculated by multiplying the number of additional shares to be distributed by the fair market value of each share.

Stock Dividends Distributable is a stockholders' equity account that substitutes for *Common Stock* until the stock can be issued. *Stock Dividends Distributable* can only be in multiples of par, just like Common Stock: the number of shares in the stock dividend times the par value per share.

Paid-in Capital in Excess of Par - Common Stock is used for any amount above par.

2.Date of Record - no journal entry

3. Date of Distribution

Issued the stock certificates. The *Stock Dividends Distributable* account balance is set to zero.

Account		Debit	Credit
Stock Dividends Distributable		4,200	
Common Stock			4,200

21,000 x 2% x $10 (par value)

- *Stock Dividends Distributable* is a **stockholders' equity** account that is **decreasing.**
- **Common Stock** is a **stockholders' equity** account that is **increasing.**

Stock Dividends Distributable is debited (zeroed out) when dividends are distributed and Common Stock is credited.

NOTE: Many times the challenge with stock dividend declarations is to first determine the number of shares outstanding.

For example, if a company issued 30,000 share of common stock, reacquired 10,000 as Treasury Stock, and then sold 1,000 shares of the Treasury Stock, there would be 21,000 shares outstanding (30,000 - 10,000 + 1,000). If a 2% stock dividend is declared, there would be 420 additional shares issued (21,000 x 2%).

6.7 STOCKHOLDERS' EQUITY SECTION OF THE BALANCE SHEET

The equation for the balance sheet is **Assets = Liabilities + Stockholders' Equity.** The stockholders' equity section of the balance sheet reports the worth of the stockholders. It has two subsections: Paid-in capital (from stockholder investments) and Retained earnings (profits generated by the corporation.)

Total paid-in capital is the sum of the first five accounts above and equals Preferred Stock plus *Paid-in Capital in Excess of Par - Preferred plus Common Stock* plus Paid-in Capital in Excess of Par - *Common plus Paid-in Capital from Sale* of Treasury Stock.

Common stock includes all shares issued, including those reacquired as treasury stock. Since treasury stock is not currently owned by stockholders, it should not be included as part of their worth. Therefore, the value of treasury stock shares is subtracted out to arrive at total stockholders' equity.

In summary, total stockholders' equity equals total paid-in capital plus retained earnings minus treasury stock. *Cash Dividends* and Stock Dividends are not reported on the balance sheet.

Sample Stockholders' Equity Section of the Balance Sheet

Paid in Capital		
Preferred Stock, $100, $100 par		$1,000,000
(80,000 shares authorized, 10,000 shares issued)		
Excess of issue price over par - preferred		10,000
Common stock, $25 par		500,000
(50,000 shares authorized, 20,000 shares issued)		
Excess of issue price over par - common		150,000
From sale of treasury stock		2,000
	Total paid in capital	$1,662,000
Retained Earnings		130,000
	Total	1,792,000
Deduct treasury stock		27,000
Total stockholders' equity		1,765,000

6.8 STOCK SPLITS

A **stock split** is when a corporation reduces the par value of each share of stock outstanding and issues a proportionate number of additional shares. This does affect the number of shares outstanding and, therefore, the number of shares dividends will be paid on. It also may affect the par value and market price per share, reducing them proportionately. However, the total dollar value of the shares outstanding does not change. No journal entry is required for a stock split.

EXAMPLE

A company has 10,000 shares outstanding. The par value is $16 per share. The fair market value per share is $20. The total capitalization (value of the shares outstanding) is $200,000 (10,000 x $20).

The company declares a 4-for-1 stock split. Multiply the number of shares by 4: there are 40,000 shares outstanding after the split. Divide the par value by 4: each share has a par value of $4 after the split. Also divide the market value per share by 4, resulting in $5 per share. The total capitalization (value of the shares outstanding) is still $200,000 (40,000 x $5).

6.9 CASH DIVIDENDS CALCULATIONS

Preferred stockholders are paid a designated dollar amount per share before common stockholders receive any cash dividends. However, it is possible that the dividend declared is not enough to pay the entire amount per preferred share that is guaranteed before common stockholders receive dividends. In that case the amount declared is divided by the number of preferred shares. Common stockholders would then receive no dividend payment.

Preferred stock may be cumulative or non-cumulative. This determines whether preferred shares will receive dividends in arrears, which is payment for dividends missed in the past due to inadequate amount of dividends declared in prior periods. If preferred stock is non-cumulative, preferred shares never receive payments for past dividends that were missed. If preferred stock is cumulative, any past dividends that were missed are paid before any payments are applied to the current period.

EXAMPLE

25,000 shares of $3 non-cumulative preferred stock and 100,000 shares of common stock. Preferred shares would receive $75,000 in dividends (25,000*$3) before common shares would receive anything.

		Preferred Stockholders		Common Stockholders		Owed to
Year	Total Dividend	Total	Per Share	Total	Per Share	Preferred
1	$0	$0	$0	$0	$0	$0
2	$20,000	$20,000	$0.80	$0	$0	$0
3	$60,000	$60,000	$2.40	$0	$0	$0
4	$175,000	$75,000	$3.00	$100,000	$1.00	$0
5	$200,000	$75,000	$3.00	$125,000	$1.25	$0
6	$375,000	$75,000	$3.00	$300,000	$3.00	$0

In years 1 through 3, dividends of less than $75,000 were declared. Since preferred stockholders are entitled to receive the first $75,000 in each year, they receive the entire amount of the dividend declared and the common shareholders receive nothing.

In years 4 through 6, dividends of more than $75,000 were declared. In each of those years, the preferred stockholders receive the first $75,000 and the common stockholders receive the remainder.

The preferred stockholders are never "caught up" for the amounts that were less than $75,000 that they missed out on in years 1 through 3.

EXAMPLE

25,000 shares of $3 cumulative preferred stock and 100,000 shares of common stock. Preferred shares would receive $75,000 in dividends (25,000 * $3) before common shares would receive anything.

Year	Total Dividend	Preferred Stockholders Total	Preferred Stockholders Per Share	Common Stockholders Total	Common Stockholders Per Share	Owed to Preferred
1	$0	$0	$0	$0	$0	$75,000
2	$20,000	$20,000	$0.80	$0	$0	$130,000
3	$60,000	$60,000	$2.40	$0	$0	$145,000
4	$175,000	$175,000	$7.00	$0	$0	$45,000
5	$200,000	$120,000	$4.80	$80,000	$0.80	$0
6	$375,000	$75,000	$3.00	$300,000	$3.00	$0

In years 1 through 3, dividends of less than $75,000 were declared. Since dividends on preferred stock are cumulative, each year that dividends are declared there is a look back to previous years to ensure that preferred shareholders received their full $75,000 for all past years before any dividends are paid to common stockholders in the current year. In this example, no dividends are paid on either class of stock in year 1.

In year 2, preferred stockholders must receive $150,000 ($75,000 for year 1 and $75,000 for year 2) before common shareholders receive anything. Since only $20,000 is declared, preferred stockholders receive it all and are still "owed" $130,000 at the end of year 2.

In year 3, preferred stockholders must receive $205,000 ($130,000 in arrears and $75,000 for year 3) before common shareholders receive anything. Since only $60,000 is declared, preferred stockholders receive it all and are still "owed" $145,000 at the end of year 3.

In year 4, preferred stockholders must receive $220,000 ($145,000 in arrears and $75,000 for year 4) before common shareholders receive anything. Since only $175,000 is declared, preferred stockholders receive it all and are still "owed" $45,000 at the end of year 4.

In year 5, preferred stockholders must receive $120,000 ($45,000 in arrears and $75,000 for year 5) before common shareholders receive anything. Since $200,000 is declared, preferred stockholders receive $120,000 of it and common shareholders receive the remaining $80,000. In year 6, preferred stockholders are not owed any dividends in arrears. Of the $375,000 that is declared, they receive the $75,000 due to them in year 6. Common shareholders receive the remaining $300,000.

The accounts that are highlighted in bright yellow are the new accounts you just learned. Those highlighted in pale yellow are the ones you learned previously.

#1

Jonick Corporation
Income Statement
For the Month Ended June 30, 2014

Operating REVENUES:			
Fees Earned		$200,000	
Sales	$150,000		
Less: Sales returns	10,000		
Less: Sales discounts	5,000		
Net sales	135,000		
Cost of merchandise sold	55,000		
Gross profit		80,000	
Gross operating revenues			$280,000
Operating EXPENSES:			
Salaries expense		$25,000	
Wages expense		22,000	
Rent expense		20,000	
Insurance expense		19,000	
Supplies expense		18,000	
Advertising expense		17,000	
Maintenance expense		16,000	
Depreciation expense		15,000	
Taxes expense		14,000	
Utilities expense		13,000	
Payroll tax expense		12,000	
Bad debt expense		11,000	
Bank card expense		10,000	
Vehicle expense		9,000	
Delivery expense		8,000	
Amortization expense		7,000	
Miscellaneous expense		6,000	
Total operating expenses			242,000
Net income from operations			$38,000
Other revenue and expenses:			
Interest revenue		$5,000	
Interest expense		(4,000)	
Gain on sale of equipment		3,000	
Loss on redemption of bonds		(2,000)	2,000
Net income			$40,000

#3

Jonick Corporation
Balance Sheet
June 30, 2014

ASSETS			
Current assets:			
Cash		$40,000	
Accounts receivable	$28,000		
Less: Allowance for doubtful accounts	3,000	25,000	
Merchandise inventory		60,000	
Supplies		18,000	
Prepaid rent		12,000	
Prepaid insurance		6,000	
Prepaid taxes		4,000	
Note receivable		2,000	
Total current assets			$167,000
Fixed assets:			
Equipment	$16,000		
Less: Accumulated depreciation	2,000	14,000	
Van	30,000		
Less: Accumulated depreciation	5,000	25,000	
Building	200,000		
Less: Accumulated depreciation	70,000	130,000	
Land		110,000	
Total fixed assets			279,000
Intangible assets:			
Patents			14,000
Total assets			$460,000

LIABILITIES			
Current liabilities:			
Accounts payable	$14,000		
Unearned fees	13,000		
Wages payable	12,000		
Salaries payable	11,000		
Taxes payable	10,000		
Interest payable	9,000		
Notes payable	8,000		
Sales tax payable	7,000		
Social security tax payable	6,000		
Medicare tax payable	5,000		
Federal withholding tax payable	4,000		
State withholding tax payable	3,000		
Federal unemployment tax payable	2,000		
State unemployment tax payable	1,000		
Total current liabilities		$105,000	
Long-term liabilities:			
Mortgage note payable	$56,000		
Bonds payable	40,000		
Less: Discount on bonds payable	(6,000)		
Total long-term liabilities		90,000	
Total liabilities			$195,000
STOCKHOLDERS' EQUITY			
Common stock		$80,000	
Paid-in-capital in excess of par - common stock		34,000	
Preferred stock		50,000	
Paid-in-capital in excess of par - preferred stock		18,000	
Paid-in-capital from sale of treasury stock		13,000	
Retained earnings		90,000	
Treasury stock		(20,000)	
Total stockholders' equity			265,000
Total liabilities and stockholders' equity			$460,000

#2

Jonick Corporation
Retained Earnings Statement
For the Month Ended June 30, 2014

Retained earnings, June 1, 2014			$60,000
Net income		$40,000	
Less: Cash dividends	$6,000		
Stock dividends	4,000	10,000	
Increase in retained earnings			30,000
Retained earnings, June 30, 2014			$90,000

At this point you have learned all of the accounts and calculated amounts that are shown below on the income statement, retained earnings statement, and balance sheet. Understanding what these accounts are and how their balances are determined provides you with a sound foundation for learning managerial accounting concepts. You will move from preparing and reading financial statements to using these results for decision making purposes in a business.

#1

Jonick Corporation
Income Statement
For the Month Ended June 30, 2018

Operating REVENUES:			
Fees Earned		$200,000	
Sales	$150,000		
Less: Sales returns	10,000		
Less: Sales discounts	5,000		
Net sales	135,000		
Cost of merchandise sold	55,000		
Gross profit		80,000	
Gross operating revenues			$280,000
Operating EXPENSES:			
Salaries expense		$25,000	
Wages expense		22,000	
Rent expense		20,000	
Insurance expense		19,000	
Supplies expense		18,000	
Advertising expense		17,000	
Maintenance expense		16,000	
Depreciation expense		15,000	
Taxes expense		14,000	
Utilities expense		13,000	
Payroll tax expense		12,000	
Bad debt expense		11,000	
Bank card expense		10,000	
Vehicle expense		9,000	
Delivery expense		8,000	
Amortization expense		7,000	
Miscellaneous expense		6,000	
Total operating expenses			242,000
Net income from operations			$38,000
Other revenue and expenses:			
Interest revenue		$5,000	
Interest expense		(4,000)	
Gain on sale of equipment		3,000	
Loss on redemption of bonds		(2,000)	2,000
Net income			$40,000

#3

Jonick Corporation
Balance Sheet
June 30, 2018

ASSETS			
Current assets:			
Cash		$40,000	
Accounts receivable	$28,000		
Less: Allowance for doubtful accounts	3,000	25,000	
Merchandise inventory		60,000	
Supplies		18,000	
Prepaid rent		12,000	
Prepaid insurance		6,000	
Prepaid taxes		4,000	
Note receivable		2,000	
Total current assets			$167,000
Fixed assets:			
Equipment	$16,000		
Less: Accumulated depreciation	2,000	14,000	
Van	30,000		
Less: Accumulated depreciation	5,000	25,000	
Building	200,000		
Less: Accumulated depreciation	70,000	130,000	
Land		110,000	
Total fixed assets			279,000
Intangible assets:			
Patents			14,000
Total assets			$460,000

LIABILITIES			
Current liabilities:			
Accounts payable	$14,000		
Unearned fees	13,000		
Wages payable	12,000		
Salaries payable	11,000		
Taxes payable	10,000		
Interest payable	9,000		
Notes payable	8,000		
Sales tax payable	7,000		
Social security tax payable	6,000		
Medicare tax payable	5,000		
Federal withholding tax payable	4,000		
State withholding tax payable	3,000		
Federal unemployment tax payable	2,000		
State unemployment tax payable	1,000		
Total current liabilities		$105,000	
Long-term liabilities:			
Mortgage note payable	$56,000		
Bonds payable	40,000		
Less: Discount on bonds payable	(6,000)		
Total long-term liabilities		90,000	
Total liabilities			$195,000
STOCKHOLDERS' EQUITY			
Common stock		$80,000	
Paid-in-capital in excess of par - common stock		34,000	
Preferred stock		50,000	
Paid-in-capital in excess of par - preferred stock		18,000	
Paid-in-capital from sale of treasury stock		13,000	
Retained earnings		90,000	
Treasury stock		(20,000)	
Total stockholders' equity			265,000
Total liabilities and stockholders' equity			$460,000

#2

Jonick Corporation
Retained Earnings Statement
For the Month Ended June 30, 2018

Retained earnings, June 1, 2018			$60,000
Net income		$40,000	
Less: Cash dividends	$6,000		
Stock dividends	4,000	10,000	
Increase in retained earnings			30,000
Retained earnings, June 30, 2018			$90,000

07 Capstone Experiences: Statement of Cash Flows & Financial Statement Analysis

7.1 FINANCIAL STATEMENTS

Businesses publish financial statements to communicate information about their operating performance and economic health. The income statement shows the profitability of a business by presenting its revenue and expenses for a period of time and summarizes its profitability in one final result: net income. The retained earnings statement reports all of the profit that a business has accumulated since it began operations. The balance sheet is a comprehensive summary report that lists a business's assets, liabilities, owner investments, and accumulated profit. Examples appear below.

Jonick Company
Income Statement
For the Year Ended December 31, 2019

Sales	$174,000	
Cost of merchandise sold	94,000	
Gross profit		$80,000
Operating expenses:		
Wages expense	$20,000	
Rent expense	10,000	
Insurance expense	6,000	
Depreciation expense	5,000	
Total operating expenses		41,000
		$39,000
Other revenue and expenses		
Gain on sale of investments	$10,000	
Loss on sale of equipment	(1,000)	9,000
Net income		$48,000

Jonick Company
Retained Earnings Statement
For the Year Ended December 31, 2019

Retained earnings, January 1, 2019		$113,000
Net income	$48,000	
Less: Cash dividends	3,000	
Increase in retained earnings		45,000
Retained earnings, December 31, 2019		$158,000

Jonick Company
Comparative Balance Sheet
December 31, 2019 and 2018

	End 2019	End 2018
Assets		
Cash	$50,000	$12,000
Accounts receivable	34,000	58,000
Merchandise inventory	112,000	80,000
Prepaid insurance	9,000	15,000
Investment in ABC Co. stock	0	80,000
Equipment	221,000	60,000
Accumulated depreciation	(50,000)	(45,000)
Land	0	100,000
Total assets	$376,000	$360,000
Liabilities		
Accounts payable	$29,000	$22,000
Wages payable	14,000	17,000
Cash dividends payable	5,000	8,000
Bonds payable	0	50,000
Stockholders' Equity		
Common stock	$140,000	$125,000
Paid-in capital in excess of par	30,000	25,000
Retained earnings	158,000	113,000
Total liabilities and stockholders' equity	$376,000	$360,000

7.2 STATEMENT OF CASH FLOWS

Managers, investors, and lenders are particularly interested in the availability of cash, where it comes from, and what it is used for in a business. However, the income statement, retained earnings statement, and balance sheet do not directly track or report the flow of cash. Therefore, businesses prepare a fourth financial statement, the statement of cash flows, to clearly provide information about the sources and uses of cash.

The statement of cash flows is based on information from the income statement, retained earnings statement, and balance sheet. Therefore, it is prepared last.

7.2.1 Types of Business Activities

All business transactions can be classified as one of three types of activities: operating, investing, or financing.

Operating activities are those involved in the day-to-day running of the business. Accounts used for operating activities include all those on the income statement as well as current assets and current liabilities on the balance sheet. (Current assets and liabilities are those that are expected to be converted to cash within one year.) Most of a business' transactions are operating activities.

Investment activities involve fixed or long-term assets that are found on the balance sheet. These are assets that are expected to last more than one year. Investment activities include buying and/or selling any of the following: equipment, vehicles, buildings, land, patents, investments in stock, and investments in bonds. **Financing activities** involve raising funds for a business and may include long-term debt or equity accounts found on the balance sheet. These include transactions involving the following: issuing common or preferred stock, issuing or redeeming bonds payable, and paying off a mortgage note payable. Buying or selling treasury stock and paying dividends are related to stock and are also financing activities.

7.2.2 Cash Inflows and Outflows

The statement of cash flows reports cash inflows and/or cash outflows in each of three sections: cash flows from operating activities, cash flows from investing activities, and cash flows from financing activities. An inflow occurs when cash is paid to a business. An outflow is when a business makes a cash payment.

Each of the three sections is summarized by one number, which is the net cash flows amount. If the summary number is positive, it means that more cash was received than was paid out for that activity during the accounting period. If the summary number is negative, more cash was paid out than was received for that activity during the period.

EXAMPLE

You receive and cash your paycheck for the week for $400. This is a cash inflow. On the same day you pay your cell phone bill and car insurance payment for a total of $210. You then go out for dinner and pay $30 cash with tip. These three payments are cash outflows. The net cash inflow on that day is $160; that is, $160 more came in than went out.

The following sample journal entries are reminders of transactions that involve cash. The Cash account is either debited or credited, to indicate a cash inflow or cash outflow, respectively.

EXAMPLE 1

When ***Cash*** is debited, there is a cash inflow. Here is an example of an investing activity that results in a cash inflow: selling equipment.

Account	Debit	Credit
Cash	50,000	
Accumulated Depreciation	1,000	
Equipment		48,000
Gain on Sale of Equipment		3,000

Cash inflow: $50,000. Notice there is a gain on this transaction.

EXAMPLE 2

When Cash is credited, there is a cash outflow. Here is an example of a financing activity that results in a cash outflow: calling bonds.

Account	Debit	Credit
Bonds Payable	100,000	
Loss on Redemption of Bonds	5,000	
Discount on Bonds Payable		3,000
Cash		102,000

Cash outflow: $102,000. Notice there is a loss on this transaction.

EXAMPLE 3

When Cash is debited, here is a cash inflow. Here is an example of a financing activity that results in a cash inflow: issuing common stock.

Account	Debit	Credit
Cash	180,000	
Common Stock		150,000
Paid-in Capital in Excess of Par - Common Stock		30,000

Cash inflow: $180,000. Notice there is no gain or loss on this transaction.

The operating activities section of the statement of cash flows appears first. It may be prepared in one of two ways, using either the indirect or the direct method. The **indirect method** begins with net income from the income statement and mathematically backs out non-cash transactions to arrive at cash flows from operating activities.The direct method itemizes all of the operating cash inflows, or receipts, followed by a list of the operating cash ouflows, or payments. Although information presented in the operating activities section is different, both methods yield the same cash flows from operating activities amount. The indirect method is more popular because the information needed to prepare the section is readily available on the income statement and balance sheet. The choice of methods pertains only to the operating activities section. The investing and financing section both are prepared using a direct method.

The following is a sample statement of cash flows that has been prepared based on the financial statements presented on page 255. The operating activities section uses the indirect method.

Jonick Company
Statement of Cash Flows
For the Year Ended December 31, 2009

Cash flows from operating activities:				
Net income		$48,000		1.
Adjustments to reconcile net income to net cash flow from operating activities:				
Depreciation		5,000		2.
Gain on sale of investments		(10,000)		3.
Loss on sale of equipment		1,000		4.
Changes in current operating assets and liabilities:				
Decrease in accounts receivable		$24,000		5.
Increase in merchandise inventory		(32,000)		6.
Decrease in prepaid insurance		6,000		7.
Increase in accounts payable		7,000		8.
Decrease in wages payable		(3,000)		9.
Net cash flow from operating activities			$46,000	10.
Cash flows from investing activities				
Cash received from sale of land	$99,000			11.
Cash received from sale of investment	90,000	$189,000		12.
Cash paid to purchase equipment		161,000		13.
Net cash flow from investing activities			28,000	14.
Cash flows from financing activities:				
Cash received from issuing common stock		$20,000		15.
Cash paid to redeem bonds	$50,000			16.
Cash paid for dividends	6,000	56,000		17.
Net cash flow from financing activities			(36,000)	18.
Increase in cash			$38,000	19.
Cash at the beginning of the year			12,000	20.
Cash at the end of the year			$50,000	21.

1. From the income statement.
2. Depreciation expense amount from the income statement.
3. Other revenues and expenses section of the income statement - deduct gains included in net income.
4. Other revenues and expenses section of the income statement - add back losses included in net income.
5. Difference between beginning-of-year and end-of-year amounts on the balance sheet: 58,000 - 34,000. Add decreases in current assets.
6. Difference between beginning-of-year and end-of-year amounts on the balance sheet: 80,000 - 112,000. Deduct increases in current assets.
7. Difference between beginning-of-year and end-of-year amounts on the balance sheet: 15,000 - 9,000. Add decreases in current assets.
8. Difference between beginning-of-year and end-of-year amounts on the balance sheet: 22,000 - 29,000. Add increases in current liabilities.
9. Difference between beginning-of-year and end-of-year amounts on the balance sheet: 17,000 - 14,000. Deduct decreases in current liabilities.
10. Total of all of the amounts in the operating activities section.
11. Cost of $100,000 given on the balance sheet minus the $1,000 loss shown on the income statement = the amount of cash received.
12. Cost of $80,000 given on the balance sheet plus the $10,000 gain shown on the income statement = the amount of cash received.
13. Increase in Equipment on the balance sheet from 60,000 to 221,000 is the cash paid for new equipment since there were no sales of equipment.
14. Total of all the cash inflows (added) and cash outflows (deducted) equals net cash flows from investing activities.
15. Increases in Common Stock and Paid-in Capital accounts on the balance sheet (140,000 - 125,000) + (30,000 - 25,000).
16. Decrease in Bonds Payable on the balance sheet from 50,000 to 0.
17. Beginning Cash Dividends Payable balance of 8,000 + cash dividends declared on the retained earnings statement of 3,000 - ending Cash Dividends Payable balance of 5,000.
18. Total of all the cash inflows (added) and cash outflows (deducted) equals net cash flows from financing activities.
19. The difference between the beginning and ending Cash balances.
20. From the balance sheet, beginning Cash balance.
21. From the balance sheet, ending Cash balance.

The following section will show you how to prepare the statement of cash flows (**indirect method** for operating activities section) on page 259 from the financial statements on page 255.

7.2.3 Basic Shell of the Statement of Cash Flows (indirect method)

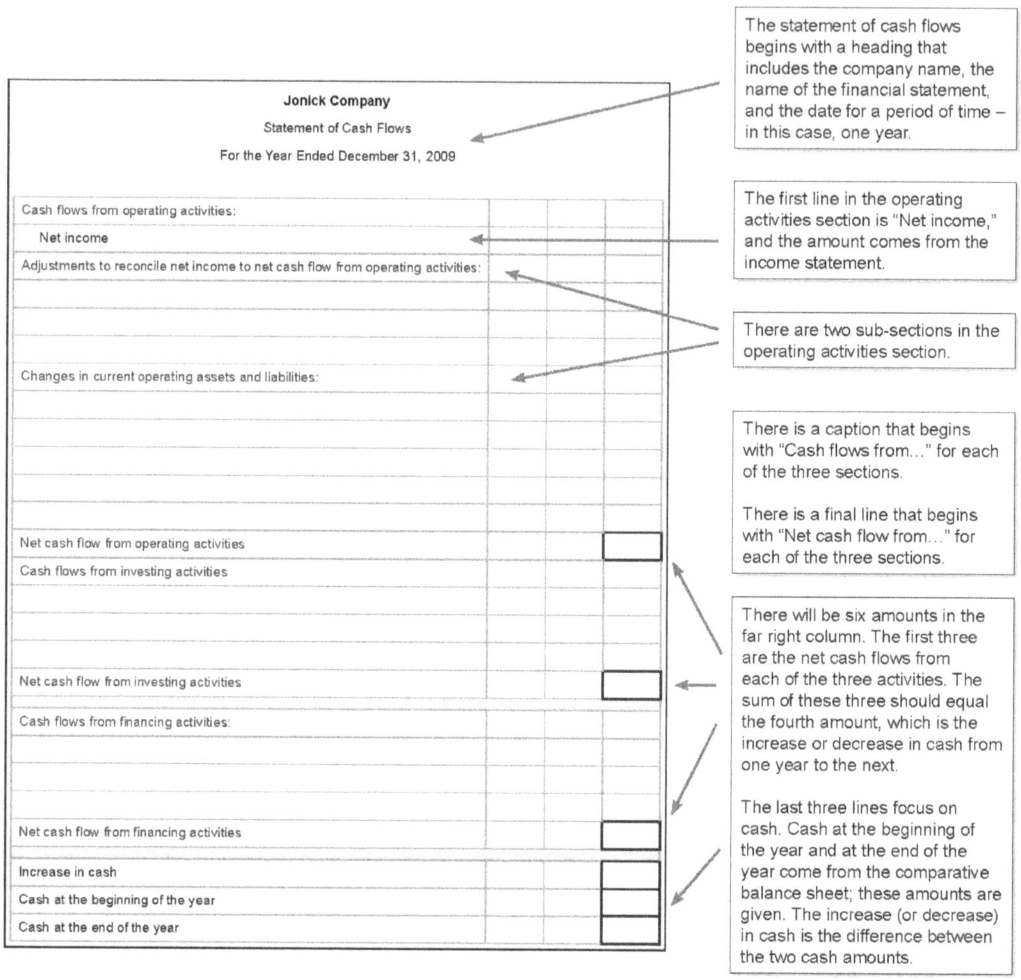

STEPS IN PREPARING THE STATEMENT OF CASH FLOWS

Using the basic shell that includes the heading and formatting captions, complete the statement of cash flows.

Operating activities section (indirect method)

Most of a business' transactions are operating activities. Some of these involve cash; some do not. There are too many transactions to make it practical to look at each one individually to determine its impact on cash flow. Therefore, the income statement and comparative balance sheet numbers will be used to efficiently remove non-cash transactions in order to arrive at the net cash flow from operating activities number. The process is described next.

1. Enter the net income amount, which is the final number on the income statement that is given.

Cash flows from operating activities:	
Net income	$48,000

2. Adjust the net income amount to remove non-cash expenses such depreciation expense and interest expense on the amortization of a bond discount. Also add back losses and deduct gains shown on the income statement since they do not pertain to operating activities and therefore do not belong in the operating activities section.

Adjustments to reconcile net income to net cash flow from operating activities:	
Depreciation	5,000
Gain on sale of investments	(10,000)
Loss on sale of equipment	1,000

3. Current assets and liabilities are used in the operation of the business and are relatively short term; less than one year before used or converted to cash. Identify the CURRENT assets (except Cash) and CURRENT liabilities on the comparative balance sheet. Calculate the amount of increase or decrease in each one between the previous year and the current year (shown in red in the far right column below.)

Comparative Balance Sheet
December 31, 2019 and 2018

	End 2019	End 2018	
Assets	34,000	58,000	24,000 decrease
Accounts receivable	112,000	80,000	32,000 increase
Merchandise inventory	9,000	15,000	6,000 decrease
Prepaid insurance			
Liabilities			
Accounts payable	29,000	22,000	7,000 increase
Wages payable	14,000	17,000	3,000 decrease

To remove non-cash operating transactions, the difference in the amount from one year and the next for each of these accounts is reported in the operating activities section of the statement of cash flows using the following rules:

Add the following to net income:

- Decreases in current assets (accounts receivable, inventory, prepaid insurance, prepaid expenses, etc.)
- Increases in current liabilities (accounts payable, wages payable, accrued expenses, etc.)

Deduct the following from net income:

- Increases in current assets (accounts receivable, inventory, prepaid insurance, prepaid expenses, etc.)
- Decreases in current liabilities (accounts payable, wages payable, accrued expenses, etc.)

Changes in current operating assets and liabilities:	
Decrease in accounts receivable	$24,000
Increase in merchandise inventory	(32,000)
Decrease in prepaid insurance	6,000
Increase in accounts payable	7,000
Decrease in wages payable	(3,000)

List these current operating assets and liabilities in the order in which they appear on the balance sheet. Be sure any deductions in the operating activities section are in parenthesis to indicate they are amounts to be subtracted.

4. Calculate net cash flows from operating activities amount by adding to and/ or subtracting from net income.

Net income		$48,000	
Adjustments to reconcile net income to net cash flow from operating activities:			
Depreciation		5,000	
Gain on sale of investments		(10,000)	
Loss on sale of equipment		1,000	
Changes in current operating assets and liabilities:			
Decrease in accounts receivable		$24,000	
Increase in merchandise inventory		(32,000)	
Decrease in prepaid insurance		6,000	
Increase in accounts payable		7,000	
Decrease in wages payable		(3,000)	
Net cash flow from operating activities			$46,000

The final summary amount indicates that $46,000 more "came in" than was paid out during this year for operating activities. (If it were a net cash outflow, use parenthesis on the number to indicate this.) This is the first of six numbers in the right-hand column.

INVESTING ACTIVITIES SECTION

There are relatively few items in the investing activities section, so it is reasonable to look at them one by one to determine if there is a cash inflow or outflow and, if so, its amount. Identify the investing activities on the comparative balance sheet. These are any fixed, long-term, or intangible assets

Jonick Company Comparative Balance Sheet December 31, 2019 and 2018		
	End 2019	End 2018
Investment in ABC Co. Stock	0	80,000
Equipment	221,000	60,000
Accumulated depreciation	(50,000)	(45,000)
Land	0	100,000

NOTE:

a. All investing and financing activities were for cash.
b. No additional investments were purchased.
c. No additional land was purchased.
d. No equipment was sold or otherwise disposed of.

If a fixed asset's balance increases from one year to the next, it means that more must have been purchased and there was a cash outflow. Similarly, if a fixed asset's balance decreases from one year to the next, it means that some or all of it was sold and there was a cash inflow. To help determine the amount of cash received or paid, refer to the journal entry for each transaction to see if Cash was debited or credited.

IMPORTANT: It is possible for one fixed asset, such as equipment, to have both a sale and a purchase of two different pieces of equipment for cash. This would have to be explained in a separate note in order to properly prepare the statement of cash flows.

When a long-term or fixed asset is sold, there may be a gain or loss. This information would be found on the income statement.

Jonick Company Income Statement For the Year Ended December 31, 2009		
Other revenue and expenses	10,000	
Gain on sale of investments	(1,000)	
Loss on sale of land		9,000
Net income		48,000

The land cost $100,000 (given on the balance sheet) and there was a loss of $1,000 when it was sold (given on the income statement). That would mean there was a $99,000 cash inflow ($100,000 - $1,000).

The investments cost $80,000 (given on the balance sheet) and there was a gain of $10,000 when they were sold (given on the income statement). That would mean there was a $90,000 cash inflow ($80,000 + $10,000).

The Equipment balance on the balance sheet at the beginning of the year was

$60,000 and at the end of the year was $221,000, an increase of $161,000. Since it was noted that no equipment was sold, this is the amount of the cash outflow for equipment.

Each investing activity transaction is listed on its own line on the statement of cash flows. Cash inflows are listed first and each begins with "Cash received from..." Cash outflows follow and each begins with "Cash paid for..." If there is more than one inflow, they are subtotaled in the middle column. The same is true for more than one outflow.

Cash flows from investing activities			
Cash received from sale of land	$99,000		
Cash received from sale of investment	90,000	$189,000	
Cash paid to purchase equipment		161,000	
Net cash flow from investing activities			28,000

Calculate net cash flows from investing activities amount by deducting cash outflows from cash inflows. This final summary amount indicates that $28,000 more "came in" than was paid out during this year for investing activities. (If it were a net cash outflow, use parenthesis to indicate this.) This is the second of six numbers in the right-hand column.

As a different possibility, an asset account such as Equipment may have experienced more than one transaction rather than just a single purchase. Using the same comparative balance sheet information as in the previous example, note that the information to its right in item d. shows that some of the equipment was also sold.

Jonick Company Comparative Balance Sheet December 31, 2019 and 2018		
	End 2019	End 2018
Investment in ABC Co. Stock	0	80,000
Equipment	221,000	60,000
Accumulated depreciation	(50,000)	(45,000)
Land	0	100,000

NOTE:

a. All investing and financing activities were for cash.
b. No additional investments were purchased.
c. No additional land was purchased.
d. Equipment that cost $15,000 was sold for its current book value of $10,000 (therefore, no

This would impact the cash flows from investing activities section since there would be an additional cash receipt.

Cash flows from investing activities			
Cash received from sale of equipment	$10,000		
Cash received from sale of land	99,000		
Cash received from sale of investment	90,000	$199,000	
Cash paid to purchase equipment		171,000	
Net cash flow from investing activities			28,000

Additional equipment still had to have been purchased since the overall Equipment balance on the balance sheet increased from year to year. The calculation to determine the amount of the purchase is as follows:

$221,000 ending balance - ($60,000 beginning balance - $10,000 cost of equipment sold given) = $171,000 purchased

The same information about the equipment that was sold could have been provided in the form of a ledger account, such as the one that follows for *Equipment:*

Equipment					
Date	Item	Debit	Credit	Debit	Credit
1/1/2012	Balance			60,000	
4/3/2012			10,000	50,000	
9/12/2012		171,000		221,000	

The beginning and ending balances that appear on the comparative balance sheet are the same as those in the Equipment ledger's debit balance column on January 1 and September 12, respectively. The $10,000 credit entry is the cost of the equipment that was sold on April 3. The $171,000 debit entry in the debit column is the cost of the equipment that was purchased on September 12. The sale results in a cash inflow, and the purchase results in a cash outflow.

FINANCING ACTIVITIES SECTION

There are relatively few items in the financing activities section, so it is reasonable to look at them one by one to determine if there is a cash inflow or outflow and, if so, its amount.

5. Identify the financing activities on the comparative balance sheet. These are found in the long-term liabilities or stockholders' equity sections of the balance sheet.

Jonick Company Comparative Balance Sheet December 31, 2019 and 2018		
	End 2019	End 2018
Liabilities		
Cash dividends payable	5,000	8,000
Bonds payable	0	50,000
Stockholders' Equity		
Common stock	140,000	125,000
Paid-in capital in excess of par	30,000	25,000
~~Retained earnings~~	~~158,000~~	~~113,000~~

If a long-term liability or stockholders' equity account balance increases from one year to the next, it means that more must have been borrowed or received from investors and there may have been a cash inflow. Similarly, if a long-term liability account balance decreases from one year to the next, it means that it was repaid and there was a cash outflow. To help determine the amount of cash received or paid, refer to the journal entry for each transaction.

Cash flows from financing activities:			
Cash received from issuing common stock		$20,000	
Cash paid to redeem bonds	$50,000		
Cash paid for dividends	6,000	56,000	
Net cash flow from financing activities			(36,000)

6. For stock issuances, add the increase in Common Stock + the increase in Paid-in Capital in Excess of Par to determine the amount of cash inflow [($140,000-$125,000) + ($30,000 - $25,000)].
7. Cash paid for dividends is calculated as follows: Beginning Cash Dividends Payable balance + Cash dividends declared – ending Cash Dividends Payable balance

Cash dividends declared is found on the retained earnings statement. In this case the calculation is $8,000 + $3,000 - $5,000 = $6,000.

Each financing activity transaction is listed on its own line on the statement of cash flows. Cash inflows are listed first and each begins with "Cash received from..." Cash outflows follow and each begins with "Cash paid for..." If there is more than one inflow, they are subtotaled in the middle column. The same is true for more than one outflow.

8. Calculate net cash flows used for financing activities amount by deducting cash outflows from cash inflows. Use parenthesis since it is a net cash outflow. This final summary amount indicates that $36,000 more was paid out than "came in" during this year for financing activities. This is the third of six numbers in the right-hand column.
9. Add the three numbers for cash flows from/used for operating, investing, and financing activities and label it as "Increase in cash" if it is positive or "Decrease in cash" if it is negative."
10. Add the net cash flows amounts from the three types of activities. **The sum should equal the increase (or decrease) in cash amount.**
11. List the amounts of cash at the beginning and the end of the year that are given on the balance sheet. The difference should equal the sum of the cash flows amounts from the three types of activities.

Net cash flow from operating activities			$46,000
Net cash flow from investing activities			28,000
Net cash flow from financing activities			(36,000)
Increase in cash			$38,000
Cash at the beginning of the year			12,000
Cash at the end of the year			$50,000

The statement of cash flows used in this example is a relatively simple one. There may be additional accounts that impact cash and therefore would also need to be included in other situations. Conversely, not all of the items on this sample statement of cash flows must be included on other statements. Only include those that are relevant to the problem or business you are working on and omit all others.

Analogy – Cash paid for dividends is calculated as follows:

Beginning Cash Dividends Payable balance + Cash dividends declared – ending Cash Dividends Payable balance

The beginning Cash Dividends Payable balance is what the company already owed stockholders from dividends it declared the previous year but did not yet pay. Cash dividends declared is additional amounts promised and owed to stockholders for the current year. Those two combined represent the total owed. The Cash Dividends Payable balance at the end of the year is what has not yet been paid. The difference between the total owed and the total not yet paid is what must have been paid out in cash.

Think of it this way. I borrowed $50 from a student last week. On the way to class today, I borrowed another $10 from him. I owe a total of $60 to this student. If we leave class today and I owe him $20, there is only one explanation: I must have paid him $40 while we were in class. That was my cash outflow during the period.

Subtotaling Tips for Investing and Financing Sections			
Three receipts; one payment example with one subtotal			
Cash flows from . . . activities:			
Cash received from . . .	$1,000		
Cash received from . . .	2,000		
Cash received from . . .	3,000	$6,000	
Cash paid for . . .		4,000	
Net cash from from . . . activities			$2,000
Two receipts; two payments example with two subtotals			
Cash flows from . . . activities:			
Cash received from . . .	$1,000		
Cash received from . . .	2,000	$3,000	
Cash paid for . . .	$4,000		
Cash paid for . . .	5,000	9,000	
Net cash flow from activities			(6,000)

The following is a sample statement of cash flows that has been prepared based on the financial statements presented on page 255. The operating activities section uses the direct method in the operating activities section.

Two-step calculation to determine cash paid for inventory

First determine the cost of inventory purchases. The determine how much of those purchases was paid in cash.

1. Beginning Inventory balance + purchases - cost of merchandise sold = ending inventory balance: solve for purchases, the unknown 80,000 + ? - 94,000 = 112,000; therefore? = 112,00 - 80,000 + 94,000 = 126,000
2. Beginning Accounts Payable + purchases - ending Accounts Payable = cash paid for purchases 22,000 + 126,000 - 29,000 = 119,000

Jonick Company Statement of Cash Flows For the Year Ended December 31, 2009				
Cash flows from operating activities:				
Cash received from sales to customers		$198,000		1.
Cash paid for inventory		(119,000)		2.
Cash paid for wages		(23,000)		3.
Cash paid for rent		(10,000)		4.
Net cash flow from operating activities			$46,000	5.
Cash flows from investing activities				6.
Cash received from sale of land	$99,000			
Cash received from sale of investment	90,000	$189,000		
Cash paid to purchase equipment		161,000		
Net cash flow from investing activities			28,000	
Cash flows from financing activities:				
Cash received from issuing common stock		$20,000		
Cash paid to redeem bonds	$50,000			
Cash paid for dividends	6,000	56,000		
Net cash flow from financing activities			(36,000)	
Increase in cash			$38,000	
Cash at the beginning of the year			12,000	
Cash at the end of the year			$50,000	

1. Beginning Accounts Receivable balance from balance sheet + Sales from income statement - ending Accounts Receivable balance from the balance sheet.
2. See two-step calculation above.
3. Beginning Wages Payable balance from balance sheet + Wages Expense from income statement - ending Wages Payable balance from the balance sheet.
4. Rent Expense amount from the income statement since it is a cash payment.
5. Total of all of the amounts in the operating acivities section.
6. The remainder of the statement of cash flows if the same as the example that used the indirect method for the operating activities section.

The following section will show you how to prepare the statement of cash flows (direct method for operating activities section) on page 270 from the financial statements on page 255.

7.2.4 Basic Shell of the Statement of Cash Flows (direct method)

Jonick Company
Statement of Cash Flows
For the Year Ended December 31, 2009

Cash flows from operating activities:			
Net cash flow from operating activities			
Cash flows from investing activities			
Cash received from sale of land	$99,000		
Cash received from sale of investment	90,000	$189,000	
Cash paid to purchase equipment		161,000	
Net cash flow from investing activities			28,000
Cash flows from financing activities:			
Cash received from issuing common stock		$20,000	
Cash paid to redeem bonds	$50,000		
Cash paid for dividends	6,000	56,000	
Net cash flow from financing activities			(36,000)
Increase in cash			$38,000
Cash at the beginning of the year			12,000
Cash at the end of the year			$50,000

The heading is already completed here since it is the same as the statement of cash flows where the indirect method is used for operating activities.

Each row in the operating activities section comes directly from the revenue and expense line items on the income statement that involve cash. The amounts for these line items are not necessarily what appear on the income statement since not all revenue and expense amounts listed there were cash transactions. Need to calculate the operating activities amounts.

The investing activities section is already completed here since it is the same as the statement of cash flows where the indirect method is used for operating activities.

The financing activities section is already completed here since it is the same as the statement of cash flows where the indirect method is used for operating activities.

The last three lines are already completed here since they are the same as the statement of cash flows where the indirect method is used for operating activities.

STEPS IN PREPARING THE STATEMENT OF CASH FLOWS

Using the basic shell that includes the heading and formatting captions, complete the statement of cash flows.

Operating activities section (direct method)

The operating activities section using the line items on the income statement that (1) relate to operations and (2) that involve cash transactions. In the sample income statement below, there are six operational accounts: Sales, Cost of Merchandise Sold, and four expense accounts that might possibly be listed on the statement of cash flows if they involve cash. The gain and loss that is listed on the income statement are the result of transactions that do not relate to the normal operations of the business, so they will not appear in the operating activities section on the statement of cash flows when using the direct method. Balance sheet accounts are needed as well to mathematically determine how much of some of the amounts are cash transactions.

Jonick Company Income Statement For the Year Ended December 31, 2009			
Sales		$174,000	
Gain on sale of investments		94,000	
Gross Profit			$80,000
Operating Expenses			
Wages expense		$20,000	
Rent expense		10,000	
Insurance expense		6,000	
Depreciation expense		5,000	
Total operating expenses			41,000
			39,000
Other revenue and expenses			
Gain on sale of investments		10,000	
Loss on sale of equipment		(1,000)	9,000
Net income			~~48,000~~

Jonick Company Comparative Balance Sheet (partial) December 31, 2019 and 2018		
	End 2019	End 2018
Assets		
Cash	$50,000	$12,000
Accounts receivable	34,000	58,000
Merchandise Inventory	112,000	80,000
Prepaid insurance	9,000	15,000
Liabilities		
Accounts payable	$29,000	$22,000
Wages payable	14,000	17,000

1. The first line item listed in the operating activities section is Cash received from sales to customers. The amount of $198,000 is determined by using the Sales amount from the income statement and the Accounts Receivable amounts on the comparative balance sheet (partial), as follows:

Beginning Accounts Receivable + Sales – Ending Accounts Receivable = cash received from sales to customers

58,000 + 174,000 – 34,000 = 198,000

Jonick Company Statement of Cash Flows For the Year Ended December 31, 2009			
Cash flows from operating activities:			
Cash received from sales to customers		$198,000	
Net cash flow from operating activities			

2. The second line item relates to cash paid for inventory. The calculation is a two-step process. The amount of $119,000 is determined by using the Cost of Merchandise Sold amount from the income statement and the Merchandise Inventory AND Accounts Payable amounts on the comparative balance sheet (partial), as follows:

   (1) Beginning Inventory + Purchases (unknown) – Cost of Merchandise Sold

   = Ending Inventory

   80,000 + x – 94,000 = 112,000

   x = 112,000 – 80,000 + 94,000 = 126,000 in purchases

   (2) Beginning Accounts Payable + Purchases – Ending Accounts Payable cash paid for inventory

   22,000 + 126,000 – 29,000 = 119,000

   The $119,000 is a deduction in the operating activities section.

Jonick Company Statement of Cash Flows For the Year Ended December 31, 2009			
Cash flows from operating activities:			
Cash received from sales to customers		$198,000	
Cash paid for inventory		(119,000)	
Net cash flow from operating activities			

3. The third line item relates to cash paid for wages. The amount of $23,000 is determined by using the Wages Expense amount from the income statement and the Wages Payable amounts on the comparative balance sheet (partial), as follows:

Beginning Wages Payable + Wages Expense – Ending Wages Payable = cash paid to employees

17,000 + 20,000 – 14,000 = 23,000

Jonick Company Statement of Cash Flows For the Year Ended December 31, 2009			
Cash flows from operating activities:			
Cash received from sales to customers		$198,000	
Cash paid for inventory		(119,000)	
Cash paid for wages		(23,000)	
Net cash flow from operating activities			

4. The fourth line item relates to cash paid for rent. Since Rent Expense is a cash transaction, the amount of $10,000 from the income statement is deducted in the operating activities section.

Jonick Company Statement of Cash Flows For the Year Ended December 31, 2009			
Cash flows from operating activities:			
Cash received from sales to customers		$198,000	
Cash paid for inventory		(119,000)	
Cash paid for wages		(23,000)	
Cash paid for rent		(10,000)	
Net cash flow from operating activities			$46,000

Insurance Expense and Depreciation Expense are non-cash items on the income statement and are therefore not included in the operating activities section. The difference in the Prepaid Insurance amounts on the balance sheets is $3,000 ($9,000 - $6,000), and that is the amount of Insurance Expense on the income statement. Therefore there was no net cash expenditure for insurance this period.

7.2.5 Comparative Operating Activities Sections – Statement of Cash Flows

INDIRECT METHOD

Jonick Company Statement of Cash Flows For the Year Ended December 31, 2009			
Cash flows from operating activities:			
Net income		$48,000	
Adjustments to reconcile net income to net cash flow from operating activities:			
Depreciation		5,000	
Gain on sale of investments		(10,000)	
Loss on sale of equipment		1,000	
Changes in current operating assets and liabilities:			
Decrease in accounts receivable		24,000	
Increase in merchandise inventory		(32,000)	
Decrease in prepaid insurance		6,000	
Increase in accounts payable		7,000	
Decrease in wages payable		(3,000)	
Net cash flow from operating activities			$46,000

DIRECT METHOD

Jonick Company Statement of Cash Flows For the Year Ended December 31, 2009			
Cash flows from operating activities:			
Cash received from sales to customers		$198,000	
Cash paid for inventory		(119,000)	
Cash paid for wages		(23,000)	
Cash paid for rent		(10,000)	
Net cash flow from operating activities			$46,000

Notice that for both methods, the net cash flow from operating activities amount is the same: $46,000.

7.3 FINANCIAL STATEMENT ANALYSIS

At this point, you have learned quite a bit about financial accounting. This includes the process of analyzing a wide variety of transactions, recording them in the journal, maintaining running account balances, and summarizing the information in the financial statements.

Businesses publish financial statements to communicate information about their operating performance and economic health. The income statement shows the profitability of a business by presenting its revenue and expenses for a period of time and summarizes its profitability in one final result: net income. The retained earnings statement reports all of the profit that a business has accumulated since it began operations. The balance sheet is a comprehensive summary report that lists a business's assets, liabilities, owner investments, and accumulated profit. Examples of basic financial statements appear below.

Once the financial statements are available, the next step is to analyze them to gleen useful information about a corporation's performance over time and its current financial health. These insights help business managers and investors make decisions about future courses of action. Areas of weakness may be identified and followed up with appropriate measures for improvement. Elements of strength should be reinforced and continued.

Much of this financial statement analysis is accomplished using ratios that reveal how one amount relates to another. One or more amounts are divided by other amount(s), yielding a decimal or percentage amount. However, no ratio is particularly meaningful by itself; it needs to be compared to something else, such as desired or expected results, previous results, other companies' results, or industry standards. This comparison lets you know where you stand in terms of whether you are doing better, worse, or the same as what you have expected or hoped for.

Once the financial statements are available, the next step is to analyze them to gleen useful information about a corporation's performance over time and its current financial health. These insights help business managers and investors make decisions about future courses of action. Areas of weakness may be identified and followed up with appropriate measures for improvement. Elements of strength should be reinforced and continued.

Much of this financial statement analysis is accomplished using ratios that reveal how one amount relates to another. One or more amounts are divided by other amount(s), yielding a decimal or percentage amount. However, no ratio is particularly meaningful by itself; it needs to be compared to something else, such as desired or expected results, previous results, other companies' results, or industry standards. This comparison lets you know where you stand in terms of whether you are doing better, worse, or the same as what you have expected or hoped for.

Jonick Company Statement of Cash Flows For the Years Ended December 31, 2019 and 2018		
	2019	**2018**
Sales	$994,000	$828,000
Cost of merchandise sold	414,000	393,000
Gross Profit	$580,000	$435,000
Operating Expenses		
Salaries expense	$77,000	$64,000
Rent expense	63,000	52,000
Insurance expense	56,000	46,000
Supplies expense	49,000	41,000
Advertising expense	42,000	35,000
Depreciation expense	35,000	29,000
Utilities expense	28,000	23,000
Total operating expenses	348,000	290,000
Net income from operations	$232,000	$145,000
Other revenue and expenses		
Gain on sale of investments	$137,000	$186,000
Interest expense	(55,000)	(50,000)
Income before income tax	$314,000	$281,000
Income tax expense	66,000	50,000
Net income	$248,000	$231,000

Jonick Company Comparative Retained Earnings Statement For the Years Ended December 31, 2019 and 2018		
	2019	2018
Retained earnings, beginning of year	$2,198,000	$1,987,000
Net income	248,000	231,000
Less: Prefered stock dividends	12,000	12,000
Common stock dividends	8,000	8,000
Increase in retained earnings	20,000	20,000
Retained earnings, end of year	$2,426,000	$2,198,000

Jonick Company Comparative Balance Sheet December 31, 2019 and 2018		
ASSETS		
Current assets:	**2019**	**2018**
Cash	$373,000	$331,000
Marketable securities	248,000	215,000
Accounts receivable	108,000	91,000
Merchandise Inventory	55,000	48,000
Prepaid insurance	127,000	115,000
Total current assets	$911,000	$800,000
Long-term investments:		
Investment in equity securities	$1,946,000	$1,822,000
Property, plant and equipment:		
Equipment (net of accumulated deprecition)	$87,000	$42,000
Building (net of accumulated depreciation)	645,000	581,000
Land	361,000	361,000
Total property, plant and equipment	$1,093,000	$984,000
Total assets	$3,950,000	$3,606,000
LIABILITIES		
Current liabilities:		
Accounts payable	$120,000	$109,000
Salaries payable	244,000	222,000
Total current liabilities	$364,000	$331,000
Long-term liabilities:		
Mortgage note payable	$83,000	$83,000
Bonds payable	828,000	745,000
Total long-term liabilities	$911,000	$828,000
Total liabilities	$1,275,000	$1,159,000
STOCKHOLDERS' EQUITY		
Preferred $1.50 stock, $20 par	$166,000	$166,000
Common stock, $10 par	83,000	83,000
Retained earnings	2,426,000	2,198,000
Total stockholders' equity	$2,675,000	$2,447,000
Total liabilities and stockholders' equity	$3,950,000	$3,606,000

ANNUAL CHECK-UP

Many people visit a doctor annually for a check-up to evaluate their overall health. This often involves a physician looking, listening, poking, prodding, weighing, and conducting tests to assess the strength and wellness of multiple body parts and the status of vital signs and chemical levels.

The results may be positive in some areas and less so in others. One deficiency or ailment may impact the body as a whole. As weaknesses are uncovered, measures such as medication, procedures, exercise, diet changes, etc. may be prescribed to assist with recovery.

For example, if high cholesterol levels and excessive weight are discovered, lifestyle changes and medication may be recommended. At the following year's visit, subsequent testing will reveal the progress made over time in these areas as well as other diagnostic results on that particular date. The goal is to continuously address deficiencies for improvement and to maintain positive outcomes on an ongoing basis.

A similar process is used for determining the operational and financial health of a corporation. The financial statements represent the current condition of an organization as a whole for a period of time. Probing, testing, and spot-checking efforts are conducted on a number of its parts to verify areas of strength and to pinpoint weaknesses. Action plans for improvement may then be prescribed to address substandard line items going forward.

7.3.1 Horizontal analysis

Important information can result from looking at changes in the same financial statement over time, both in terms of dollar amounts and percentage differences. Comparative financial statements place two years (or more) of the same statement side by side. **A horizontal analysis** involves noting the increases and decreases both in the amount and in the percentage of each line item. The earlier year is typically used as the base year for calculating increases or decreases in amounts.

A horizontal analysis of a firm's 2018 and 2019 income statements appears to the left. The first two columns show income statement amounts for two consecutive years. The amount and percentage differences for each line are listed in the final two columns, respectively.

The presentation of the changes from year to year for each line item can be analyzed to see where positive progress is occuring over time, such as increases in revenue and profit and decreases in cost. Conversely, less favorable readings may be isolated using this approach and investigated further.

Jonick Company Statement of Cash Flows For the Years Ended December 31, 2019 and 2018				
	2019	**2018**		
Sales	$994,000	$828,000	166,000	20.0%
Cost of merchandise sold	414,000	393,000	21,000	5.3%
Gross Profit	$580,000	$435,000	145,000	33.3%
Operating Expenses:				
Salaries expense	$77,000	$64,000	13,000	20.3%
Rent expense	63,000	52,000	11,000	21.2%
Insurance expense	56,000	46,000	10,000	21.7%
Supplies expense	49,000	41,000	8,000	19.5%
Advertising expense	42,000	35,000	7,000	20.0%
Depreciation expense	35,000	29,000	6,000	20.7%
Utilities expense	28,000	23,000	5,000	21.7%
Total operating expenses	348,000	290,000	58,000	20.0%
Net income from operations	$232,000	$145,000	87,000	60.0%
Other revenue and expenses				
Gain on sale of investments	$137,000	$186,000	(49,000)	-26.3%
Interest expense	(55,000)	(50,000)	5,000	10.0%
Income before income tax	$314,000	$281,000	33,000	11.7%
Income tax expense	66,000	50,000	16,000	32.0%
Net income	$248,000	$231,000	17,000	7.4%

In this sample comparative income statement, sales increased 20.0% from one year to the next, yet gross profit and income from operations increased quite a bit more at 33.3% and 60.0%, respectively. However, the final net income amount increased only 7.4%. Changes between the income from operations and net income lines can be reviewed to identify the reasons for the relatively lower increase in net income.

Likewise, the following is a horizontal analysis of a firm's 2018 and 2019 balance sheets. Again, the amount and percentage differences for each line are listed in the final two columns, respectively.

Jonick Company Comparative Balance Sheet December 31, 2019 and 2018				
	2019	**2018**	**Amount**	**Percentage**
	ASSETS			
Current assets:				
Cash	$373,000	$331,000	42,000	12.7%
Marketable securities	248,000	215,000	33,000	15.3%
Accounts receivable	108,000	91,000	17,000	18.7%
Merchandise Inventory	55,000	48,000	7,000	14.6%
Prepaid insurance	127,000	115,000	12,000	10.4%
Total current assets	$911,000	$800,000	111,000	13.9%
Long-term investments:				
Investment in equity securities	$1,946,000	$1,822,000	124,000	6.8%
Property, plant and equipment:				
Equipment (net of accumulated depreciation)	$87,000	$42,000	45,000	107.1%
Building (net of accumulated depreciation)	645,000	581,000	64,000	11.0%
Land	361,000	361,000		
Total property, plant and equipment	$1,093,000	$984,000	109,000	11.1%
Total assets	$3,950,000	$3,606,000	344,000	9.5%
	LIABILITIES			
Current liabilities:				
Accounts payable	$120,000	$109,000	11,000	10.1%
Salaries payable	244,000	222,000	22,000	9.9%
Total current liabilities	$364,000	$331,000	33,000	10.0%
Long-term liabilities:				
Mortgage note payable	$83,000	$83,000		
Bonds payable	828,000	745,000	83,000	11.1%
Total long-term liabilities	$911,000	$828,000	83,000	10.0%
Total liabilities	$1,275,000	$1,159,000	116,000	10.0%
	STOCKHOLDERS' EQUITY			
Preferred $1.50 stock, $20 par	$166,000	$166,000		
Common stock, $10 par	83,000	83,000		
Retained earnings	2,426,000	2,198,000	228,000	10.4%
Total stockholders' equity	$2,675,000	$2,447,000	228,000	9.3%
Total liabilities and stockholders' equity	$3,950,000	$3,606,000	344,000	9.5%

The horizontal analysis to the left uses a firm's 2018 and 2019 balance sheets. Again, the amount and percentage differences for each line are listed in the final two columns, respectively.

The increase of $344,000 in total assets represents a 9.5% change in the positive direction. Total liabilities increased by 10.0%, or $116,000, from year to year. The change in total stockholders' equity of $228,000 is a 9.3% increase. There seems to be a relatively consistent overall increase throughout the key totals on the balance sheet.

7.3.2 Vertical Analysis

A vertical analysis may also be conducted to each financial statement to report the percentage of each line item to a total amount. On the comparative income statement, the amount of each line item is divided by the sales number, which is the largest value.

Jonick Company Comparative Income Statement For the Years Ended December 31, 2019 and 2018				
	2019	**2019**	**2018**	**2018**
Sales	$994,000	100.0%	$828,000	100.0%
Cost of merchandise sold	414,000	41.6%	393,000	47.5%
Gross Profit	$580,000	58.4%	$435,000	52.5%
Operating Expenses:				
Salaries expense	$77,000	7.7%	$64,000	7.7%
Rent expense	63,000	6.3%	52,000	6.3%
Insurance expense	56,000	5.6%	46,000	5.6%
Supplies expense	49,000	4.9%	41,000	5.0%
Advertising expense	42,000	4.2%	35,000	4.2%
Depreciation expense	35,000	3.5%	29,000	3.5%
Utilities expense	28,000	2.8%	23,000	2.8%
Total operating expenses	348,000	35.0%	290,000	35.0%
Net income from operations	$232,000	23.3%	$145,000	17.5%
Other revenue and expenses				
Gain on sale of investments	$137,000	13.8%	$186,000	22.5%
Interest expense	(55,000)	5.5%	(50,000)	6.0%
Income before income tax	$314,000	31.6%	$281,000	33.9%
Income tax expense	66,000	6.6%	50,000	6.0%
Net income	$248,000	24.9%	$231,000	27.9%

On the comparative balance sheet, the amount of each line item is divided by the total assets amount, which is the largest value (and which equals total liabilities and stockholders' equity.)

Jonick Company Comparative Balance Sheet December 31, 2019 and 2018				
	2019	2019	2018	2018
ASSETS				
Current assets:				
Cash	$373,000	9.4%	$331,000	9.2%
Marketable securities	248,000	6.3%	215,000	6.0%
Accounts receivable	108,000	2.7%	91,000	2.5%
Merchandise Inventory	55,000	1.4%	48,000	1.3%
Prepaid insurance	127,000	3.2%	115,000	3.2%
Total current assets	$911,000	23.1%	$800,000	22.2%
Long-term investments:				
Investment in equity securities	$1,946,000	49.3%	$1,822,000	50.5%
Property, plant and equipment:				
Equipment (net of accumulated depreciation)	$87,000	2.2%	$42,000	1.2%
Building (net of accumulated depreciation)	645,000	16.3%	581,000	16.1%
Land	361,000	9.1%	361,000	10.0%
Total property, plant and equipment	$1,093,000	27.7%	$984,000	27.3%
Total assets	$3,950,000	100.0%	$3,606,000	100.0%
LIABILITIES				
Current liabilities:				
Accounts payable	$120,000	3.0%	$109,000	3.0%
Salaries payable	244,000	6.2%	222,000	6.2%
Total current liabilities	$364,000	9.2%	$331,000	9.2%
Long-term liabilities:				
Mortgage note payable	$83,000	2.1%	$83,000	2.3%
Bonds payable	828,000	21.0%	745,000	20.7%
Total long-term liabilities	$911,000	23.1%	$828,000	23.0%
Total liabilities	$1,275,000	32.3%	$1,159,000	32.1%
STOCKHOLDERS' EQUITY				
Preferred $1.50 stock, $20 par	$166,000	2.1%	$166,000	2.3%
Common stock, $10 par	83,000	4.2%	83,000	4.6%
Retained earnings	2,426,000	61.4%	2,198,000	61.0%
Total stockholders' equity	$2,675,000	67.7%	$2,447,000	67.9%
Total liabilities and stockholders' equity	$3,950,000	100.0%	$3,606,000	100.0%

On both financial statements, percentages are presented for two consecutive years so that the percent changes over time may be evaluated.

7.3.3 Common-size Statements

The use of percentages converts a company's dollar amounts on its financial statements into values that can be compared to other companies whose dollar amounts may be different.

Common-size statements include only the percentages that appear in either a horizontal or vertical analysis. They often are used to compare one company to another or to compare a company to other standards, such as industry averages.

The following compares the performance of two companies using a vertical analysis on their income statements for 2019.

The common-size income statements for Jonick Corporation and Schneider Corporation show that Schneider has lower gross profit and net income from operations percentages to sales. Yet Schneider has a higher overall net income due to much greater gains on the sale of investments.

Jonick Company Comparative Balance Sheet For the Year Ended December 31, 2019		
	Jonick	**Schneider**
ASSETS		
Sales	100%	100%
Cost of merchandise sold	41.6%	47.5%
Gross Profit	58.4%	52.5%
Total operating expenses	35.0%	35.0%
Net income from operations	23.3%	17.5%
Other revenue and expenses		
Gain on sale of investments	13.8%	22.5%
Interest expense	5.5%	6.0%
Income before income tax	31.6%	33.9%
Income tax expense	6.6%	6.0%
Net income	24.9%	27.9%

7.3.4 Ratio Analysis

Horizontal and vertical analyses present data about each line item on the financial statements in a uniform way across the board. Additional insight about a corporation's financial performance and health can be revealed by calculating targeted ratios that use specific amounts that relate to one another. Again, as stated earlier, no ratio is meaningful by itself; it needs to be compared to something, such as desired or expected results, previous results, other companies' results, or industry standards. There are a series of ratios that are commonly used by corporations. These will be classified as liquidity, solvency, profitability, and return on investment.

Liquidity analysis looks at a company's available cash and its ability to quickly convert other current assets into cash to meet short-term operating needs such as paying expenses and debts as they become due. Cash is the most liquid asset; other current assets such as accounts receivable and inventory may also generate cash in the near future.

Creditors and investors often use liquidity ratios to gauge how well a business is performing. Since creditors are primarily concerned with a company's ability to repay its debts, they want to see if there is enough cash and equivalents available to meet the current portions of debt.

Six liquidity ratios follow. The current and quick ratios evaluate a company's ability to pay its current liabilities. Accounts receivable turnover and number of days' sales in receivables look at the firm's ability to collect its accounts receivable. Inventory turnover and number of days' sales in inventory gauge how effectively a company manages its inventory.

CURRENT RATIO

What it measures: The ability of a firm to pay its current liabilities with its cash and/or other current assets that can be converted to cash within a relatively short period of time.

Interpretation: This company has 2.5 times more in current assets than it has in current liabilities. The premise is that current assets are liquid; that is, they can be converted to cash in a relatively short period of time to cover short-term debt. A current ratio is judged as satisfactory on a relative basis. If the company prefers to have a lot of debt and not use its own money, it may consider 2.5 to be too high – too little debt for the amount of assets it has. If a company is conservative in terms of debt and wants to have as little as possible, 2.5 may be considered low – too little asset value for the amount of liabilities it has. For an average tolerance for debt, a current ratio of 2.5 may be considered satisfactory. The point is that whether the current ratio is considered acceptable is subjective and will vary from company to company.

$$\text{Calculation}: \frac{\text{Current assests}}{\text{Current liabilities}} = \frac{911{,}000}{364{,}000} = 2.5$$

Jonick Company Comparative Balance Sheet December 31, 2019 and 2018	
	2019
ASSETS	
Current assets:	
Cash	$373,000
Marketable securities	248,000
Accounts receivable	108,000
Merchandise Inventory	55,000
Prepaid insurance	127,000
Total current assets	$911,000

Jonick Company Comparative Balance Sheet December 31, 2019 and 2018	
	2019
ASSETS	
Current liabilities:	
Accounts payable	$120,000
Salaries payable	244,000
Total current liabilities	$364,000

QUICK RATIO

What it measures: the ability of a firm to pay its current liabilities with its cash and other current assets that can be converted to cash within an extremely short period of time. Quick assets include cash, accounts receivable, and marketable securities but do not include inventory or prepaid items.

Interpretation: This company has 2.0 times more in its highly liquid current assets, which include cash, marketable securities, and accounts receivable, than it has in current liabilities. The premise is these current assets are the most liquid and can be immediately converted to cash to cover short-term debt. Current assets such as inventory and prepaid items would take too long to sell to be considered quick assets. A quick ratio is judged as satisfactory on a relative basis. If the company prefers to have a lot of debt and not use its own money, it may consider 2.0 to be too high – too little debt for the amount of assets it has. If a company is conservative in terms of debt and wants to have as little as possible, 2.0 may be considered low – too little asset value for the amount of liabilities it has. For an average tolerance for debt, a current ratio of 2.0 may be considered satisfactory. The point is that whether the quick ratio is considered acceptable is subjective and will vary from company to company.

$$\text{Calculation}: \frac{\text{Quick assets}}{\text{Current liabilities}} = \frac{373{,}000 + 248{,}000 + 108{,}000}{364{,}000} = 2.0$$

Jonick Company Comparative Balance Sheet December 31, 2019 and 2018	
	2019
ASSETS	
Current assets:	
Cash	$373,000
Marketable securities	248,000
Accounts receivable	108,000
Merchandise Inventory	55,000
Prepaid insurance	127,000
Total current assets	$911,000

Jonick Company Comparative Balance Sheet December 31, 2019 and 2018	
	2019
ASSETS	
Current liabilities:	
Accounts payable	$120,000
Salaries payable	244,000
Total current liabilities	$364,000
Merchandise Inventory	55,000

ACCOUNTS RECEIVABLE TURNOVER

What it measures: the number of times the entire amount of a firm's accounts receivable, which is the monies owed to the company by its customers, is collected in a year.

Interpretation: *The higher the better.*

The more often customers pay off their invoices, the more cash available to the firm to pay bills and debts and less possibility that customers will never pay at all.

$$\text{Calculation}: \frac{\text{Sales}}{\text{Average accounts receivable}} = \frac{994{,}000}{(108{,}000 + 91{,}000)\ /2} = 10.0$$

Jonick Company Comparative Income Statement For the Years Ended December 31, 2019 and 2018		
	2018	2019
ASSETS		
Sales	$994,000	$828,000
Cost of merchandise sold	414,000	393,000
Gross Profit	$580,000	$435,000

Jonick Company Comparative Balance Sheet December 31, 2019 and 2018	
	2019
ASSETS	
Current assets:	
Cash	$373,000
Marketable securities	248,000
Accounts receivable	108,000
Merchandise Inventory	55,000
Prepaid insurance	127,000
Total current assets	$911,000

NUMBER OF DAYS' SALES IN RECEIVABLES

What it measures: the number of days it typically takes for customers to pay on account.

Interpretation: *The lower the better.*

The less time it takes customers to pay off their invoices, the more cash available to the firm to pay bills and debts and less possibility that customers will never pay at all.

$$\text{Calculation}: \frac{\text{Average account receivable}}{\text{Sales}\ /\ 365} = \frac{(108{,}000 + 91{,}000)\ /\ 2}{994{,}000\ /365} = 36.5\ \text{days}$$

The denominator of "Sales / 365" represents the dollar amount of sales per day in a 365-day year.

Jonick Company Comparative Balance Sheet December 31, 2019 and 2018		
	2019	2018
ASSETS		
Current assets:		
Cash	$373,000	$331,000
Marketable securities	248,000	215,000
Accounts receivable	108,000	91,000
Merchandise Inventory	55,000	48,000
Prepaid insurance	127,000	115,000
Total current assets	$911,000	$800,000

Jonick Company Comparative Income Statement For the Years Ended December 31, 2019 and 2018		
	2019	2018
ASSETS		
Sales	$994,000	$828,000
Cost of merchandise sold	414,000	393,000
Gross Profit	$580,000	$435,000

INVENTORY TURNOVER

What it measures: the number of times the average amount of a firm's inventory is sold in a year.

Interpretation: *The higher the better.*

The more often inventory is sold, the more cash generated by the firm to pay bills and debts. Inventory turnover is also a measure of a firm's operational performance. If the company's line of business is to sell merchandise, the more often it does so, the more operationally successful it is.

$$\text{Calculation}: \frac{\text{Cost of merchandise}}{\text{Average inventory}} = \frac{414{,}000}{(55{,}000 + 48{,}000)/2} = 8.0$$

Jonick Company Comparative Income Statement For the Years Ended December 31, 2019 and 2018		
	2019	2018
ASSETS		
Sales	$994,000	$828,000
Cost of merchandise sold	414,000	393,000
Gross Profit	$580,000	$435,000

Jonick Company Comparative Balance Sheet December 31, 2019 and 2018		
	2019	2018
ASSETS		
Current assets:		
Cash	$373,000	$331,000
Marketable securities	248,000	215,000
Accounts receivable	108,000	91,000
Merchandise Inventory	55,000	48,000
Prepaid insurance	127,000	115,000
Total current assets	$911,000	$800,000

NUMBER OF DAYS' SALES IN INVENTORY

What it measures: the number of days it typically takes for a typical batch of inventory to be sold.

Interpretation: *The lower the better.*

The less time it takes for the inventory in stock to be sold, the more cash available to the firm to pay bills and debts. There is also less of a need to pay storage, insurance, and other holding costs and less of a chance that inventory on hand will become outdated and less attractive to customers.

Jonick Company Comparative Balance Sheet December 31, 2019 and 2018		
	2019	2018
ASSETS		
Current assets:		
Cash	$373,000	$331,000
Marketable securities	248,000	215,000
Accounts receivable	108,000	91,000
Merchandise Inventory	55,000	48,000
Prepaid insurance	127,000	115,000
Total current assets	$911,000	$800,000

Jonick Company Comparative Balance Sheet For the Years Ended December 31, 2019 and 2018		
	2019	**2018**
Current assets:		
Sales	$994,000	$828,000
Cost of merchandise sold	414,000	393,000
Gross Profit	$580,000	$435,000

Solvency analysis evaluates a company's future financial stability by looking at its ability to pay its long-term debts. Both investors and creditors are interested in the solvency of a company. Investors want to make sure the company is in a strong financial position and can continue to grow, generate profits, distribute dividends, and provide a return on investment. Creditors are concerned with being repaid and look to see that a company can generate sufficient revenues to cover both short and long-term obligations. Four solvency ratios follow.

RATIO OF LIABILITIES TO STOCKHOLDERS' EQUITY

What it measures: the ability of a company to pay its creditors.

$$\text{Calculation}: \frac{\text{Total liabilities}}{\text{Total stockholder's equity}} = \frac{1{,}275{,}000}{2{,}675{,}000} = 5$$

Jonick Company Comparative Balance Sheet December 31, 2019 and 2018	
	2019
Current liabilities:	
Accounts payable	$120,000
Salaries payable	244,000
Total current liabilities	$364,000
Long-term liabilities:	
Mortgage note payable	$83,000
Bonds payable	828,000
Total long-term liabilities	$911,000
Total liabilities	$1,275,000
STOCKHOLDERS' EQUITY	
Preferred $1.50 stock, $20 par	$166,000
Common stock, $10 par	83,000
Retained earnings	2,426,000
Total stockholders' equity	$2,675,000
Total liabilities and stockholders' equity	$3,950,000

Interpretation: *Favorable vs. unfavorable results are based on company's level of tolerance for debt*

Assets are acquired either by investments from stockholders or through borrowing from other parties. Companies that are adverse to debt would prefer a lower ratio. Companies that prefer to use "other people's money" to finance assets would favor a higher ratio. In this example, the company's debt is about half of what its stockholders' equity is. Approximately 1/3 of the assets are paid for through borrowing.

RATIO OF FIXED ASSETS TO LONG-TERM LIABILITIES

What it measures: the availability of investments in property, plant, and equipment that are financed by long-term debt and to generate earnings that may be used to pay off long-term debt. The denominator of "Cost of merchandise sold / 365" represents the dollar amount of cost per day in a 365-day year.

$$\text{Calculation}: \frac{\text{Book value of fixed assets}}{\text{Long-term liabilities}} = \frac{1{,}093{,}000}{911{,}000} = 1.2$$

Jonick Company Comparative Balance Sheet December 31, 2019 and 2018	
	2019
ASSETS	
Property, plant and equipment:	
Equipment (net of accumulated depreciation)	$87,000
Building (net of accumulated depreciation)	645,000
Land	361,000
Total property, plant and equipment	$1,093,000

Jonick Company Comparative Balance Sheet December 31, 2019 and 2018	
	2019
LIABILITIES	
Long-term liabilities:	
Mortgage note payable	$83,000
Bonds payable	828,000
Total long-term liabilities	$911,000

Interpretation: *The higher the better.*

The more that has been invested in fixed assets, which are often financed by long- term debt, the more potential there is for a firm to perform well operationally and generate the cash it needs to make debt payments.

NUMBER OF TIMES INTEREST CHARGES ARE EARNED

What it measures: the ability to generate sufficient pre-tax income to pay interest charges on debt.

$$\text{Calculation}: \frac{\text{Income before income tax} + \text{interest expense}}{\text{Interest expense}} = \frac{314{,}000 + 55{,}000}{55{,}000} = 6.7$$

Jonick Company Comparative Income Statement For the Years Ended December 31, 2019 and 2018	
	2019
ASSETS	
Other revenue and expenses	
Gain on sale of investments	$137,000
Interest expense	(55,000)
Income before income tax	$314,000
Income tax expense	66,000
Net income	$248,000

Since interest expense had been deducted in arriving at income before income tax on the income statement, it is added back in the calculation of the ratio.

Interpretation: *The higher the better.*

The ratio looks at income that is available to pay interest expense after all other expenses have been covered by the sales that were generated. The number of times anything is earned is always more favorable when it is higher since it impacts the margin of safety and the ability to pay as earnings fluctuate, particularly if they decline.

NUMBER OF TIMES PREFERRED DIVIDENDS ARE EARNED

What it measures: the ability to generate sufficient net income to pay dividends to preferred stockholders

$$\text{Calculation}: \frac{\text{Net income}}{\text{Preferred dividends}} = \frac{248{,}000}{12{,}000} = 20.7$$

Jonick Company Comparative Income Statement For the Years Ended December 31, 2019 and 2018	
	2019
Income before income tax	$314,000
Income tax expense	66,000
Net income	$248,000

Jonick Company Comparative Retained Earnings Statement For the Years Ended December 31, 2019 and 2018	
	2019
Retained earnings, beginning of year	$2,198,000
Net income	248,000
Less: Prefered stock dividends	12,000
Common stock dividends	8,000
Increase in retained earnings	20,000
Retained earnings, end of year	$2,426,000

Interpretation: *The higher the better.*

The ratio looks at net income that is available to pay preferred dividends, which are paid on an after-tax basis, and after all expenses have been covered by the sales that were generated. The number of times anything is earned is always more favorable when it is higher since it impacts the margin of safety and the ability to pay as earnings fluctuate

Profitability analysis evaluates a corporation's operational ability to generate revenues that exceed associated costs in a given period of time.

Profitability ratios may incorporate the concept of **leverage,** which is how effectively one financial element generates a progressively larger return on another element. Thes first five ratios that follow look at how well the assets, liabilities, or equities in the denominator of each ratio are able produce a relatively high value in the respective numerator. Ths final two ratios evaluate how well sales translate into gross profit and net income.

ASSET TURNOVER

What it measures: how effectively a company uses its assets to generate revenue.

$$\text{Calculation}: \frac{\text{Sale}}{\text{Average total assets}} = \frac{994{,}000}{(3{,}950{,}000 - 1{,}946{,}000 + 3{,}606{,}000 - 1{,}822{,}000)\,/\,2} = 52.5\%$$

(excluding long - term investments)

Long-term investments are not included in the calculation because they are not productivity assets used to generate sales to customers.

Jonick Company Comparative Income Statement For the Years Ended December 31, 2019 and 2018		
		2019
Sales	$994,000	$828,000
Cost of merchandise sold	414,000	393,000
Gross Profit	$580,000	$435,000

Jonick Company Comparative Income Statement December 31, 2019 and 2018		
	2019	**2018**
Total current assets	$911,000	$800,000
Long-term investments:		
Investment in equity securities	$1,946,000	$1,822,000
Property, plant and equipment:		
Total property, plant and equipment	$1,093,000	$984,000
Total assets	$3,950,000	$3,606,000

Interpretation: *The higher the better.*

The ratio looks at the value of most of a company's assets and how well they are leveraged to produce sales. The goal of owning the assets is that they should generate revenue that ultimately results in cash flow and profit.

RETURN ON TOTAL ASSETS

What it measures: how effectively a company uses its assets to generate net income.

$$\text{Calculation:}\ \frac{\text{Net income} + \text{Interest expense}}{\text{Average total assets}} = \frac{248{,}000 + 55{,}000}{(3{,}950{,}000 + 3{,}606{,}000)/2} = 8.0\%$$

Interest expense relates to financed assets, so it is added back to net income since how the assets are paid for should be irrelevant.

Jonick Company Comparative Income Statement For the Years Ended December 31, 2019 and 2018	
	2019
Other revenue and expenses	$137,000
Gain on sale of investments	(55,000)
Interest expense	
	$314,000
Income before income tax	66,000
Income tax expense	$248,000
Net income	$984,000

Jonick Company Comparative Balance Sheet December 31, 2019 and 2018		
	2019	**2018**
ASSETS		
Total current assets	$911,000	$800,000
Long-term investments:		
Investment in equity securities	$1,946,000	$1,822,000
Property, plant and equipment:		
Total property, plant and equipment	$1,093,000	$984,000
Total assets	$3,950,000	$3,606,000

Interpretation: *The higher the better.*

The ratio looks at the value of a company's assets and how well they are leveraged to produce net income. The goal of owning the assets is that they should generate cash flow and profit.

RETURN ON STOCKHOLDERS' EQUITY

What it measures: how effectively a company uses the investment of its owners to generate net income.

$$\text{Calculation}: \frac{\text{Net income}}{\text{Average total stockholder's equity}} = \frac{248{,}000}{(2{,}675{,}000 + 2{,}447{,}000)/2} = 9.7\%$$

Jonick Company Comparative Balance Sheet For the Years Ended December 31, 2019 and 2018	
	2019
Income before income tax	$314,000
Income tax expense	66,000
Net income	$248,000

Jonick Company Comparative Balance Sheet December 31, 2019 and 2018		
	2018	**2019**
STOCKHOLDERS' EQUITY		
Preferred $1.50 stock, $20 par	$166,000	$166,000
Common stock, $10 par	83,000	83,000
Retained earnings	2,426,000	2,198,000
Total stockholders' equity	$2,675,000	$2,447,000
Total liabilities and stockholders' equity	$3,950,000	$3,606,000

Interpretation: *The higher the better.*

The ratio looks at how well the investments of preferred and common stockholders are leveraged to produce net income. One goal of investing in a corporation is for stockholders to accumulate additional wealth as a result of the company making a profit.

RETURN ON COMMON STOCKHOLDERS' EQUITY (ROE)

What it measures: how effectively a company uses the investment of its common stockholders to generate net income; overall performance of a business.

$$\text{Calculation: } \frac{\text{Net income - Preferred dividends}}{\text{Average common stockholder's } equity} = \frac{248{,}000-12{,}000}{(83{,}000+2{,}426{,}000+83{,}000+2{,}198{,}000)/2} = 9.9\%$$

Preferred dividends are removed from the net income amount since they are distributed prior to common shareholders having any claim on company profits.

In this example, shareholders saw a 9.9% return on their investment. The result indicates that every dollar of common shareholder's equity earned about $.10 this year.

Jonick Company Comparative Balance Sheet For the Years Ended December 31, 2019 and 2018	
	2019
Income before income tax	$314,000
Income tax expense	66,000
Net income	$248,000

Jonick Company Comparative Balance Sheet For the Years Ended December 31, 2019 and 2018	
	2019
Retained earnings, beginning of year	$2,198,000
Net income	248,000
Less: Prefered stock dividends	12,000
Common stock dividends	8,000
Increase in retained earnings	20,000
Retained earnings, end of year	$2,426,000

Interpretation: *The higher the better.*

The ratio looks at how well the investments of preferred and common stockholders are leveraged to produce net income. One goal of investing in a corporation is for stockholders to accumulate additional wealth as a result of the company making a profit.

Jonick Company Comparative Balance Sheet December 31, 2019 and 2018		
	2019	**2018**
STOCKHOLDERS' EQUITY		
Preferred $1.50 stock, $20 par	$166,000	$166,000
Common stock, $10 par	83,000	83,000
Retained earnings	2,426,000	2,198,000
Total stockholders' equity	$2,675,000	$2,447,000
Total liabilities and stockholders' equity	$3,950,000	$3,606,000

EARNINGS PER SHARE ON COMMON STOCK

What it measures: the dollar amount of net income associated with each share of common stock outstanding.

$$\text{Calculation}: \frac{\text{Net income - Preferred stock dividends}}{\text{Number of shares of common stock outstanding}} = \frac{248{,}000-12{,}000}{83{,}000/\$10} = \$28.43\%$$

Preferred dividends are removed from the net income amount since they are distributed prior to common shareholders having any claim on company profits.

The number of common shares outstanding is determined by dividing the common stock dollar amount by the par value per share given.

Jonick Company Comparative Balance Sheet For the Years Ended December 31, 2019 and 2018	
	2019
Income before income tax	$314,000
Income tax expense	66,000
Net income	$248,000

Jonick Company Comparative Retained Earnings Statement For the Years Ended December 31, 2019 and 2018	
	2019
Retained earnings, beginning of year	$2,198,000
Net income	248,000
Less: Prefered stock dividends	12,000
Common stock dividends	8,000
Increase in retained earnings	20,000
Retained earnings, end of year	$2,426,000

Jonick Company Comparative Balance Sheet December 31, 2019 and 2018	
STOCKHOLDERS' EQUITY	
Preferred $1.50 stock, $20 par	$166,000
Common stock, $10 par	83,000
Retained earnings	2,426,000
Total stockholders' equity	$2,675,000
Total liabilities and stockholders' equity	$3,950,000

Interpretation: *The higher the better.*

The ratio is critical in reporting net income at a micro level – per share – rather than in total. A greater net income amount will result in a higher earnings per share given a fixed number of shares.

GROSS PROFIT PERCENTAGE

What it measures: how effectively a company generates gross profit from sales or controls cost of merchandise sold.

$$\text{Calculation}: \frac{\text{Gross profit}}{\text{Sales}} = \frac{580{,}000}{944{,}000} = 58.4\%$$

Jonick Company Comparative Balance Sheet For the Years Ended December 31, 2019 and 2018	
	2019
Sales	$994,000
Cost of merchandise sold	414,000
Gross Profit	$580,000
Net income	$248,000

Interpretation: *The higher the better.*

The ratio looks at the main cost of a merchandising business – what it pays for the items it sells. The lower the cost of merchandise sold, the higher the gross profit, which can then be used to pay operating expenses and to generate profit.

PROFIT MARGIN

What it measures: the amount of net income earned with each dollar of sales generated.

$$\text{Calculation}: \frac{\text{Net Income}}{\text{Sales}} = \frac{248{,}000}{944{,}000} = 24.9\%$$

Jonick Company Comparative Balance Sheet For the Years Ended December 31, 2019 and 2018	
	2019
Sales	$994,000
Cost of merchandise sold	414,000
Gross Profit	$580,000
Net income	$248,000

Interpretation: *The higher the better.*

The ratio shows what percentage of sales are left over after all expenses are paid by the business.

Finally, a Dupont analysis breaks down three components of the return on equity ratio to explain how a company can increase its return for investors. It may be evaluated on a relative basis, comparing a company's Dupont results with either another company's results, with industry standards, or with expected or desired results.

DUPONT ANALYSIS

What it measures: a company's ability to increase its return on equity by analyzing what is causing the current ROE.

Calculation: Proft margin x Total asset turnover x Financial leverage

OR

(Net income / Sales) x (Sales / Average total assets) x (Total assets / Total equity)

Example of a simple comparison of two similar companies with the same return on investment of 30%.

	Profit margin	x Total asset turnover	x Financial leverage
Company A	.30	.5	2.0
Company B	.15	4.0	.5

Results indicate that Company A has a higher profit margin and greater financial leverage. Its weaker position on total asset turnover as compared to Company B is what brings down its ROE. The analysis of the components of ROE provides insight of areas to address for improvement.

Interpretation: Investors are not looking for large or small output numbers from this model. Investors want to analyze and pinpoint what is causing the current ROE to identify areas for improvement. This model breaks down the return on equity ratio to explain how companies can increase their return for investors.

Return-on-investment analysis looks at actual distributions of current earnings or expected future earnings.

DIVIDENDS PER SHARE ON COMMON STOCK

What it measures: the dollar amount of dividends associated with each share of common stock outstanding.

$$\text{Calculation}: \frac{\text{Common stock dividends}}{\text{Number of shares of common stock outstanding}} = \frac{8{,}000}{83{,}000\ \$10} = \$0.96$$

The number of common shares outstanding is determined by dividing the common stock dollar amount by the par value per share given.

Jonick Company Comparative Retained Earnings Statement For the Years Ended December 31, 2019 and 2018	
	2019
Retained earnings, beginning of year	$2,198,000
Net income	248,000
Less: Prefered stock dividends	12,000
Common stock dividends	8,000
Increase in retained earnings	20,000
Retained earnings, end of year	$2,426,000

Jonick Company Comparative Balance Sheet December 31, 2019 and 2018	
	2019
STOCKHOLDERS' EQUITY	
Net income	248,000
Preferred $1.50 stock, $20 par	$166,000
Common stock, $10 par	83,000
Retained earnings	2,426,000
Total stockholders' equity	$2,675,000
Total liabilities and stockholders' equity	$3,950,000

Interpretation: *If stockholders desire maximum dividends payouts, then the higher the better. However, some stockholders prefer to receive minimal or no dividends since dividend payouts are taxable or because they prefer that their returns be reinvested. Then lower payouts would be better.*

The ratio reports distributions of net income in the form of cash at a micro level – per share – rather than in total. A greater dividends per share amount will result from a higher net income amount given a fixed number of shares.

DIVIDENDS YIELD

What it measures: the rate of return to common stockholders from cash dividends.

Assume that the market price per share is $70.00.

$$\text{Calculation}: \frac{\text{Common dividends / Common shares outstanding}}{\text{Market price per share}} = \frac{\$0.96}{\$70.00} = 1.4\%$$

The number of common shares outstanding is determined by dividing the common stock dollar amount by the par value per share given.

Jonick Company Comparative Retained Earnings Statement For the Years Ended December 31, 2019 and 2018	
Retained earnings, beginning of year	**$2,198,000**
Net income	248,000
Less: Prefered stock dividends	12,000
Common stock dividends	8,000
Increase in retained earnings	20,000
Retained earnings, end of year	$2,426,000

Jonick Company Comparative Balance Sheet December 31, 2019 and 2018	
	2019
Preferred $1.50 stock, $20 par	$166,000
Common stock, $10 par	83,000
Retained earnings	2,426,000
Total stockholders' equity	$2,675,000
Total liabilities and stockholders' equity	$3,950,000

Interpretation: *If stockholders desire maximum dividend payouts, then the higher the better. However, some stockholders prefer to receive minimal or no dividends since dividend payouts are taxable or because they prefer that their returns be reinvested. Then lower payouts would be better.*

The ratio compares common stock distributions to the current market price. This conversion allows comparison between different companies and may be of particular interest to investors who wish to maximize dividend revenue.

PRICE EARNINGS RATIO

What it measures: the prospects of future earnings. Assume that the market price per share is $70.00.

$$\text{Calculation}: \frac{\text{Market price pershare}}{\text{Common stock earnings per share}} = \frac{\$70.00}{\$28.43} = 2.5$$

Recall that earnings per share is (Net income – Preferred stock dividends) / Number of shares of common stock.

Jonick Company Comparative Retained Earnings Statement For the Years Ended December 31, 2019 and 2018	
	2019
Retained earnings, beginning of year	$2,198,000
Net income	248,000
Less: Prefered stock dividends	12,000
Common stock dividends	8,000
Increase in retained earnings	20,000
Retained earnings, end of year	$2,426,000

Jonick Company Comparative Balance Sheet December 31, 2019 and 2018	
	2019
STOCKHOLDERS' EQUITY	
Preferred $1.50 stock, $20 par	$166,000
Common stock, $10 par	83,000
Retained earnings	2,426,000
Total stockholders' equity	$2,675,000
Total liabilities and stockholders' equity	$3,950,000

Interpretation: *The higher the better.*

The more the market price exceeds earnings, the greater the prospect of value growth, particularly if this ratio increases over time.

All the analytical measures discussed, taken individually and collectively, are used to evaluate a company's operating performance and financial strength. They are particularly informative when compared over time to expected or desired standards. The ability to learn from the financial statements makes the processes of collecting, analyzing, summarizing, and reporting financial information all worthwhile.

7.4 SUMMARY

Most of this document has been a discussion of **financial** accounting, which relates to preparing the four financial statements - the income statement, retained earnings statement, balance sheet, and statement of cash flows – for a company as a whole. These reports are prepared according to generally accepted accounting principles (GAAP) to ensure consistency from company to company and period to period. The financial statements are published on a regular basis, such as monthly or annually, primarily for external users such a stockholders, creditors, investors, and government/tax entities.

7.5 ACCOUNTING AS A PROFESSION

At this point you have seen the process of accounting in terms of identifying, recording, and summarizing financial transactions for a business. Much of what you have learned so far involves the basics of financial accounting, which involves producing reports to inform external groups – investors, boards of directors, creditors, and government/tax agencies – about the company's financial status. It is an excellent start, but the scope of the accounting profession is much more broad and diverse and is covered in other textbooks.

A good stopping point for this text is to summarize the value of the material in this book and to look forward to what you might learn at more advanced levels. We'll do this by briefly discussing the different areas of practice that an accounting professional may become involved in.

First, it is fair to say that any business person should have a background in accounting as part of their general business management skills. Accounting is the language of business, and professionals will necessarily plan, make decisions, and evaluate the progress of their firms based on financial information. A sound understanding of accounting adds to a professional's credentials and effectiveness. Whether you work for a company or own your own business, you will need to analyze and act on information prepared through the accounting process.

You may also choose a career in accounting, where you have the opportunity to work in almost any industry imaginable. An accountant is a professional who performs accounting functions such as financial statement analysis and audits. Accountants may be employed by an accounting firm, work for a company with an internal accounting department, or set up an individual practice of their own. There are five major fields of accounting. The kind of work these professionals do is determined by the field they choose:

Management accountants provide company executives with the information and analyses they need to make decisions related to general company operations. Companies also use this information to prepare the financial reports that are distributed to shareholders, creditors, regulatory agencies and the Internal Revenue Service (IRS).

Public Accountants are part of the broadest accounting field. They provide accounting, tax, auditing and/or consulting services to corporations, individuals, governments, and nonprofits. Public accountants assist individuals and corporations with a variety of financial tasks, including computing and filing income taxes, reviewing financial records, staying up to date on fiscal regulations, creating financial statements and providing general accounting advice.

A certified public accountant, or CPA, is a person who has passed the difficult CPA Exam administered by the American Institute of Certified Public Accountants (AICPA) and has been licensed by one of the states in the U.S. Most state boards of accountancy, including Georgia, require candidates to have 150 college credits in order to sit for the CPA Exam. The **CPA's** license is then renewed if the state's requirements continue to be met, including earning continuing professional education credits annually.

Internal auditors review a company's financial documents for accuracy and compliance with laws and regulations. They examine the internal controls of the organization and attempt to discover and prevent inaccuracy, mismanagement and fraud. They identify potential risks and propose preventative measures for increased operational efficiency, risk management and regulatory compliance.

Forensic accountants are examiners who analyze financial records to ensure they are compliant with standards and laws. Conversely, forensic accountants are brought in to uncover errors, omissions or outright fraud. They typically work in either investigation or litigation support.

Government accountants/auditors are employed by federal, state and local governments. They do the books for government agencies and manage budgets, expenses and revenues at the federal, state, county and city levels for organizations such as the military, law enforcement and public schools. They also audit businesses and individuals who are required to conform to government regulations or pay tax.

The following Accounts Summary Table includes all accounts covered in this document.

ACCOUNTS SUMMARY TABLE

ACCOUNT TYPE	ACCOUNTS	TO INCREASE	TO DECREASE	NORMAL BALANCE	FINANCIAL STATEMENT	CLOSE OUT?
Asset (*temporary)	Cash Accounts Receivable Notes Receivable Supplies Prepaid Rent Prepaid Insurance Prepaid Taxes Merchandise Inventory Purchases * Freight-In * Equipment Furnishings Truck Land Building Patent Copyright Trademark Goodwill Organization Costs Investment in ABC Stock Investment in ABC Bonds	debit	credit	debit	Balance Sheet	NO
Contra Asset (*temporary)	Estimated Inventory Returns Purchases Returns * Purchases Discounts * Allowance for Doubtful Accounts Accumulated Depreciation	credit	debit	credit	Balance Sheet	NO

ACCOUNT TYPE	ACCOUNTS	TO INCREASE	TO DECREASE	NORMAL BALANCE	FINANCIAL STATEMENT	CLOSE OUT?
Liability	Accounts Payable Wages Payable Salaries Payable Taxes Payable Interest Payable Unearned Fees Unearned Rent Note Payable Sales Tax Payable Federal Income Tax Payable State Income Tax Payable Social Security Tax Payable Medicare Tax Payable Federal Unemployment Tax Payable State Unemployment Tax Payable Bonds Payable Premium on Bonds Payable Cash Dividends Payable	credit	debit	credit	Balance Sheet	NO
Contra Liability	Discount on Bonds Payable	debit	credit	debit	Balance Sheet	NO
Stockholders' Equity	Common Stock (CS) Paid-in Capital in Excess of Par - CS Preferred Stock (PS) Paid-in Capital in Excess of Par - PS Paid-in Capital from Sale of Treasury Stock Stock Dividends Distributable Retained Earnings Unrealized Holding Gain - Available-for-Sale Securities	credit	debit	credit	Balance Sheet	NO

ACCOUNT TYPE	ACCOUNTS	TO INCREASE	TO DECREASE	NORMAL BALANCE	FINANCIAL STATEMENT	CLOSE OUT?
Contra Stockholders' Equity	Treasury Stock Unrealized Holding Loss - Available-for-Sale Securities	debit	credit	debit	Balance Sheet	NO
Contra Stockholders' Equity	Cash Dividends Stock Dividends	debit	credit	debit	Retained Earnings Statement	YES
Revenue or Gain	Fees Earned Rent Revenue Sales Interest Revenue Dividends Revenue Investment Income Gain on Disposal of Fixed Asset Gain on Sale of Investment Gain on Redemption of Bonds Unrealized Holding Gain - Net Income	credit	debit	credit	Income Statement	YES
Contra Revenue	Allowance for Sales Returns Sales Discounts Sales Discounts Not Taken Sales Returns	debit	credit	debit	Income Statement	YES

ACCOUNT TYPE	ACCOUNTS	TO INCREASE	TO DECREASE	NORMAL BALANCE	FINANCIAL STATEMENT	CLOSE OUT?
Expense or Loss	Cost of Merchandise Sold Wages Expense Salaries Expense Rent Expense Utilities Expense Supplies Expense Insurance Expense Advertising Expense Maintenance Expense Depreciation Expense Taxes Expense Interest Expense Truck Expense Delivery Expense Bank Card Expense Bad Debt Expense Payroll Tax Expense Miscellaneous Expense Loss on Disposal of Fixed Asset Loss on Sale of Investment Loss on Redemption of Bonds Unrealized Holding Loss - Net Income	debit	credit	debit	Income Statement	YES

INDEX

A

Ability 312, 320

Account 2, 4-9, 11, 16-18, 23-27, 31-34, 5-98, 106-108, 111, 116, 132-149, 152, 207, 209-227, 231-236, 238-239, 243, 245-247, 249-252, 261, 263, 266, 268-275

Accrual 49

Allowance 142, 144-145, 147, 167, 174-178

Amount 4-5, 7-8, 18, 30, 34, 58-59, 61-62, 64-65, 67-69, 73, 76-77, 81, 83-84, 86, 97-98, 108-109, 117, 126, 135-136, 142, 144, 153, 155-156, 159, 161, 171, 173, 178, 188, 192, 194, 197, 202-203, 205-207, 214, 217, 222, 226, 228, 230, 234-236, 238, 240-242, 244-249, 251-254, 257, 267, 277, 287, 289-290, 292, 295, 300-301, 303, 309, 325, 328

Annual 83, 204, 236

Assets 2, 28-29, 32, 36, 40, 70, 152, 180-181, 186, 261, 267, 284, 287, 289-290, 312-313, 319, 321-322

B

Balance 7, 9, 11-12, 17-18, 20, 34, 39-40, 42, 58-59, 61-62, 64-65, 68-69, 71-73, 167-171, 174, 209, 215-216, 220-221, 223-224, 226, 287, 291-295, 297

Billed 101

Business 1-3, 17, 23-26, 28-30, 32, 43, 56, 59, 62, 65-66, 68-69, 82, 91, 93-94, 133-134, 166, 180, 233, 254, 261-262, 283-284, 303, 331

C

Charge 265

Company 25, 27, 31, 58, 74-76, 81-82, 85, 100, 115, 124, 126, 130, 133-135, 139-140, 144, 153, 156, 160, 162-163, 166-167, 174-177, 180, 185, 232-233, 238, 253, 261, 265, 311-314, 318, 324, 327, 331

Computer 2

Contra 34, 142

Contract 240, 243

Corporate 185, 240

Credit 4-9, 11, 18, 25, 29, 31, 35, 71, 73, 146, 148, 154, 169-171, 174, 178, 251-253, 265

Current 174, 186, 284, 287, 289-290, 312-313

Customer 23-25, 73-76, 85, 135-138, 140-143

D

Debited 5, 78, 234-235, 285

Decreasing 18, 33, 54, 56, 70, 95, 97-98, 107, 111, 132, 137-139, 141, 143, 172, 175-177, 179, 199, 210, 233-234, 236, 238, 243, 247, 251

Deduct 287

Deferrals 54, 73

Discount 97-98, 203, 205, 208, 212-213, 245-247

Dupont 327

E

Employee 228-230

Equation 36-37, 261

Equipment 31, 70-71, 73, 152-154, 161, 167-168, 287, 291-293

Equity 30, 33, 36-37, 40, 42-44, 111, 189-190, 195, 201, 261-264, 266, 268-272, 274-275, 327

Exchange 174

Expense 15, 17-19, 25, 27, 32, 37, 50, 54-60, 62, 64-71, 79-84, 111, 132-134, 140-142, 145-146, 148-149, 152, 154, 156, 168, 180, 234-235, 238, 246, 251, 301

Expert 46

F

Federal 232

Financial 3, 14-15, 40-41, 51-52, 220, 283, 303, 306, 327, 330-332

Financing 284, 293, 295

G

Government 332

H

Health 303

I

Income 2-3, 14-17, 22, 28, 39, 41-42, 44, 49, 58, 62, 65, 69, 77, 81, 84, 86, 93-94, 152, 166, 179, 189-193, 195-198, 200-201, 216, 220, 223, 226, 231, 283, 287, 289, 297-298, 301, 307, 311, 320, 324, 326

Increases 270, 287, 306

Inflow 284-285, 294

Insurance 59-62, 232, 301

Intangible 180

Interest 79, 135-138, 185, 202, 204-205, 210-212, 214, 217-218, 233-236, 238, 240-244, 246, 249-251, 320

Inventory 91, 93, 95-98, 106, 108-109, 115-127, 296, 300, 312, 316-317

Invest 185, 202

Investment 186-189, 191-194, 196-199, 201-203, 205-210, 212-214, 216, 222, 225-226

Investor 43, 185, 202, 212, 216

Invoice 97

L

Ledger 6-9, 11-12, 130-131, 198, 200, 206, 209, 215, 221, 223-224, 226

Liability 29, 54, 75, 77, 79, 95, 231-234, 236, 238-239, 245, 247, 249

Locate 230

Losses 166, 179

M

Market 125, 203, 240, 242-245, 248-250, 269, 274, 276

Medicare 232

O

Operating 284-286, 288-290, 297

Owners 29, 262

Ownership 30, 100, 185

P

Paid-in 266, 275

Payable 26-27, 29, 54, 79, 81-84, 95, 231-236, 238, 245-247, 250-253, 257, 273, 287, 295, 300-301

Paying 241, 272

Payment 36, 69, 97, 211, 236, 238

Payouts 328-329

Payroll 228

Percent 147

Percentage 189-190, 195, 306

Period 3, 6, 11, 14-17, 20, 28, 49, 51, 79, 98, 106, 122, 154, 180, 228

Periodic 106, 122-123

Perpetual 95

Prepaid 54, 60-68, 76

Product 25, 27, 91, 94, 124

Profit 17, 32, 94, 116, 121, 262, 326

Property 82

Purchase 95, 97, 117, 122-123, 152, 203, 244, 270-271

Purchaser 101-102

Purchases 31, 106, 108, 118-120, 296, 300

R

Ratios 312, 321

Rebate 244

Record 104, 272, 274

Redemption 253

Reduction 238

Reports 190, 195, 331

Resale 115

Results 3, 121, 124, 166, 285, 303, 312, 327

Revenue 2-3, 14-15, 17-18, 23, 34, 37, 49-50, 54, 73-74, 77-78, 85, 111, 136-139, 166, 189, 205, 211-213, 218

S

Securities 185-186, 202-203, 207, 216, 218-220, 222-223, 225

Seller 98, 100-103, 214

Service 23, 25, 27, 73-74, 76, 91

Shares 185, 187-189, 192-194, 197-199, 265, 267, 269-278

Solvency 318

Statement v, viii, 14-16, 22, 28, 39, 41-42, 58, 62, 65, 77, 81, 84, 86, 93, 130-132, 179, 192, 197, 226, 283-284, 287-289, 291, 297-298, 301, 303, 306, 331

System 95, 106-108, 122-123

T

Timekeeper 17

Traded 175

Trade-in 167, 174-178

Trading 202, 216, 218, 222-223

Transfers 100

Transit 100, 126

Treasury 270-272, 275

www.ingramcontent.com/pod-product-compliance
Lightning Source LLC
LaVergne TN
LVHW062114200926
848484LV00007B/1664